The Laminated Wood Boatbuilder

The Laminated Wood Boatbuilder

A Step-by-Step Guide
for the Backyard Builder

Hub Miller

International Marine
Camden, Maine

Published by International Marine®

10 9 8 7 6 5 4 3 2

Library of Congress Cataloging-in-Publication Data

Miller, Hub.
The laminated wood boatbuilder/Hub Miller.
    p. cm.
  Includes bibliographical references (p.) and index.
  ISBN 0-87742-386-5 (alk. paper)
  1. Boatbuilding—Amateurs' manuals. 2. Laminated wood—
Amateurs' manuals. I. Title.
VM321.M54 1993
623.8'202—dc20   93-20741
                                 CIP

Questions regarding the content of this book should be addressed to:
International Marine
P.O. Box 220
Camden, ME 04843

Questions regarding the ordering of this book should be addressed to:
McGraw-Hill, Inc.
Customer Service Department
P.O. Box 547
Blacklick, OH 43004
Retail customers: 1-800-822-8158
Bookstores: 1-800-338-3987

Printed by R.R. Donnelley, Harrisonburg, VA
Design and Production by Faith Hague
Edited by Jim Babb, Pamela Benner, and Paula Blanchard

Contents

Introduction

This book is about building boats by bending relatively small pieces of wood and bonding them together in a process normally called lamination, or cold-molding. It does not deal with mechanical and electrical systems or rigging because these topics deserve books of their own. This book relies on a graphic depiction of the process; the story is told in pictures accompanied by words. (It's not easy. Try facing a blank piece of paper and coming up with illustrations like these.) It also discusses some alternative ideas about how to reduce the use of metal fasteners.

Laminated wood construction is the best way to go for builders who like to watch a beautiful, curvaceous object evolve from their labors. The result can be a yacht that is lighter, stronger, more durable, and more impervious to penetration by moisture and marine borers than a plank-on-frame yacht. The builder experiences the pleasure of working with wood, but the process is less complex than traditional boatbuilding methods. There is also the undeniable pleasure of owning a finished product that will last through the years with relatively little maintenance.

Compound curved laminated plywood boats date from the development of PT boats during World War II, but the materials and complex procedures (involving high heat and great pressures) used then would not be of much use to a private boatbuilder today. In the meantime, oil and chemical companies developed adhesives that required only the spark of genius to illuminate their possibilities for boatbuilding. That spark was supplied by the Gougeon Brothers of Bay City, Michigan, in the late 1960s, and has been fanned by them and numerous others ever since.

The breakthrough for the new material came with the development of adhesives that would cure without the application of heat and pressure. Modern two-part adhesives consisting of an epoxy resin and hardener require only that the bonded parts be held or fixed in position until the resin has had time to cure. Once combined, these epoxies have a pot life of 20 to 90 minutes, depending on air temperature and the type of hardener used. They will begin to set in three to seven hours and will reach full cure in three to seven days. Modern epoxies are also used as coatings on wood to seal out moisture and marine borers.

Strictly as a matter of semantics, the term *cold molding* sounds like something one might do in the Arctic, as in, "Dear, I'm going to begin cold molding our new igloo for winter." To say "cold-molded wood" is to belie the warmth and workability of the material, as if it would crack into a thousand pieces at the tap of a mallet. After all, it isn't necessary to refrigerate the project any more than it's necessary to put it under intense heat. I won't use the term *cold molding,* preferring instead *laminated wood* boatbuilding—because that's what it really is.

All these relatively small pieces of wood we are bending and bonding must be formed over something if we are to arrive at the shape of a boat. Much of the criticism of this boatbuilding methodology centers on the perceived waste in building a "something" (a mold) that must be discarded. While there is some justification to this criticism, it must be pointed out that it is possible to incorporate the mold into the permanent structure of the hull so that nothing is wasted. In real life it is usually more practical to build a "disposable" mold for boats under about 30 feet in length. It is also possible to build a mold durable enough to allow the construction of a number of hull shells.

For purposes of this text, the word *mold* refers to the shape of the "something." *Mold frame* refers to a structure that will not be a part of the hull shell, and *shell frame* refers to a structure that *will* be a permanent part of the hull shell. In this story, we follow the construction of three boats. A 12-foot skiff and a 28-foot powerboat illustrate the mold frame method, and a 32-foot sailboat illustrates the shell frame method. At the end we'll see a series of variations of these three boats.

I came to the world of boats by way of my father, who designed and built them in the Pacific Northwest. He started instructing me when I was eight, and his methods were rather detail oriented. At one point, having designed and built a boat, he designed and built an engine for it, actually designing the individual castings, making the sand forms, casting the iron, and assembling a working one-cylinder engine.

"Okay," he said, "first you create the vocabulary of details." I tended to follow that in my career as a terrestrial architect, then in boat design, starting with traditional plank-on-frame, then in sheet plywood. For a while there was a romance with ferrocement. Beautiful work is possible in that medium, but it is very labor intensive. Prospective boatbuilders were enticed by the prospect of owning a world-girdling ocean yacht for about the price of a medium-size outboard motor—that is, if their time was worth nothing. As is so often the case with people whose time is worth nothing, the wreckage of their projects litters the waterways and byways of life.

Steel is surely the best material for large projects, being not only the strongest but also the cheapest. Plank-on-frame construction is for those who want to keep a tradition alive, or want to be the curator of a one-boat museum. Fiberglass gained ascendancy early in the manufactured boat market and is entrenched to the point that it is difficult to challenge. That's not altogether bad: there are good examples of the kind as well as bad ones. It does not seem to me, however, that it's the best way for the individual boatbuilder to go for one-off construction. Building a mold for the lay-up of a fiberglass hull is costly and requires advanced skills.

Some professional designer-builders have a sophistication with sheet plywood boat construction that is amazing. Well-thought-out plans are available, some with full-size paper patterns to speed things along. This can be a very good way for an individual to build a boat.

But I prefer the delight of making compound curved shapes in wood that is possible only with laminated wood. I'm not opposed to full-size paper patterns for larger shaped pieces of the mold or frames, but I don't agree that lofting is dead. I prefer lofting the lines of such a boat full size, in the traditional manner. There are so many curves that it would be difficult to supply patterns for everything, and it is easier to work out these shapes right on the job, using the lofting as a reference the entire time.

After reading the books I could find on the subject of boatbuilding, I determined to develop my own vocabulary of details. All the texts were good, I thought, although one author seemed to think of the "amateur" builder as both physically weak and slightly mentally retarded. Another was a mine of information but seemed curiously wordy and hard to follow at times. For the guide to accompany my construction plans, I was determined to avoid the word *amateur* altogether. As for the rest of it, I was to sit up nights with a sharp knife, excising words, sentences, and paragraphs. Goodness knows I'm capable of creating sentences that rise into the heavens only to explode into multitudinous, diverse, and parallel lines of conflicting imagery, philosophical conjecturing, and gesticulation, ultimately to cascade down the page like the lingering afterglow of summer fireworks. Not here. This text reads in short choppy sentences that say, in essence: Begin by doing this, then do this, then this, then this, and, finally, do that.

Why can't they say, "Turn out the lights when you leave," instead of, "Please extinguish all illumination prior to departing the premises"? (FDR)

CHAPTER 1

Materials

WOOD

When it comes to boatbuilding, wood has certain strengths and weaknesses: Wood can be strong, light, stable, durable, flexible, or stiff, and can hold fastenings. It can also rot, warp, shrink and swell, soak up water, and be attacked by borers. None of its negative qualities has prevented wood from being probably the most satisfactory boatbuilding material throughout history. It still can be, provided these problems are dealt with.

Rot is unknown in wood having a moisture content below 20 percent. Rot caused by fungus growth is aided by warm temperatures (76 to 86 degrees F) and the presence of oxygen. Bonding strength and crushing strength are affected by moisture content as well. A reduction from 25 percent moisture content to 5 percent can double these strengths. Structural wood should be cured to about 12 percent moisture content. The work space should not be so hot and humid that wood absorbs moisture. For example, if the work space is 70 degrees F, the wood begins absorbing moisture when the relative humidity of the air rises above about 55 percent. This means that cooler and dryer air is better. Rot growth in the completed boat is prevented by treatments, coatings, or complete encapsulation, which eliminates moisture buildup and oxygen supply. These also lock out borers.

Strength, weight, dimensional stability, stiffness or flexibility, and ability to hold fastenings are properties that vary among species of wood and must be considered when selecting wood for any given application. Local lumberyards carry material for the commercial building industry and are not likely to stock wood suitable for boatbuilding. There are large mail-order specialty houses that supply boatbuilding woods nationally. Areas where wooden boatbuilding is practiced, such as New England and the Pacific Northwest, have specialty firms that supply boatbuilding materials. Check ads in nautical magazines. If you live where timber is cut, you may be able to get top-quality lumber directly from a sawmill. All green wood has to be stored until its moisture content is 12 percent or less.

Lumber is ordered by length in feet, width in inches, and thickness in multiples of a quarter inch. A thickness of ¼ inch is called one-quarter, 1-inch thickness is called four-quarter, etc. Rough lumber is usually true to the given dimensions. Lumber planed smooth on two sides (S2S) and four sides (S4S) will be less than the given dimensions. For boatbuilding purposes, it's best to buy rough lumber.

Lumber that is not to become a part of the boat structure can be purchased at local lumber companies in finished sizes. For example, a 2 x 4 will actually measure 1½ inches by 3½ inches, and a 1 x 4 will be ¾ inch by 3½ inches.

It is best to see the wood before taking delivery. The solid timber should be quarter sawn or vertical grain (labeled VG). The end view of the lumber should reveal grain running across it from about 45 degrees to straight across the short dimension. If the grain is running straight up and down the long dimension, it is called flat grain. Flat-grain lumber will also display widely spaced, looping grain on the sides. The sides of the boards should show grain that runs more or less evenly in parallel lines from end to end, rather than running out toward one end. Flat-grain lumber tends to warp and is not as strong as vertical-grain wood. It is also more difficult to finish smoothly.

Plywood should be marine AA ext., or, if it is to be finished bright or natural, marine NA ext. This means that "B" quality or better (marine) inner plys were used, and that the adhesive used in the manufacture of the plywood is for exterior use (ext.). *AA* means that the quality of the surfaces on both sides is "A" (or best) quality. *NA* means that one of the two faces has a "natural" side.

Douglas fir plywood panels have a lot of built-in stress, and are difficult to finish to the uniform surfaces needed for boatbuilding. Better choices are Philippine mahogany (lauan), Gaboon (okoume), Sipo (utile), Meranti, and Mecore plywood panels, usually imported from the

LUMBER CUTS

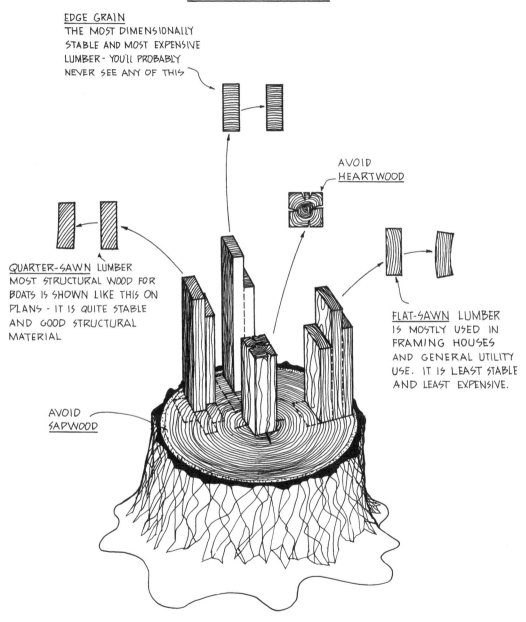

EDGE GRAIN
THE MOST DIMENSIONALLY STABLE AND MOST EXPENSIVE LUMBER - YOU'LL PROBABLY NEVER SEE ANY OF THIS

AVOID **HEARTWOOD**

QUARTER-SAWN LUMBER
MOST STRUCTURAL WOOD FOR BOATS IS SHOWN LIKE THIS ON PLANS - IT IS QUITE STABLE AND GOOD STRUCTURAL MATERIAL

FLAT-SAWN LUMBER IS MOSTLY USED IN FRAMING HOUSES AND GENERAL UTILITY USE. IT IS LEAST STABLE AND LEAST EXPENSIVE.

AVOID **SAPWOOD**

Netherlands, United Kingdom, or West Germany. In England, the plywood should be stamped BSS1088WBP.

Veneers sliced off a quartered log generally come in lengths up to 17 feet and widths between 6 and 12 inches. The thickest veneer is ⅛ inch. It is best to purchase these veneers directly from manufacturers on a per-square-foot basis.

No set of plans could specify wood for each component of the boat that would be meaningful everywhere in the world. The availability and suitability of wood vary with location, so the following list of woods and their uses is included.

Predominant Woods Used in Boatbuilding

Alder

Red alder grows in the northwestern United States and western Canada. This wood is moderately strong and light but low in shock resistance. It is straight-grained, works easily, and is stable when seasoned. Used mostly for interior cabinetry, molding, and furnishings. It is not rot resistant and needs preservative treatment.

Ash

American ash (*tough ash* and *soft ash*) grows in the eastern United States. Tough ash has a hard texture of long, tough fibers that have high shock resistance. Used for paddles, tillers, and boat hooks. It glues well and is suitable for laminated structural parts. Not rot resistant.

European ash grows throughout much of Europe. It is a straight-grained, somewhat coarse wood that is moderately hard, works fairly easily, and glues and finishes well. Suitable for small laminated structural members and decorative trim. Not rot resistant.

Beech

European beech grows throughout Europe. It has a fine, even texture and is hard and moderately heavy. It glues easily and finishes well. Used primarily for interior furnishings and plywood. Requires preservative treatment.

Birch

Yellow birch grows in the eastern United States and Canada. It is hard, heavy, uniform, and fine-grained, with a subdued figure that gives an attractive finish. Its curly grain requires sharp tools for working. Used for plywood and for interior cabinetry and finish. Not rot resistant.

Cedar

Alaska yellow cedar grows in Alaska and British Columbia, and is one of just a few trees that could be used to construct an entire vessel. The wood is strong in bending, compression, and shock resistance. It is uniformly dense and stable with low shrinkage, works well with hand and power tools, and glues and varnishes well. Often seen as planking and decking, and good for laminated structural members. Rot resistant.

Spanish cedar, or *cedro*, grows in wide areas of tropical Central and South America from southern Mexico to northern Argentina. It is straight-grained, easily worked, light, strong, and durable. It has about the same strength as mahogany, but it is harder and stronger in compression across the grain. Easily worked, glues well, and can be used for laminated structural members. Rot resistant.

Western red cedar is from the western slopes of the Pacific Northwest and British Columbia. It provides the best wood for veneers used in laminated wood boat construction. Light, strong, and durable, but requires care in working because of its softness. Rot resistant.

White Cedar

Northern white cedar grows in the northeastern United States. Atlantic cedar (*juniper, southern white cedar,* and *swamp cedar*) grows along the Atlantic and eastern Gulf coasts. It is light and very resistant to rot, glues well, and is stable. It is not as strong and hard as western cedars, however, and tends to have knots. Most often used as planking.

Cypress

Bald cypress grows in the southeastern United States. It is moderately heavy, strong, hard, and very durable, and is available in long, wide boards with clear, straight grain. Used for exterior joinery, planking, and decking. If not waterproofed, the wood will soak up copious quantities of water. Extremely rot resistant.

Elm

Rock elm grows in the northeastern United States and eastern Canada. It is straight-grained and stringy, and hard to work with hand tools, but works well with power tools. It glues, paints, and varnishes well and is easy to bend. Used as pianking and for frames and laminated structural parts. Moderately rot resistant.

Fir

Douglas fir grows in the coastal northwestern United States and British Columbia. It is moderately soft, straight-grained, and strong, and is easily worked with hand and power tools. It holds fastenings well and glues well. Fir could be used for the construction of entire vessels but is most often seen as planking and decking. It could be used for laminated structural members. Moderately rot resistant.

Western true fir (*subalpine, California red, grand, noble, Pacific silver,* and *white*) grows in the western United States. It is a light, soft, but firm wood suitable for interior finish work. For marine use it must be prime stock, carefully dried. It is not rot resistant and should be treated with preservative.

Hemlock

Western hemlock (*Alaska pine, Prince Albert fir, hemlock spruce,* and *Pacific hemlock*) grows in the northwestern United States and Canada. It is a moderately hard, straight-grained wood with a medium to fine texture that machines well. Prime stock is required for marine use. Because it glues well, it is suitable for laminated structural parts. It should be used on the interior; it is not as strong as other softwoods and is not rot resistant.

Larch

European larch grows throughout Europe. It is straight-grained with medium texture and hardness. It glues and holds fastenings well but is difficult to work with hand tools. Rot resistant. It can be used as planking and for laminated structural parts.

Mahogany

African mahogany grows in west central Africa. It is a popular boatbuilding lumber, with an interlocked grain that works easily and glues well. Available in wide, clear boards. Used for planking, interior and exterior joinery, and finish trim. Could be used for laminated structural parts. Moderately rot resistant.

Honduras mahogany grows from southern Mexico to Bolivia. It is a dimensionally stable wood with fairly straight grain that is easy to work and is capable of taking a very beautiful finish. The heavier, darker species grow in the upper Amazon area. It glues very well. The wood is used for interior and exterior joinery, decking, and planking. Considered the best of the mahoganies. Moderately rot resistant.

Philippine mahogany (*lauan, dark red,* and *light red*) comes, not surprisingly, from the Philippines. It is not a true mahogany but is close to the cedar family. The wood has interlocked grain. The light red variety is not suitable for boatbuilding. The darker variety is easy to work; it glues, paints, and varnishes well, and is used for planking and interior and exterior joinery. Moderately rot resistant.

Maple

Eastern hard maple (*sugar maple* and *rock maple*) grows in North America. It is generally straight-grained, heavy, strong, and stiff, with good resistance to shock. The wood shrinks a great deal and glues only moderately well; it does not work easily with hand tools. Used for plywood paneling and interior joinery. Not rot resistant.

Oak

Red oak (*northern red oak* and *southern red oak*) grows in North America and Europe. It is a hard, strong, shock-resistant wood that bends well and is easily worked and finished. It holds fastenings well. Its open, porous end grain needs filling to protect it from water absorption. Most often used for framing, flooring, and interior joinery. Moderately rot resistant. Stains black when wet.

White oak grows in North America and Europe. It is a tough, durable wood, very easily bent when green. The wood works well when seasoned and paints and glues easily. When fully dried, it makes excellent structural members and cabinetwork. It holds fastenings extremely well. It does not soak up water like red oak and is much stronger. Rot resistant. Stains black when wet.

Pine

Eastern white pine (*Weymouth pine* and *soft pine*) grows in the northeastern United States. It is a light but firm, straight-grained wood of uniform texture, easily kiln-dried with little shrinkage. It is easy to work and glues well, which makes it suitable for laminated structural parts. It tends to be knotty, so prime stock is needed for marine work. Used for pattern making and general trim. Not rot resistant.

Kauri pine grows in New Zealand. It is the strongest softwood in the world, and has a tightly packed, even grain. It is one of the best boatbuilding woods and could be used to build the entire vessel, but is increasingly difficult to obtain. The wood works easily with hand and machine tools, glues well, and is suitable for laminated structural parts. It is durable and takes paint and varnish very well.

Malayan kauri pine comes from Malaysia. It is a straight-grained, fine-textured wood that is easy to work with hand and power tools. It glues well and can be used for laminated structural parts but is not nearly as strong as New Zealand kauri pine It is suitable for planking. It finishes beautifully and is most often seen in cabinetwork. Not rot resistant.

Parana pine grows in southeastern Brazil and parts of Paraguay and Argentina. It is a relatively straight-grained, strong wood that paints and glues well. It has great shearing strength but crushes easily across the grain. Works easily with hand and power tools and holds fastenings well. Its applications in marine use are for doors, interior trim, and cabinetwork. Not rot resistant.

Southern pine (*longleaf pine, shortleaf pine, loblolly pine, slash pine,* and *pitch pine*) grows in the southern United States. It is heavy, strong, stiff, hard, and a little difficult to work. Shortleaf and loblolly pines are somewhat lighter. The wood is stable after it thoroughly seasons. It holds fastenings well and takes glue moderately well. It is good for planking, decking, and laminated structural members, and is used for structural-grade plywood. Rot resistant.

Western white pine (*silver pine* and *Idaho pine*) grows in the northwestern United States and British Columbia. It is a moderately soft, easily worked wood that glues well and does not split readily. Due to its characteristic tight, red knots, it does not bend well, nor does it hold fastenings well. Used for interior furnishings and finish. Not rot resistant.

Redwood

Redwood grows in western California. It is a moderately strong, stiff wood that is light in weight and easily worked. It is generally straight-grained, glues well, and is very stable, but has little shock resistance and does not bend well. The wood is beautiful when finished clear. Used most often for cabinetwork and interior paneling. Very rot resistant.

Spruce

Eastern spruce (*white spruce, black spruce,* and *red spruce*) grows in the Appalachian Mountains and New England. It is a light, strong, fine-grained wood that works and glues well, and is stable once thoroughly seasoned. It usually has many knots and is not available in long, clear lengths. Used in decking and planking; select material is suitable for laminated structural parts. Not rot resistant.

Sitka spruce grows in coastal areas of British Columbia and Alaska. Its wood is straight-grained with long, even, woolly fibers that demand very sharp tools for working. It is light and very strong and glues and varnishes beautifully. It is suitable for laminated structural parts and is the best material for stringers in laminated wood boat construction. Available in long, clear stock and is the best choice for spar construction. Not rot resistant.

More Woods from Africa

Abura grows in tropical Africa. A medium-hard wood, it works fairly easily and glues and stains well. The grain is slightly interlocked; to prevent splitting, guide holes are a must for fastenings. Suitable for laminated structural parts. Not rot resistant.

Afara limba grows in central West Africa. It is a fairly straight-grained wood of uniform but coarse texture. It is stable, works easily, and glues well but requires filling and staining before varnishing. Used for interior joinery. Not rot resistant.

Afromosia (*kokrodua*) grows in West Africa. It is a strong, durable, and stable wood that works well with hand and power tools. The wood has a fine grain, glues well, and finishes beautifully with varnish. Used for interior joinery and planking and could be used for laminated structural parts. Very rot resistant.

Agba grows in tropical Africa. It is a straight-grained wood that works easily, glues well, and is suitable for many boatbuilding applications, such as planking, joinery, and laminated structural components. Very rot resistant.

Gaboon grows in western central Africa. It is a lightweight wood that works, glues, and finishes well. It is used for plywood and is suitable for laminated structural parts and interior joinery. Not rot resistant.

Iroko grows in tropical Africa. It is a tough, durable wood with coarse, interlocking grain that is not easy to work with hand tools. It glues only moderately well. Used for planking, decking, and exterior trim, as well as for interior joinery; the wood finishes beautifully. Extremely rot resistant.

Obeche (*samba* and *wawa*) grows in western central Africa. It is a fairly soft wood that can have either straight or interlocked grain of uniform texture; lightweight, stable, and works easily. It glues well, and is used as a core stock in plywood; can be used for laminated structural parts. Not rot resistant.

More Woods from South America

Angelique (*Guiana teak*) grows in Brazil's Amazon Territory. This hardwood is difficult to work but is tough and durable. It holds fastenings well. Used for decking, planking, and laminated structural parts. Very rot resistant.

Balsa grows from southern Mexico to southern Brazil and Bolivia, and is the lightest and softest wood on the market. It has little strength or durability but readily absorbs resins and shows surprising compression strength when laid with the end grain up as a filler in various composite structures. It works and glues easily. Used as a core material in lightweight yacht construction.

Greenheart grows in Guyana, and is very strong, stiff, and heavy with a uniform, fine texture. It is very difficult to work with hand tools and requires carbide-tipped power tools for cutting. It is stronger than teak and can be finished to an even more impressive luster. Used for guards, beltings, rail caps, and sheathings because of its ability to withstand abrasion. Very rot resistant.

Ishpingo (*amburana*) grows in the upper reaches of the Amazon Basin. It is a stable wood with interlocked grain that glues only moderately well. Used as planking, decking, and structural parts, as well as for interior and exterior joinery. Very rot resistant.

Lignum vitae grows in the West Indies and along the northwestern coast of South America to the west coast of Mexico, and is one of the hardest, heaviest, and most close-grained woods known. The grain is interlocked and impossible to work with hand tools. Used wherever high impact resistance is needed, such as for mallet heads, tool handles, and high-quality blocks. Because of its oily nature, it is almost impossible to glue. Very rot resistant.

More Woods from the Pacific and Asia

Apitong (*apitong panau* and *hagakhak*) grows in the Philippines. Other members of the species include *keruinq* in Malaysia, *yang* in Thailand, and *gurjun* in India and Burma. These are fairly straight-grained, strong, hard, and heavy woods that can be coarse- to fine-textured. The wood is hard to work with hand tools but machines well. It takes glue and paint moderately well and is suitable for all the structural parts of the boat. Rot resistant.

Blackbutt grows in eastern Australia. It is a generally straight-grained hardwood that is easily worked and bends well. It is tough and strong and takes a long time to season. Used primarily as a planking material. Durable.

Coachwood grows in eastern Australia. It is a straight-grained, fine-textured wood that is relatively easy to work and glues easily. It seasons quickly and holds fastenings well. Used for marine-quality plywood and interior joinery. Not rot resistant.

Ironbark grows in northern New South Wales and southern Queensland, Australia. It is a very dense hardwood with interlocking grain and takes a long time to season. Used for sheathing, beltings, and guards, as well as for keels and stem assemblies. Sometimes used as mast steps, shoes, and floor timbers. Very rot resistant.

Jarrah grows on the southwestern coast of Australia, and is heavy, hard, and strong with straight to interlocked grain that is even to moderately coarse. Difficult to work with hand and power tools. Used for guards and rail caps. Very rot resistant.

Jelutong comes from Malaysia, the Philippines, Thailand, and Burma, and is moderately fine- and even-textured with straight grain. Easy to work, and finishes and glues satisfactorily. Used mainly for interior joinery. Not rot resistant.

Karri, which grows in Western Australia, is quite strong and available in long, clear sizes. It takes a long time to season and is hard to work with hand or power tools. Does not glue well. Used where strength and abrasion resistance are required, as in beltings, guards, and caps. Rot resistant.

Koa is from the Hawaiian Islands. It is a hard and stable wood that works relatively easily and takes glue moderately well. Used primarily for interior joinery. Rot resistant.

Meranti (*shorea*) comes from southeastern Asia. It has a moderately coarse but even texture, with interlocked grain. It works easily with hand and power tools and glues relatively easily. Used in the manufacture of plywood, and can be used for laminated structural components and other structural parts of the boat. Fairly rot resistant.

Ramin grows in Malaysia and Indonesia. Its wood has a straight or shallowly interlocked grain and a moderately fine texture. It is moderately heavy and hard, easy to work and finish, and takes glue well. Used for plywood and fine interior joinery. Not rot resistant.

Teak grows in Southeast Asia. Latin America and Africa are now producing teak as well. It is the most sought-after wood for high-quality nautical joinery, decking, and trim. The wood has great natural durability and does not stain when weathered. Carbide cutters are needed to work the material satisfactorily. It does not glue particularly well but can be glued if degreased. Very rot resistant.

Although an individual boatbuilder uses a very small quantity of wood compared with other wood consumers, it's always a good idea to purchase what North Americans consider "exotic" woods from plantation-raised stock to help reduce pressure on wild forests.

ADHESIVES

At this writing, it is pretty well universally agreed that epoxy resin is a better adhesive for laminated wood boat construction than resorcinol-type glues or others. The type of construction discussed in this book requires that adhesives have both bonding and sealing properties. Wood surfaces exposed to the atmosphere in the completed boats are sealed with resin to lock out both moisture and oxygen, thereby preventing the growth of rot fungus in the wood fibers. Needless to say, the wood must be very dry to prevent locking in moisture. For this reason, the wood should be dried and maintained at a moisture content of 12 percent or less. (That means that the water in the wood weighs 12 percent or less of what the wood alone weighs.)

Epoxy adhesives have an advantage over resorcinol-type glues in that they can be applied successfully in a cooler, drier environment, which is more conducive to favorable wood maintenance conditions. Epoxy resins can also fill small voids that are likely to occur between the various layers of hull-shell planking. It fills these gaps without any apparent loss of strength.

In this book, the word *resin* means a resin–hardener mixture. *Adhesive mixture* refers to resin that is applied to the bonding surfaces, whether or not it contains additives. There are additives for both speeding and slowing cure; others impart color or provide an ultraviolet-ray shield. These are added to the basic resin–hardener mixture in each batch. *Thickened adhesive mixture* means that carbon or glass fibers have been added to the resin–hardener mixture to increase its gap-filling capacity; it can also mean that silica has been added to reduce runniness so that the adhesive can be applied to vertical or overhead surfaces. Other fillers, such as microballoons or microspheres, can be added to the resin–hardener mixture to produce a strong, low-density adhesive used for fills and fillets.

If WEST System products are used, it is best to obtain a current copy of the WEST System Products Technical Manual from Gougeon Brothers, Inc., of Bay City, Michigan. They are constantly improving and updating their products. Systems Three Resins of Seattle, Washington, offers products for builders of laminated wood boats. Their informational book is called *The Epoxy Book.*

Adhere strictly to manufacturers' instructions when mixing and applying epoxy adhesives. The toxic effects of epoxies have been greatly reduced in recent years, but precautions are still required. Use a barrier cream on any area of the skin that might be exposed to epoxies, and wear disposable surgical gloves. Resin should not be removed from the skin with solvents, because they add a drying effect that worsens the condition of any rash that may be present. Epoxy manufacturers offer or can recommend a solution for the purpose. Resin spilled on clothing should be removed with a solvent before the clothing becomes bonded to the skin. The best policy is to wear a disposable shop apron when handling these chemicals.

The shop should have adequate ventilation to remove fumes given off during the application and cure of epoxies. This is doubly true in boat interiors, where forced-air circulation is required.

FASTENINGS

While a goal of laminated boatbuilding is to minimize the use of metal fastenings, they cannot be eliminated altogether. Fastenings are required to attach various items of hardware to the boat and to hold lead ballast, chainplates, and engines in place. Sometimes wood-to-wood fastening is also needed.

For boats constructed of laminated wood, fastenings can be divided into two broad categories: temporary fastenings to hold portions of the construction together while the epoxy adhesive cures, and fastenings that are to remain a part of the completed structure.

Temporary fastenings are primarily staples, small nails, and wood screws used in lamination and scarfing processes. In most other instances, clamps are used to hold parts for cure. Temporary fastenings can be plain steel because they will be removed. Wide-crown staples are easy to remove if they are driven through strapping tape; with a pull on the tape, an entire row of staples can be lifted. Staples with legs up to $\frac{9}{16}$ inch in length can be used in hand-operated staple guns to fasten wood up to about $\frac{1}{4}$ inch thick. Compressed-air staple guns are available that can shoot staples with 1³⁄₁₆-inch legs and a crown width of ¼ inch.

Fastenings that become permanent parts of the structure include wood screws, machine screws, threaded rods, studs, and bolts. These must be bronze, Monel, or hot-dipped galvanized steel. Stainless steel will corrode badly if it is in constant contact with salt water, but it is superb for use up and away from the water. Screw sizes useful for laminated wood boatbuilding are #8, #10, #12, and #14, in various lengths. Bolts and rods are generally from ¼ inch to about ⅝ inch in diameter, with lengths as long as required.

SOLVENTS

Common solvents used for cleaning operations are acetone, methylene chloride, perchloroethylene, methyl-ethyl-ketone (MEK), toluene, turpentine, and xylene. All of these solvents must be used in power-ventilated spaces if exposure to concentrated fumes is to last more than just a few minutes. Canister-type face masks may be required. Methylene chloride and perchloroethylene are not flammable. Turpentine gives off flammable vapor at temperatures above 93 degrees F. Acetone, on the other hand, gives off flammable vapor above 0 degrees F. The others range in between. The presence of wood dust in a confined space, at high temperatures, and with a lack of air circulation creates the possibility of spontaneous explosions when mixed with high concentrations of these solvent vapors. Manufacturers of epoxy resins usually offer solvents that are suitable for use with their products. Follow the manufacturers' directions carefully.

SHEATHING

A more durable surface is obtained with a sheathing of glass cloth. This is particularly true with relatively soft wood, such as the popular western red cedar veneers. Glass cloth not only provides some strength but also supports an adequate thickness of resin over the surface. Glass cloth of 6-ounce to 10-ounce weight is usually specified. Two layers of cloth are sometimes used to cover areas of high wear, such as on stem and transom edges. Four-ounce cloth is used on surfaces that are finished bright so the weave won't show through. Even varnished hulls are usually painted below the boottop, so heavier glass cloth is used on the bottom.

Other sheathing materials, such as Dynel and polypropylene, are strong in themselves but do not strengthen or stiffen the laminated wood hull. Due to the stretchability of these materials, the underlying wood would have to break before their strength came into play. Glass cloth has only about a 3 percent stretch factor, which allows it to deform locally about the same extent as wood.

COATINGS

Oil-based paint can be used on bare wood; because it is more flexible, it will move with the wood. On surfaces that have been encapsulated with resin or covered with glass-cloth sheathing that has been encapsulated in resin, a linear polyurethane (LP) paint is best.

The highest-quality varnish you can find is also the cheapest in the long run. Normally called spar varnishes, these usually have a phenolic resin base that is mixed with tung and linseed oil, and have an added ultraviolet (UV) filter.

Tools

The tool list for laminated wood boat construction is somewhat less extensive than for traditional plank-on-frame construction. If you don't build boats for a living, purchase or lease tools and equipment only when specific uses and needs become apparent. The fewer tools and the higher their quality, the better. There are three general categories of tools: *hand tools, portable power tools,* and *stationary power tools.*

HAND TOOLS

The quality of hand tools has declined somewhat, possibly because reliance on power tools has increased. Some builders say modern hand tools are mostly rubbish, while others feel that quite reliable hand tools are available. In any case, the tools to have are ones that don't break and don't cause arm and hand fatigue. Cutting tools must hold a sharp edge. Some boatbuilding tasks can be done best (or can only be done) with hand tools.

A claw hammer and some saws are considered the classic hand tools and, indeed, they are necessary. A claw hammer sets and extracts nails on the lofting floor and when temporarily fastening together various glued parts for curing. A hammer doesn't have to be heavy; it is normally used for nails 1½ inches or less in length. A 16-ounce hammer is easier on the arm, particularly when it's swung all day fixing planking for cure. Builders report that fiberglass or steel handles covered with rubber hold up well and feel good to grip. Some boatbuilders like handles made of compressed leather washers. A small sledge hammer is useful for driving stakes into the ground and nudging large objects into position. Some builders use them to drive large bolts and as backing for nailing.

Everyone needs a crosscut saw about 26 inches long with about 10 teeth to the inch. Some builders prefer a coarser ripsaw, with about 6 teeth to the inch, although most ripping is done with power equipment. For finish work, a backsaw about a foot long with 12 to 14 teeth to the inch is needed. A pistol-grip adjustable hacksaw with various 12-inch blades is useful. An adjustable handle makes it possible to use in awkward locations. More common is a coping saw with its handle in line with the blade.

A saw can be sharpened using a set of small files and a clamp with jaws long enough to hold the full length of the saw. Nevertheless, saws should be sharpened professionally from time to time.

Some screwdrivers are needed: a short, stubby one, for tight places; a small one, about 9 inches long with a $\frac{3}{16}$-inch-wide blade; a heavy one, about a foot long with a $\frac{3}{8}$-inch-wide blade; and, maybe, a pump screwdriver about 14 inches long with a variety of bits. Also needed are some standard pliers, needlenose pliers, and a wire cutter.

Drilling normally is done with power equipment, so the traditional brace and bit is not considered cost or time effective.

A jack plane is a necessity. Jack planes are mostly steel bodied, but occasionally wood-bodied ones can be found. Wood-bodied planes are lighter, but steel planes are easier to set and adjust. They should be about 10 inches long, with a blade about $2\frac{5}{8}$ inches wide. Smaller block and smoothing planes are useful. Planes with long beds of 20 inches or more speed the shaping of long surfaces such as keels. A small block plane 6 inches long, with a blade $1\frac{1}{2}$ inches wide, works well on bevels and interior joinery. Construction plans may call for concave or convex surfaces; if so, a compass plane is useful. A spokeshave is used for tighter radiuses.

Chisels are needed, although to a lesser degree than in traditional plank-on-frame construction. They are used for notching in the preliminary phase of some fairing processes and for shaping some members in interior joinery. The most important criteria for selecting chisels are that the handles remain intact and that the cutting edges hold sharp edges. Many chisels available today cannot hold an edge. A ½-inch and a 1-inch chisel are needed, and, perhaps, a ¼-inch and a ⅜-inch one as well.

Builders earning a living from boatbuilding tend to sharpen tools often. A sign of a novice is persistent work with dull tools. Life is much easier when the oil stone is used often. Artificial stones of about 2 by 8 inches are available. These must be provided with a closely fitting wooden box to protect them from breaking. Place a new stone in oil for a day or so before using it. Wedge some wood shims between the box and stone to prevent the stone from moving during use. A medium to coarse surface is needed to remove the first stage of dullness, and a fine surface to develop the final cutting edge. Some builders say to use a double-faced stone, coarse on one side and fine on the other. Other builders insist that this is a bad practice and that two stones are required because the oil runs off when a double-faced stone is turned over. In any case, the surface must be lubricated with oil and must be level and at a convenient working height.

To achieve the proper edge, the tool must be held at the correct angle to the stone. A sharpening gauge, either purchased or handmade, helps determine the correct angle. Most tools show about a 25-degree angle at the cutting edge. When the edge is finished, remove any metal at the outer edges of the blade that might cause ridges in the work. Also, turn the blade over and gently remove any burrs from the back of the edge, using the stone.

Eventually, a tool will reach the point where grinding is necessary to restore its shape. You'll need to buy (or borrow) a modern grinding wheel. Tools must be kept cool during grinding by repeatedly immersing them in water to prevent loss of temper. If temper is lost, the tools won't hold an edge. Always wear goggles when working at the grinding wheel.

A framing square about 16 by 24 inches and a 12-inch adjustable combination square are needed. A large square is sometimes fabricated from lumber and plywood to aid lofting. An 8-inch bevel gauge is handy for transferring bevel angles from lofting to the work and from part to part. Other hand tools needed include a spirit level about 24 inches to 30 inches long, a marking gauge, a protractor, a hand-held stapler, and an awl or ice pick.

Measuring devices include non-stretching tape measures of steel or fiberglass—one long enough to reach over the length of the boat, and a smaller one, about 10 feet long. Some builders like to use a 3-foot-long wooden folding rule. During lofting and construction, measuring sticks and straightedges are made from lumber as needed.

Lots and lots of clamps are needed. Bar clamps are the most useful because of their quick action, which helps prevent "twister's wrist" when many clamps are needed. Bar clamps are made up to 72 inches long. There are applications, however, for C-clamps and spring clamps.

Suppliers of epoxy products offer resin pumps, which ensure the proper proportioning of resin and hardeners, in several versions.

PORTABLE POWER TOOLS

The most useful portable power tool is a drill motor. It would be a horrendous task to drill the numerous holes required for fastenings, plugs, and dowels with a brace and bit. Some builders feel that the popular ¼-inch drill motor is a bit lightweight for boatbuilding and prefer the ⁵⁄₁₆- or ⅜-inch size. These turn about 2,000 rpm. If there are large-bore and long holes to be drilled, a ½-inch drill motor that turns about 400 rpm can be used. You'll need a selection of spade bits, as well as standard bits.

The next most important tool is an electric sabersaw. Good quality is important in a sabersaw because it gets a lot of use cutting out templates, frames, and bulkheads. Some can be set to various speeds to suit different materials and have a guard to prevent the blade from messing up plywood edges. Others have oil attachments for use in cutting metals.

A hand-held electric circular saw with a 7-inch tungsten carbide-tipped blade will rip planking and cut abrasive hardwoods. A finer-toothed blade is used for crosscutting. A small, lightweight saw with a 4¼ inch-diameter blade is useful for making accurate cuts in plywood up to ⅜ inch thick.

If an air compressor is available, a little 2-inch-diameter air-powered saw is useful for cutting ⅛-inch-thick veneers (and for a planking process that will be described later).

On larger projects, a hand-held electric plane saves a great deal of time. These are the adzes of our day. For removing a large volume of wood from a keel or sheer clamp, a power plane with an 18-inch bed is useful. It can speed the process of forming scarfs in plywood but must be selected carefully. Some are tiring to use and others throw chips in your face.

A power sander is the next choice. The best ones turn about 3,000 rpm and use a foam disc to which sandpaper is applied with a special

HAND TOOLS

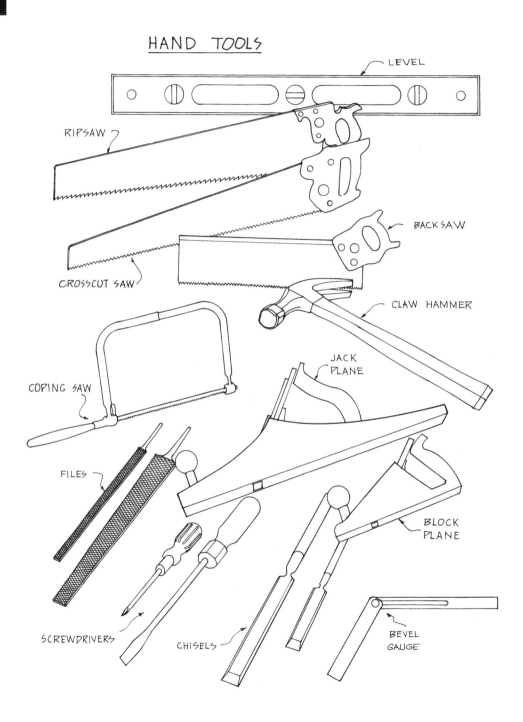

LEVEL

RIPSAW

BACK SAW

CROSSCUT SAW

CLAW HAMMER

JACK PLANE

COPING SAW

FILES

BLOCK PLANE

SCREWDRIVERS

CHISELS

BEVEL GAUGE

POWER TOOLS

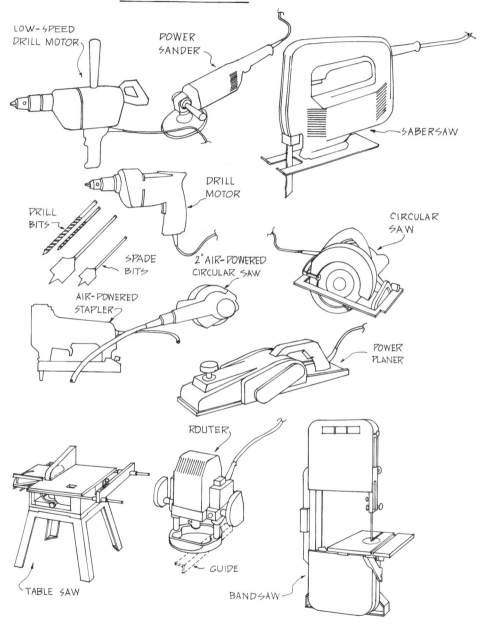

LOW-SPEED DRILL MOTOR

POWER SANDER

SABERSAW

DRILL MOTOR

DRILL BITS

SPADE BITS

2" AIR-POWERED CIRCULAR SAW

CIRCULAR SAW

AIR-POWERED STAPLER

POWER PLANER

ROUTER

GUIDE

TABLE SAW

BANDSAW

adhesive. These will be used in sanding the hull, among other things. Air-powered sanders with 4-inch foam disc pads are available for finish sanding. Circular sanders are recommended over belt sanders for boatbuilding.

A hand-held router with a variety of cutters is used for grooving, shaping, cutting dadoes, and rounding edges. It can cut a window recess, plough a rabbet, or cut a notch. Routers turn at about 20,000 rpm; exercise caution to protect against objects zinging about. It is usually best to bolt a guide to the work; the router moves along it when shaping the wood. A small model with fly-cutting knives and a ball-bearing guide can be used to trim edges of veneer and plywood.

STATIONARY POWER TOOLS

Most builders agree that a table saw is the one indispensable stationary power tool. A radial-arm saw is not considered as good a choice for boatbuilding. A few builders prefer a hand-held circular saw; however, only the table saw cuts rough lumber to exact specifications, tapers, bevels, provides a straightedge, and can be used as a shaper with special attachments. With a sliding miter gauge, it can work as a cut-off saw. Look for a 10-inch tilting arbor saw (or a 14-inch saw for a large project) with an easily adjustable rip fence.

After a table saw, some boatbuilders feel that a bandsaw is the most important tool for a boat shop. Others consider it unnecessary, preferring an electric saber saw. For cutting curves and bevels, a bandsaw is the most accurate tool available. The reach, or swallow (the horizontal dimension from the supporting post for the upper wheel to the saw blade), determines the size of material a bandsaw can handle. For smaller projects, 18 inches is enough. For larger ones, 2 feet or more may be necessary. Modern bandsaw blades are usually of the "disposable" variety, so it is best to have several on hand. Thick timber requires a broad blade; tighter curves a thin blade.

More mechanized shops under large projects will add a drill press, a joiner, and maybe a grinder.

Consider buying or leasing an air compressor to operate such tools as staplers and tackers, sanders, saws, files, and nailers. It can save time in the stapling operation, as well as prevent "stapler's wrist." Staple guns are available that can shoot anything from ¼-inch wire staples all the way up to wide-crown staples over 1½ inches long. Quality air tools are often less expensive and more durable than their electric counterparts.

CHAPTER 3

Work Space

B oat fantasy images of curvaceous framework rising on faraway beaches won't do for laminated wood boat construction. Shelter is required for the tiniest dinghy or the largest ocean traveler for protection from rain, dust, wind, and cold. Shelter is also needed to protect supplies and building materials, particularly wood used in the lamination process, from the elements. Any structural wood must be maintained at low moisture levels.

Professional builders have fabrication shops, storage buildings, and yards organized for the products they build. An individual boatbuilding project must be organized on a smaller scale. It is not necessary that all functions be in the same space. For example, lumber could be stored in one space and fluids in another, with fabrication space nearby. Minor fabrication projects could be undertaken in separate locations.

There is no advantage to being on or near a waterway. Provided there's adequate access, the completed boat can be loaded onto a trailer and moved easily to a distant launching site. There might even be a disadvantage to a waterfront location: most are higher-priced real estate.

For the individual builder, a work space at home is the best of all possible worlds. Tiny craft can be built in the basement or garage. Assuming there is enough land around the house, a temporary free-standing work space might be constructed in a side yard or rear yard. If there is already a workshop, a temporary fabrication shelter can be

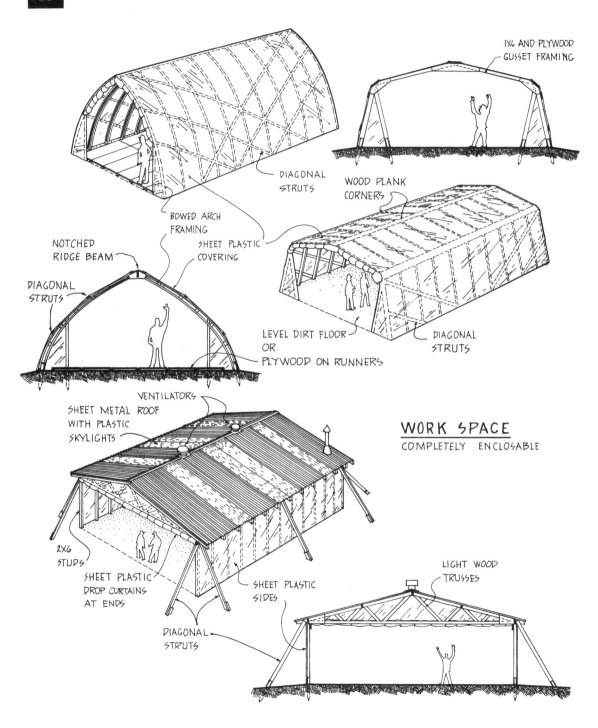

1X6 AND PLYWOOD
GUSSET FRAMING

DIAGONAL
STRUTS

BOWED ARCH
FRAMING

NOTCHED
RIDGE BEAM

SHEET PLASTIC
COVERING

DIAGONAL
STRUTS

WOOD PLANK
CORNERS

LEVEL DIRT FLOOR
OR
PLYWOOD ON RUNNERS

DIAGONAL
STRUTS

VENTILATORS

SHEET METAL ROOF
WITH PLASTIC
SKYLIGHTS

WORK SPACE
COMPLETELY ENCLOSABLE

2X6
STUDS

SHEET PLASTIC
DROP CURTAINS
AT ENDS

SHEET PLASTIC
SIDES

LIGHT WOOD
TRUSSES

DIAGONAL
STRUTS

constructed alongside. Neighbor and zoning objections are sometimes overcome if the temporary shelter is attached to a permanent one, with the understanding that it will not become permanent. Temporary shelters constructed on dirt must have level sites, with surrounding terrain ditched or sloped to conduct water away.

Builders in rural areas with acreage have a better chance of building a temporary shelter or converting a barn or some other outbuilding without causing a disturbance. City dwellers living in apartments have to lease shop space, or, better, lease some industrial or rural land for a construction site.

The building site requires electric service or a generator. Temporary service at construction sites is called "saw service" in most cities and towns in the United States. Twenty- to 30-amp service is required for most projects, more if extensive lighting or stationary power tools are used. Use heavy-duty extension cords to avoid voltage drop. Generator leads should be long enough to reduce noise without starving tools. Shop wiring, along with extension cords and the tools themselves, should be double-grounded. Natural gas is nice for heating where available, but any heat other than electric will have to be vented safely. Water should be available for cleaning and cooling purposes (to say nothing of drinking). It can be hauled in and stored, if necessary. A portable toilet is also needed.

The floor area of the temporary fabrication shelter should be about three times the nominal area of the boat. If the boat is 30 feet long by 8 feet wide, then the nominal area of the boat is 240 square feet; the shelter should be about 720 square feet. This allows for some storage to be included. For boats 30 feet long or shorter, there should be a minimum of 4 feet of clearance on one side and one end, with more on the other side and end. The overall dimensions (including height) of the work space cannot interfere with the turning over or removal of the hull. For our 30-footer, 18 feet by 40 feet of work space is about right.

The workbench, built of lumber, should be from 6 feet to 8 feet long and from 30 inches to 36 inches high (depending on the builder's height), and 30 inches to 40 inches from front to back. It is made stable with cross-bracing or splayed legs made of 2 x 4s. It should have a vise at its left end (for right-handed people) and some means of support at the other end for stock. Cheek pieces of wood inside the steel jaws of the vise protect stock as it is being worked. Shelves and bins for storage of tools and bench stock should be handy. The table saw should be positioned so that long material can be run through it without hitting anything. This

WORK SPACE

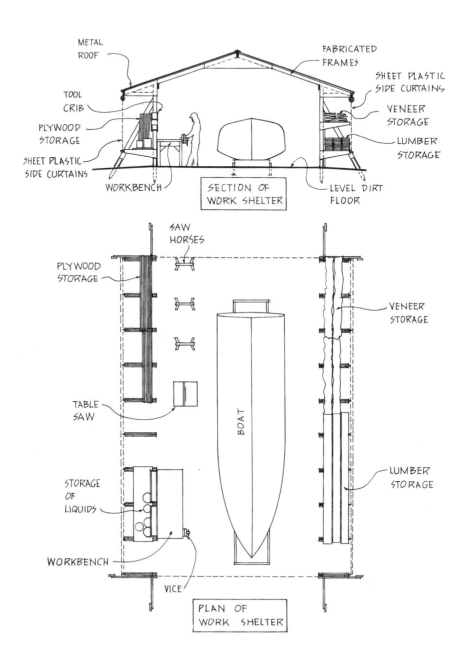

METAL ROOF

FABRICATED FRAMES

SHEET PLASTIC SIDE CURTAINS

TOOL CRIB

VENEER STORAGE

PLYWOOD STORAGE

LUMBER STORAGE

SHEET PLASTIC SIDE CURTAINS

WORKBENCH

SECTION OF WORK SHELTER

LEVEL DIRT FLOOR

SAW HORSES

PLYWOOD STORAGE

VENEER STORAGE

TABLE SAW

BOAT

STORAGE OF LIQUIDS

LUMBER STORAGE

WORKBENCH

VICE

PLAN OF WORK SHELTER

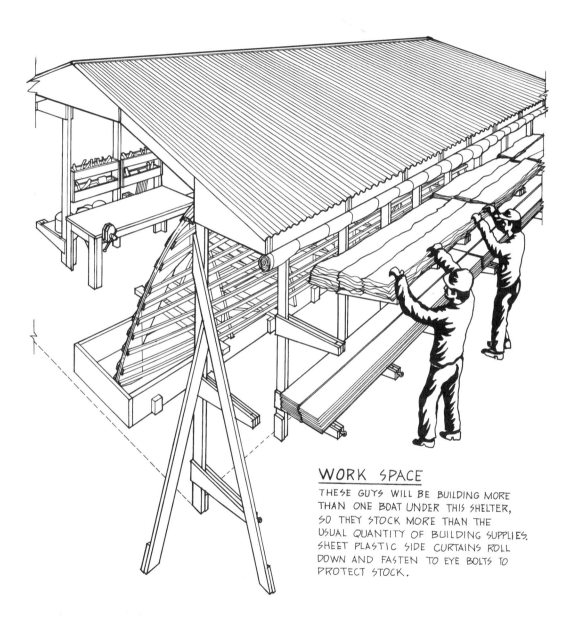

WORK SPACE

THESE GUYS WILL BE BUILDING MORE
THAN ONE BOAT UNDER THIS SHELTER,
SO THEY STOCK MORE THAN THE
USUAL QUANTITY OF BUILDING SUPPLIES.
SHEET PLASTIC SIDE CURTAINS ROLL
DOWN AND FASTEN TO EYE BOLTS TO
PROTECT STOCK.

usually means the lumber is fed into the saw along one side of the boat and emerges out the other side through openings at the end of the building. Several sawhorses are needed to position the lumber in line with the table saw.

Lumber and plywood stored in the shop should be isolated from the ground or floor with sheet plastic and 1 x 2s. Building materials may also be stored overhead.

For the structure of the shelter itself, the easiest way to go is to erect a series of frames about 4 feet apart that support a polyethylene covering. The frames are bolted to wood stakes about 4 feet long that have been driven into the ground at the angle of the lower leg of the frame. The frames can be gambrel- or barn-shaped, bowed, arched, or any shape that is easily fabricated. All frames must be braced diagonally, either within the structure or at the ends, to keep the whole thing from slumping over. Usually, 1 x 4s are used, but 1 x 6s are sometimes needed for longer spans. This lumber is joined by plywood gussets. Arches can be fabricated quickly from pairs of 1 x 4s with 2 x 4 spacers between them, formed around a mold on the ground.

The plastic covering is usually 6 mm polyethylene, available in large black or translucent sheets. Regular polyethylene can be expected to last about a year. For greater longevity, laminated material consisting of two layers of polyethylene around a layer of nylon mesh with about a ½-inch grid is available. This material lasts about two years. Sheeting is applied to the entire structure (except for the ends) as a unit. An inner liner of polyethylene increases the insulation value of the walls and ceiling.

CHAPTER 4

Lofting

The lofting is the full-size representation of the lines drawing of the hull. The lines represent the hull's various curves in such a way that they can be used to manufacture hull components. If the hull were shaped like a bread box, it would be a simple matter to indicate its dimensions by length, width, and height measurements. With the hull's complex curves (particularly with round-bilge craft), a method must be devised to pin down the multitudinous dimensions that determine its shape. This is done by taking imaginary slices through the hull in various directions and dividing these slices into parts that can be dimensioned.

If the hull were a loaf of bread of which you made a lines drawing, normal slices of bread would be called *stations.* These slices of bread are spaced along the loaf in an even and regular manner to describe its shape. But more information is needed to pin down their dimensions. If slices of bread were cut vertically, end to end from the loaf, the resulting oddly shaped pieces of bread would be called *butt lines* on a lines drawing. Slices can also be made horizontally through the loaf of bread, from end to end. The resulting slices, like layers in a layer cake, would be called *waterlines* on a lines drawing. On the actual hull, these would appear like bathtub rings left on the outside of the hull as it is pushed progressively deeper into the water.

There is one other set of lines, harder to visualize. If the loaf of bread

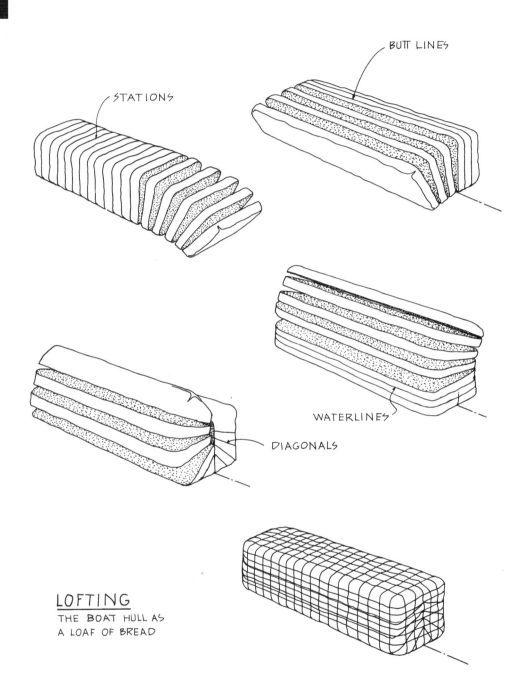

STATIONS

BUTT LINES

WATERLINES

DIAGONALS

LOFTING
THE BOAT HULL AS
A LOAF OF BREAD

were picked up and cut at an angle to the center of the loaf from end to end, the resulting slice would be called a *diagonal* on the lines drawing. These lines serve the useful function of fairing up all the other lines. So much for the culinary aspect of lofting.

No matter how curvaceous the hull, all lines will appear straight from some points of view, while they appear curved from others. The assumption is made that both sides of the hull are the same, so only one side is represented on the lines drawing. When this half-hull is observed from the top (or, better yet, from the bottom), what is seen is called the *plan view*. When looked at from the side, it is called the *profile view*. The view from the ends is usually called the *body plan*. Since that term has no specific meaning in the real world, *bow view* or *stern view* is used in this text. These end views are usually stuck together so the hull looks as if it's both coming and going at the same time.

All that is lacking in our description is a common reference to tie it all together. In a hull's profile view, a line is drawn below the keel, parallel to the waterlines on the drawing, called the *baseline*. From it, all vertical dimensions are measured. On the plan view, this line becomes the *centerline*, since it represents the middle of the hull. From it, all of the dimensions of the curved waterlines of the plan view can be taken where they cross the stationlines. On the bow-view/stern-view picture, this line appears as a dot. A vertical line is constructed on it that becomes the centerline of that view. This centerline, together with the centerlines on the plan view, describe the centerline plane—something like an imaginary partition down the exact middle of the hull. The bow view is shown on one side of the centerline and the stern view on the other.

The profile view is usually shown on the upper part of the lines drawing, with the bow-view/stern-view shown right in the middle of it. The plan view is depicted below the profile view. The diagonals are projected below the plan view, using the same centerline as the plan view.

Because of the limited space of most lofting floors, all these views are drawn on top of each other, using different colors for each set of lines. The baseline of the profile also serves as the centerline of the plan.

The distance that the various intersections of hull lines are offset from a reference line is called an *offset* and is placed in a separate table on the lines-drawing page. This is to prevent the lines drawing itself from looking as if it were crawling with bugs. The offsets are given in feet, inches, and eighths of inches; "1-2-3," for example, means 1 foot, 2⅜ inches. Hopefully, the metric system will soon become universal, thereby simplifying this archaic system of measurement.

PREPARATION FOR LOFTING

The lines and table of offsets contain all the information necessary to loft the hull shape full size. Now you need a flat place large enough to draw it. A level concrete or wooden floor needs only a suitable covering to become a drawing surface. A dirt floor is fine if it is leveled and covered with a grid of lumber topped with 4- by 8-foot sheets of plywood painted white. Before building the foundation for the mold, take the lofting up off the floor so that it is handy for reference without being hidden underneath the evolving hull. Plywood used for lofting can be used in the final stages of construction after the lofting is no longer needed.

Fabricate some drawing aids before beginning the lofting process. Scarf together some long, flexible battens that extend the overall length of the hull plus several feet. These are used to draw the waterline curves. Since a smooth curve without hard spots is needed, make the scarf joint a little longer than usual; a 12-to-1 angle is about right. Next, make some shorter, flexible battens to loft the stationlines. These should be long enough to reach from the keel to beyond the sheerline and be flexible enough to bend around the sharpest curve of the hull. Three-quarter-inch square stock is usually used for battens, unless the boat is large, in which case 1-inch square stock is used. In addition, a dozen or so stiff measuring sticks are needed for transferring dimensions. These can be 1 x 2 stock (actual size: ¾ inch by 1½ inches). It is helpful if one side is beveled to produce a sharper edge on the measuring side. Make some sticks long enough to reach from the baseline to the top of the hull and some long enough to reach from the centerline out to the edge of the deck.

Make a straightedge that reaches from the baseline to the top of the hull. Clear-grain, 1 x 4 stock is used for straightedges up to about 16 feet in length. Dress edges with a plane to a straight line. Draw a line using the straightedge as a guide, then flip it over and place it up against the line from the opposite side. Any discrepancies will show up.

For smaller boats, use a carpenter's square for roughing out 90-degree corners. For larger boats, make a square from 1 x 4s. The long leg of the square should reach from the baseline to the highest part of the hull; the short leg is about half that length. Verify its squareness by placing the short leg along a straight line and drawing a perpendicular line along the long edge. Flip the square over and place the short leg once again on the first straight line. The long edge should match the vertical line exactly.

Construct the precise 90-degree angles needed in the lofting process

LINES AND OFFSETS

FOR GOSLING-2 A 12' SKIFF

> THERE WILL BE A PAGE IN YOUR PLANS THAT LOOKS LIKE THIS IT MUST BE CONVERTED TO A FULL SIZE 'LOFTING'

TABLE OF OFFSETS
IN FEET INCHES & EIGHTS

STATION	1	2	3	4	5	T
HEIGHTS ABOVE BASELINE						
KEEL	2 - 8 - 0	2 - 9 - 5	2 - 10 - 0	2 - 10 - 0	2 - 8 - 2	2 - 6 - 0
B - I	2 - 2 - 4	2 - 8 - 2	2 - 8 - 7	2 - 8 - 7	2 - 7 - 2	2 - 4 - 6
B - II	1 - 2 - 2	2 - 6 - 2	2 - 7 - 7	2 - 8 - 0	2 - 5 - 7	2 - 2 - 1
B - III		1 - 11 - 2	2 - 5 - 5	2 - 5 - 5	2 - 1 - 4	0 - 9 - 4
SHEER	0 - 9 - 3	1 - 0 - 4	1 - 2 - 0	1 - 2 - 0	1 - 0 - 3	0 - 9 - 4
HALFBREADTHS FROM CENTERLINE						
WL - 1	0 - 4 - 6	1 - 3 - 0	1 - 7 - 7	1 - 7 - 3	1 - 3 - 5	0 - 9 - 0
WL - 2	0 - 8 - 5	1 - 6 - 5	1 - 11 - 2	1 - 11 - 3	1 - 8 - 0	1 - 2 - 4
WL - 3	0 - 11 - 5	1 - 8 - 6	2 - 1 - 1	2 - 1 - 0	1 - 10 - 0	1 - 4 - 5
SHEER	1 - 1 - 5	1 - 9 - 6	2 - 1 - 4	2 - 1 - 4	1 - 10 - 6	1 - 6 - 0
DIAGONALS						
D - 1	0 - 3 - 3	0 - 6 - 2	0 - 7 - 2	0 - 7 - 0	0 - 4 - 7	0 - 2 - 7
D - 2	0 - 7 - 5	1 - 1 - 5		1 - 3 - 3	1 - 1 - 0	0 - 10 - 0
D - 3	0 - 10 - 6	1 - 7 - 0	1 - 10 - 6	1 - 10 - 6	1 - 8 - 1	1 - 4 - 2

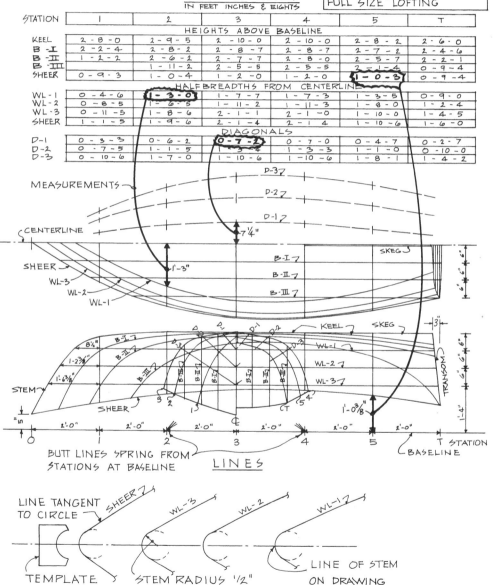

MEASUREMENTS

D-3 D-2 D-1

CENTERLINE

7¼"

SHEER WL-3 WL-2 WL-1

1'-3"

B-I B-II B-III

SKEG

6" 6"

STEM

8½" 1-2⅜" 1-6⅜"

B-I B-II B-III

SHEER

KEEL SKEG 3"

WL-1 WL-2 WL-3

TRANSOM

6" 6" 6" 1'-4"

1'-0⅜"

BUTT LINES SPRING FROM STATIONS AT BASELINE

LINES

2'-0" 2'-0" 2'-0" 2'-0" 1'-0" 2'-0"

0 1 2 3 4 5 T STATION

BASELINE

LINE TANGENT TO CIRCLE

SHEER WL-3 WL-2 WL-1

TEMPLATE STEM RADIUS ½" LINE OF STEM ON DRAWING

LOFTING

DRAWING AIDS

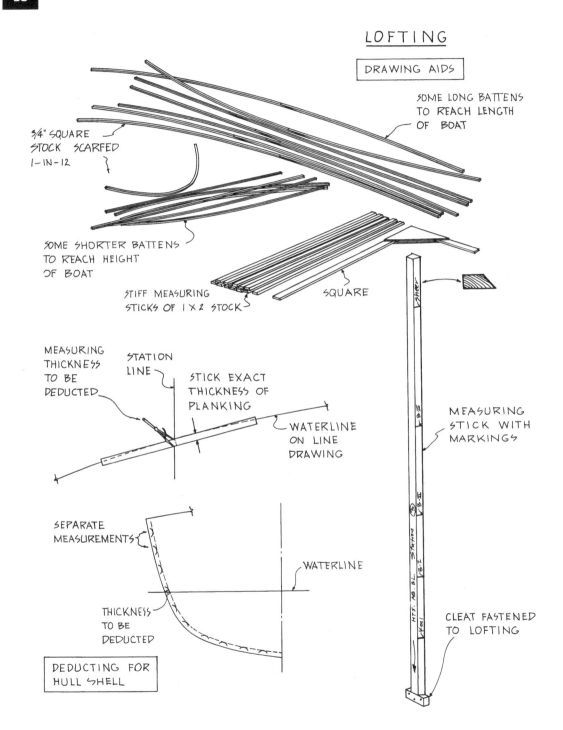

SOME LONG BATTENS TO REACH LENGTH OF BOAT

3/4" SQUARE STOCK SCARFED 1–IN–12

SOME SHORTER BATTENS TO REACH HEIGHT OF BOAT

STIFF MEASURING STICKS OF 1 X 2 STOCK

SQUARE

MEASURING THICKNESS TO BE DEDUCTED

STATION LINE

STICK EXACT THICKNESS OF PLANKING

WATERLINE ON LINE DRAWING

MEASURING STICK WITH MARKINGS

SEPARATE MEASUREMENTS

WATERLINE

THICKNESS TO BE DEDUCTED

DEDUCTING FOR HULL SHELL

CLEAT FASTENED TO LOFTING

by using a bar compass. These can be purchased at drafting supply businesses, or they can be made from slotted wood, wing nuts, and washers. To construct a line at 90 degrees to a given dot on a line, place the point of the compass on that dot. Draw two short arcs on the given line, to the right and to the left of the dot. Next, extend the compass to a larger radius, and draw two intersecting arcs above the line, using as radius points the two dots where the small arcs intersect the line. The intersection of these last two arcs will define a dot directly over the first dot. When these two dots are connected using a straightedge, a 90-degree angle will result.

Alternatively, a measurement of 3 feet can be laid out on a line to one side of the dot to define a second dot. Swing an arc 4 feet above the line using the first dot as a radius point. Next, swing a 5-foot arc above the line using the second dot as a radius point. Where the two arcs intersect, a third dot will be defined directly above the first one. When the first and third dots are connected using a straightedge, a 90-degree intersection will result.

Some means are required to hold the battens temporarily in the desired curve for drawing a line on the plywood. Some #6 nails will do the job, but if holes in the plywood are to be avoided, you'll need some kind of weights. Lead pigs, such as those used to hold a spline in drafting the lines, can be used to hold the batten. Any kind of weight that will hold the batten will do, as long as it doesn't scratch the lofting.

A supply of ballpoint pens in various colors of waterproof ink is useful in marking permanent lines. Key each color to a letter; for example, red is color "A," blue is color "B," green is color "C," and so on. Red ink could be used for sheerlines, butt lines, and the profile; blue ink for plan sheer and waterlines, green for diagonals, and so forth. Felt-tip marker pens can be used for labels. Use hard-lead pencils to draw the initial curves because these lines often need revision during the lofting process.

THE LOFTING PROCESS

Step One: Straight Lines

Draw all of the straight lines of the lofting first. A carpenter's chalkline would seem ideal for this, but this method simply is not accurate enough.

Tightly stretch a string or wire across the floor where the baseline is to go, fixing each end with a wood screw or nail. The available floor space should be long enough to permit centering of the lofting with about equal

LOFTING RIGHT ANGLES

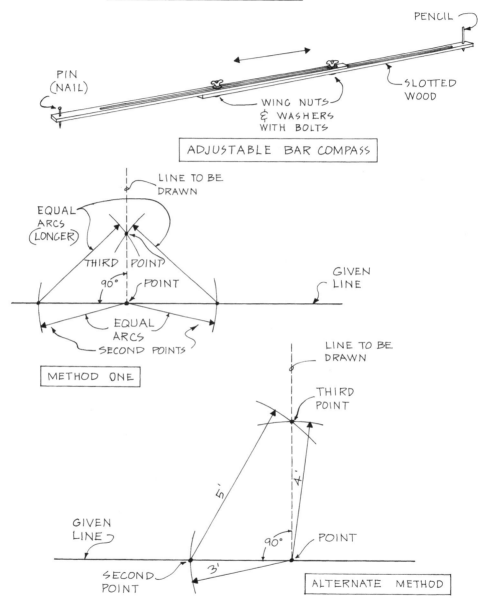

PENCIL

PIN
(NAIL)

SLOTTED
WOOD

WING NUTS
& WASHERS
WITH BOLTS

ADJUSTABLE BAR COMPASS

LINE TO BE
DRAWN

EQUAL
ARCS
(LONGER)

THIRD POINT

90° POINT

GIVEN
LINE

EQUAL
ARCS

SECOND POINTS

METHOD ONE

LINE TO BE
DRAWN

THIRD
POINT

5'

4'

GIVEN
LINE

90° POINT

3'

SECOND
POINT

ALTERNATE METHOD

LOFTING
12' SKIFF GOSLING-2

FOR BOATS TO BE BUILT UPSIDE DOWN
THE BASELINE IS USUALLY SHOWN OVER
THE HULL. IT IS ALSO THE CENTERLINE
OF THE PLAN VIEW. (BLACK)

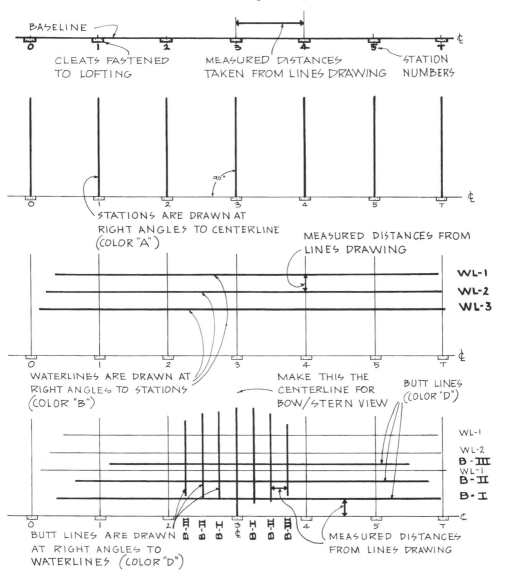

BASELINE

CLEATS FASTENED
TO LOFTING

MEASURED DISTANCES
TAKEN FROM LINES DRAWING

STATION
NUMBERS

90°

STATIONS ARE DRAWN AT
RIGHT ANGLES TO CENTERLINE
(COLOR "A")

MEASURED DISTANCES FROM
LINES DRAWING

WL-1
WL-2
WL-3

WATERLINES ARE DRAWN AT
RIGHT ANGLES TO STATIONS
(COLOR "B")

MAKE THIS THE
CENTERLINE FOR
BOW/STERN VIEW

BUTT LINES
(COLOR "D")

WL-1
WL-2
B-III
WL-1
B-II
B-I

BUTT LINES ARE DRAWN
AT RIGHT ANGLES TO
WATERLINES (COLOR "D")

MEASURED DISTANCES
FROM LINES DRAWING

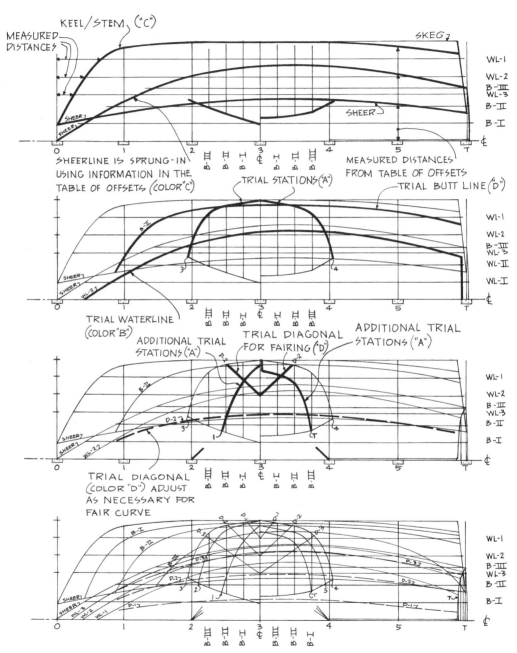

KEEL/STEM ("C")

MEASURED DISTANCES

SKEG

WL-1
WL-2
B-III
WL-3
B-II
B-I
℄

SHEERLINE IS SPRUNG-IN USING INFORMATION IN THE TABLE OF OFFSETS (COLOR "C")

SHEER

MEASURED DISTANCES FROM TABLE OF OFFSETS

TRIAL BUTT LINE ("D")

TRIAL STATIONS ("A")

WL-1
WL-2
B-III
WL-3
WL-II
WL-I
℄

TRIAL WATERLINE (COLOR "B")

TRIAL DIAGONAL FOR FAIRING ("D")

ADDITIONAL TRIAL STATIONS ("A")

ADDITIONAL TRIAL STATIONS ("A")

WL-1
WL-2
B-III
WL-3
B-II
B-I
℄

TRIAL DIAGONAL (COLOR "D") ADJUST AS NECESSARY FOR FAIR CURVE

WL-1
WL-2
B-III
WL-3
B-II
B-I
℄

COMPLETED LOFTING DRAWN FULL SIZE

spaces clear at each end, and wide enough to accommodate the profile, half breadth, and diagonals, all drawn full size. Draw dash marks on the floor directly under the wire, taking pains not to deflect it. Remove the wire and connect the dashes, using black ink and a long straightedge. This line will be the primary reference line of the lofting, being both the baseline of the profile and the centerline of the plan view.

Mark the points where the stationlines run on the baseline, using the dimensions shown on the lines drawing. Use a steel tape the entire length of the boat to prevent compounding errors, and precisely mark a point where each stationline is to be located. Be careful: Any error here will cause all the lines to be off.

Incidentally, it will speed things along in later stages of lofting if a cleat (say, a 6-inch piece of 1 x 2) is fixed with one edge against the baseline at each station. This allows a measuring stick to be butted against it so that the bottom of the stick is exactly against the baseline/centerline.

Erect lines at 90 degrees to the baseline at each of these points, and label them with their individual station numbers (0, 1, 2, 3, etc.); use color "A." Draw the waterlines of the profile view by measuring up each stationline and marking a precise point for each waterline as shown on the lines drawing. The corresponding points are connected, using the straightedge and ink color "B." These lines will be marked at each end with WL-1, WL-2, etc., as indicated on the lines drawing.

The central stationline of the profile view serves as the centerline of the bow-view/stern-view picture. Butt lines will appear as vertical lines in this view. They will be parallel to the centerline, and their spacing is given on the lines drawing. Use this spacing to measure out at 90 degrees on either side of the centerline to establish a series of points. Draw a vertical line through each point and label them B-I, B-II, etc. to match the notations on the lines drawing. Use color "C." Use the same interval dimensions and measure out from the plan centerline on each stationline to locate rows of points. Connect these with the help of a straightedge to form the butt lines in the plan view. Label these B-I, B-II, etc.; use color "C."

Most of the straight lines have been drawn in ink and coded with color. The whole thing should look like a road map for a town in Kansas.

Step Two: Adding Curved Lines

The first curved line drawn is the profile sheerline. The points used to draw this line can be found at each station by looking at the table of offsets for "heights from baseline." One row will say "sheer." Beside it are the heights at various stations. It might read, for example, at an imaginary station #2: 6-5-4. This means the point where the sheerline crosses station #2 is 6 feet 5⅛ (that is 5½) inches above the baseline. After plotting all of the points on the lofting, weight down or fix the long flexible batten along these points and draw a line along it in color "C." To achieve a fair curve, move the batten ever so slightly if any point seems out of line.

Plot the keel, stem, and transom profiles by transferring dimensions from the lines drawing by using the offset dimensions. Use color "C" to connect the points and complete the profile outline on the lofting.

Draw the plan sheerline next. The offsets for it are given under "half-breadths from centerline." One row will say "sheer"; beside it is a row of half-breadths, one for each stationline. At station #6 it may read 7-6-5. That means that the point where the sheerline crosses station #6 is 7 feet, 6⅝ inches from the centerline. When the points are located at each station, use the flexible batten and color "C" to draw a fair curve around them.

Next, plot the sheerline on the bow-view/stern-view picture. Use a measuring stick long enough to reach over the boat's half-beam to pick up the measurements at each station from the plan sheer just drawn. It's less confusing to use one stick for the forward half of the boat and another for the after part. Let's start with a hypothetical station #2. Put the base of the measuring stick at the centerline with the beveled edge of the stick up against the stationline. Place a mark exactly where the sheerline meets it. Label that spot #2. Pick up all the other sheerline crossings and label them #4, #5, etc. Label the stick *plan sheer forward* or *aft*, as the case may be. Place an arrow to indicate the end of the stick that was against the centerline.

Prepare a similar set of marked sticks to get the height of the sheer above the baseline at the various stations. Transfer these heights to the centerline of the bow-view/stern-view picture, and label them #1, #2, #3, etc. Use the square you made earlier and a pencil to draw a light line at 90 degrees to each of these points, far enough out to catch the sheer. Use the half-breadth sticks to transfer the corresponding dimension at each light pencil line. Verify the heights of these points, using the height sticks. When connected, these points show the sheerline as seen in the bow-view/stern-view picture. Use color "C" to connect them. These are the last lines to be inked at this point. The others will be drawn temporarily in pencil until they can be faired fully.

Using a pencil, run in a few waterlines on the plan view taking half-breadths from the offset table. Then draw a butt line on the profile, using the heights-from-baseline offsets.

Now there is enough information to mark a couple of points on a stationline in the bow-view/stern-view picture. Select the last station in the bow view and the first station in the stern view as trial points. These points will be the half-breadths for the two waterlines just drawn and can be transferred with measuring sticks. The balance of the half-breadths for these two stations can be located using a steel tape and dimensions from the offset table. Connect these points by tracing along one of the flexible battens prepared for the purpose. Check to see how fair the line is. If a dot or two is out of line, adjust the curve ever so slightly to create a fair curve.

It should be noted that where there is a choice, dimensions should be transferred from the other parts of the lofting rather than from the table of offsets. This is because the lofting is full size and will be more accurate than the small-scale lines drawing. Every change in a curve on the lofting will precipitate an adjustment in the other lines.

This is the time to check the agreement among the curves drawn so far. The points where the butt line intersects the two waterlines in the plan view may be projected straight up to see where they intersect those two waterlines in the profile view. The point where the butt line intersects the sheerline in the plan view can be projected straight up to see if it agrees with where the butt line intersects the sheerline in the profile view. If these agree, then they can be projected straight across to see if they agree with where these events take place in the bow-view/stern-view picture. This is where the square you constructed earlier comes in handy. Do this at several sites around the lofting. If one line has to be adjusted to be fair, adjust the others to agree.

When all is in agreement, start weaving a basket of lines, using dimensions already generated on the lofting when possible. Use the offsets only when needed. Perhaps a few more waterlines will be drawn, followed by a few more stations in the bow-view/stern-view picture. After each fresh batch of lines has been completed, check up and down, as well as back and forth, to make sure that all line intersections are in agreement. The further the lofting progresses, the better the odds of agreement.

At some point you'll have enough stations completed to start testing your drawing with diagonals. Diagonals are the final device used to fair-up the other lines. Measure these out on the diagonal from the centerline to the stationline on the bow-view/stern-view picture. If you have enough room on the lofting floor, plot these lines below the baseline. If there isn't enough room, they must be placed up with the other lines, perhaps drawn with long dash lines to distinguish them. Transfer the missing dimensions from the table of offsets and try to fair these points. Chances are they won't fair. Don't despair. Any adjustments anywhere will prevent the points from being fair. This is the acid test of lofting.

Draw the final stations on the bow-view/stern-view picture. Transfer the diagonal measurements from these stations to the diagonal plot on the lofting. The points will probably be much closer to a fair curve than the previous ones were. If the lines were faired periodically as the lofting progressed, these dots might even be right on target. If they're still off, then adjust the diagonals ever so slightly to create a fair curve, and make all the other lines agree. Draw any lines not yet completed.

The stem is usually not a knife edge but rounded, and its radius is shown someplace on the lines or construction plan. Simply draw a circle of that radius so that the forward edge of the circle lies on the stem line of the plan view. If the radius is different for different places on the stem, draw circles of the various sizes at their corresponding locations along the stem in plan view. The waterlines in plan view are faired in tangentially at each of these circles.

The transom may be flat and vertical or flat and sloped; curved and vertical or vertical and sloped. It may slope forward or aft. This will be clearly evident from the lines drawing. Flat transoms are easy to deal with. They are simply hinged out at 90 degrees to their centerline and drawn on the lofting, using information already available. The drawing will represent the transom's actual shape and can be used in making templates for the transom framing.

Curved transoms must be rolled out flat, like so much dough with a rolling pin. This is called *development,* and the resulting picture is called an *expanded transom.* Project the profile centerline of the transom up enough for the subsequent construction lines to be clear of the other lines of the lofting. Construct a new plan centerline at 90 degrees to this extended profile centerline. Lay out butt lines B-I, B-II, etc., parallel to the new plan centerline at the intervals given on the lines drawing. Swing the transom radius as indicated on the lines drawing using a long batten pinned to the new plan centerline at the radius point. This arc intersects all the butt lines just drawn. A plan sheerline is then drawn on this new plan view. Extend diagonals from the profile stationlines where they meet

LOFTING

FLATTENING OUT A RAKED AND CURVED TRANSOM

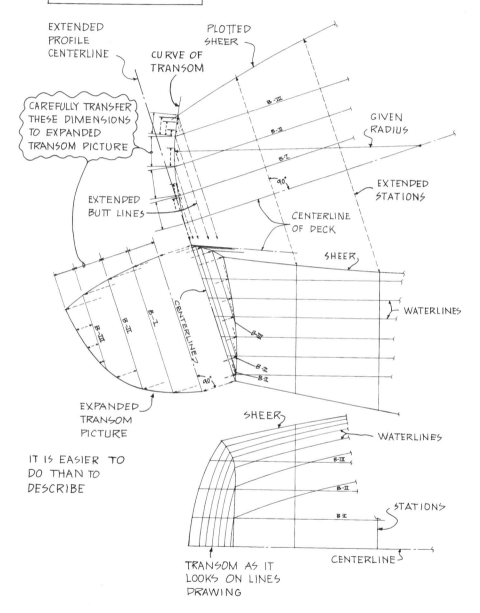

EXTENDED PROFILE CENTERLINE

PLOTTED SHEER

CURVE OF TRANSOM

CAREFULLY TRANSFER THESE DIMENSIONS TO EXPANDED TRANSOM PICTURE

B-III

B-II

B-I

90°

GIVEN RADIUS

EXTENDED STATIONS

EXTENDED BUTT LINES

CENTERLINE OF DECK

SHEER

WATERLINES

B-III

B-II

B-I

CENTERLINE

90°

EXPANDED TRANSOM PICTURE

IT IS EASIER TO DO THAN TO DESCRIBE

SHEER

WATERLINES

B-III

B-II

B-I

STATIONS

CENTERLINE

TRANSOM AS IT LOOKS ON LINES DRAWING

the profile sheerline, parallel to the extended transom centerline. Extend these far enough to catch the new sheerline to be plotted. Lay off the half-breadths for just the last couple of stations from the plan view to the new plan view, and draw in the new deck edge. Extend the line across the transom curve. This new picture gives a canted view of the after portion of the hull. It also gives an accurate representation of the transom curve.

It is necessary to draw the centerline of the deck on the profile view. This can be done using deck camber information given on the construction plan. The deck centerline crosses the extended profile centerline to define the top of the transom at the center of the hull.

Extend lines from each butt line intersection with the transom arc parallel to the extended profile centerline, so that they intersect the butt lines in the profile view. This defines the edge of the transom in the profile view. From the points just found, erect lines at 90 degrees to the transom profile centerline. Across these lines draw a line parallel to the transom profile centerline to serve as a centerline for the expanded transom picture.

Go back to the transom arc and very carefully transfer the distances between the butt lines, as measured along the curve, to a measuring stick. Pick up the edge of the deck also. The butt lines will appear slightly spread out from what they were originally. Transfer these spacings to the expanded transom picture, and draw these butt lines parallel to the centerline. Where the new butt lines intersect the lines that have been extended from the butt lines on the profile, points will be generated. Fair these points together and an outline of the expanded transom appears. Project a line at 90 degrees from where the deck centerline meets the transom in profile and the camber of the top line of the transom is determined. The expanded transom picture is used to generate transom framing and assists in its installation in the shell lay-up.

When you've finished fairing the hull lofting, the remaining pencil lines can be redrawn in ink.

Hull lines are drawn to the outside of planking. Lines drawn to the inside of the planking would complicate things immeasurably in the areas of the keel, skeg, stem, and possibly others. Therefore, the thickness of the shell planking must be deducted from the lofted lines to arrive at the shapes to be fabricated for the mold and hull. This is done right on the lofting at any place where this information is needed, such as all the stations in the bow-view/stern-view picture.

Where the shell planking runs across the frames at a low angle, deduct the actual thickness of the planking. Where the shell planking runs across the frames at a higher angle, such as toward the ends of the hull, a little more than the actual thickness is deducted. This is because the planking is a little thicker when measured across at an angle than when measured straight across.

Cut a stick to the exact thickness of the planking. Place this on the lofting at the various stationlines where it will be most useful. For the topsides, for example, the plan waterlines work best. For the bottom, maybe the butt lines or diagonals will work better. Lay the stick along the chosen line at the chosen station. Mark a line across the stick that is an extension of the stationline underneath. The length of that line is equal to the amount to be deducted at that point. Transfer these dimensions to the corresponding place on the stationlines in the bow-view/stern-view picture. A series of dots emerges. When these are faired together, using a flexible batten so that a curve roughly parallel to the lofted stationline appears, the inside face of the hull shell is revealed. This information is used in preparing templates for the fabrication of mold frames, shell frames, and bulkheads. If frames and bulkheads occur on stationlines, their shapes are already shown on the lofting. If these members are not located on stationlines, it is a simple matter to locate them on the lofting. Simply draw them as a straight line on the profile and plan views at the location shown on the construction plan. Points where the line crosses the various curved lines are marked on a measuring stick and transferred to the corresponding positions on the bow-view/stern-view picture. The resulting dots are faired together, using a flexible batten, deducting the hull shell thickness as before.

One final note about measuring sticks: These are handy throughout the job to transfer dimensions from the lofting. They are, in fact, much handier than dragging a steel tape all over the lofting. Each stick bears only one set of marks. If new marks are put on it, first paint out the old marks to prevent confusion. Clearly label all marks. For example, let's say we want to pick up all the height measurements above the baseline on station #6. Place one end of the stick against the cleat at the base of stationline #6 on the profile view, and place the beveled edge of the stick against the stationline. Mark the keel location, and label it "keel." Mark and label the butt lines "B-1," "B-2," etc. Mark the sheerline and labeled it "sheer." Label the stick "Hts. above baseline #6." Draw an arrow pointing toward the end of the stick that was against the cleat. The marks should be fine and right to the point, and the labels should be bold and easily read. This process speeds the work along greatly, and the measuring sticks are available for future reference.

Lead Ballast

Most sailboats and a few powerboats carry an outside ballast casting, usually made of lead. To make ballast for the keel, heat a quantity of lead equal in volume to the ballast, and pour it into a hole in the ground exactly the shape of the finished ballast. Usually, the lead is melted in an old boiler or a bathtub propped up on steel supports. Fanned by a blower and contained by corrugated metal, the wood-fueled fires of hell roar underneath. Slip lead pigs into the vessel to add to the liquid mass, which is conducted to the form through a steel pipe. The lead tends to congeal in the pipe, blocking the flow. When more lead is needed in the form, use a propane torch or some other heat source to heat the pipe sufficiently to get things flowing. A pig or two can be placed in the form to ease the first shock of flowing metal. These will melt and become part of the mass.

As you can imagine, there is great potential for injury in this process, but there are things you can do to minimize risk. The vessel must be securely propped and braced to prevent tipping. Don't use concrete blocks to support the vessel, since they can explode. Use steel. Moisture in the vessel or form will cause popping and splattering of the molten lead. The pipe must be threaded, or otherwise securely fastened, to the vessel's drain, and it must be leakproof all the way to the mold. Fleeing a rising tide of molten lead spreading through the work area can

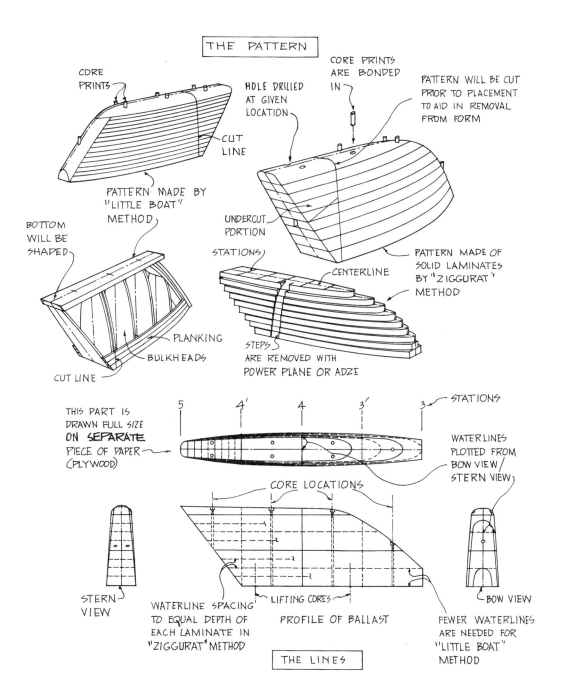

THE PATTERN

CORE PRINTS

CORE PRINTS ARE BONDED IN

HOLE DRILLED AT GIVEN LOCATION

PATTERN WILL BE CUT PRIOR TO PLACEMENT TO AID IN REMOVAL FROM FORM

CUT LINE

PATTERN MADE BY "LITTLE BOAT" METHOD

UNDERCUT PORTION

CENTERLINE

PATTERN MADE OF SOLID LAMINATES BY "ZIGGURAT" METHOD

BOTTOM WILL BE SHAPED

STATIONS

PLANKING

BULKHEADS

CUT LINE

STEPS ARE REMOVED WITH POWER PLANE OR ADZE

THIS PART IS DRAWN FULL SIZE ON SEPARATE PIECE OF PAPER (PLYWOOD)

5   4'   4   3'   3   STATIONS

WATERLINES PLOTTED FROM BOW VIEW / STERN VIEW

CORE LOCATIONS

STERN VIEW

WATERLINE SPACING TO EQUAL DEPTH OF EACH LAMINATE IN "ZIGGURAT" METHOD

LIFTING CORES

PROFILE OF BALLAST

BOW VIEW

FEWER WATERLINES ARE NEEDED FOR "LITTLE BOAT" METHOD

THE LINES

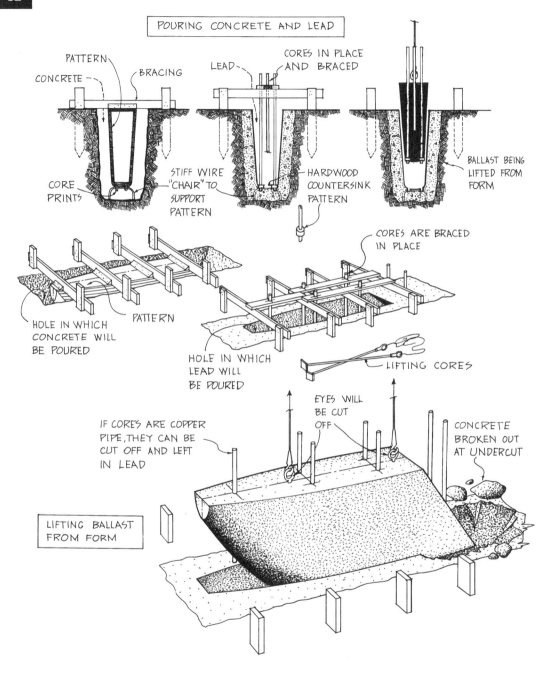

POURING CONCRETE AND LEAD

PATTERN
CONCRETE
BRACING

LEAD
CORES IN PLACE AND BRACED

CORE PRINTS

STIFF WIRE "CHAIR" TO SUPPORT PATTERN

HARDWOOD COUNTERSINK PATTERN

BALLAST BEING LIFTED FROM FORM

CORES ARE BRACED IN PLACE

HOLE IN WHICH CONCRETE WILL BE POURED

PATTERN

HOLE IN WHICH LEAD WILL BE POURED

LIFTING CORES

IF CORES ARE COPPER PIPE, THEY CAN BE CUT OFF AND LEFT IN LEAD

EYES WILL BE CUT OFF

CONCRETE BROKEN OUT AT UNDERCUT

LIFTING BALLAST FROM FORM

be hazardous to life and limb. Lead fumes are toxic. Ensure adequate ventilation, and consider wearing a fume mask.

Alternatively, the less adventurous boatbuilder can opt for the equally plausible tactic of having a foundry cast the thing. In either case, the builder must create a three-dimensional pattern from which the hole in the ground (the form) will be made. The form can be made of sand or concrete, or it can be a female form made of wood.

For a form of rammed sand or of concrete, the pattern must be strong enough to hold its shape while the ramming or pouring is going on. Concrete should be vibrated during the pour to eliminate honeycombing. Add sufficient weight to the top of the pattern to prevent its floating out of the excavation as concrete flows in.

The pattern can be made of timber that has been cut to shape and stack-laminated together to look like a ziggurat. Smooth the steps with an adze or power plane, then plane the whole shape to final contour. Alternatively, the pattern can be framed and planked like a small boat, with solid bulkhead frames covered with 1-inch (⅞-inch) planking. The covering can also be several diagonal layers of ⅛-inch or ¼-inch plywood strips, edge-glued. A female form is simply a pattern made up in reverse that will itself receive the liquid metal.

Undercut shapes require patterns that are split so they can be removed from the form in pieces. Sometimes part of the pattern will have to be cut up to get it out.

Provision must be made for the long bolts that hold the ballast to the keel. This is usually done by building bumps on the bottom of the pattern that cause indentations in the bottom of the form. These imprints will serve as centering sites for pipes or hardwood dowels that are placed in the form to displace lead in the bolt hole locations. These pipes or dowels must be braced securely across the top to prevent their floating out of the form as the lead is poured in. When sand forms are used, bumps on top of the pattern provide centering sites in the mold ceiling that stabilize the upper ends of these pipes or dowels (the cores). A couple of additional cores can be added for the attachment of lifting eyes, which aid in removing and transporting the heavy ballast.

The indentations are usually called *core prints* and are located precisely from information in the plans. The core prints at the bottom of the form will have provisions for countersinks, which contain the bolt heads and washers.

A template of the keel bolt pattern must be made and the information transferred to the keel platform on the inverted hull.

Hopefully, when holes are drilled they will emerge inside the boat where they are supposed to be.

The waterlines of the pattern are taken directly from the lofting and plotted on a separate piece of paper. To define the shape properly, there will have to be more waterlines across the ballast portion of the keel than the lines drawing has. Simply draw them on the profile, spaced as desired. They are drawn parallel to the existing waterlines only if the top of the ballast is parallel to them. Otherwise, the new waterlines are drawn sloped to match the top of the ballast. If the pattern is made of stack-laminated wood, the new waterlines are spaced apart a distance exactly equal to the thickness of the wood laminates. This way, when the waterlines are plotted on the separate piece of paper in plan view, the exact shape of each laminate in the pattern is revealed.

If the pattern is built like a little boat, then the bulkheads for it are plotted using the half-breadths from these waterlines. It is necessary to add a few stations between the existing ones to achieve and hold fair curves.

With the hull rightside up and sufficiently elevated, the completed ballast keel, with keel bolts in place, will be rolled underneath and elevated on jacks to be fastened and bonded to the boat structure.

CHAPTER 6

The Foundation

A foundation structure is needed to support the mold during shell lay-up. Begin the structure by placing two 2 x 12s edgewise on the floor, parallel to each other and about two-thirds the beam dimension of the boat apart. The boards should be slightly longer than the boat. Close the ends of the rectangle with two short 2 x 12s. For smaller hull shells, it may be convenient to elevate the foundation on blocks or legs. The resultant foundation must be secure; it cannot shift, rock, or settle during lay-up. Use a spirit level to determine that the foundation is absolutely level in both length and beam directions.

Run a $\frac{1}{16}$-inch or $\frac{3}{32}$-inch wire from a wood screw on the outside face of one of the short 2 x 12s, over the top and across the middle of the foundation to a similar fastening on the opposite end. These fastenings are placed in the measured center of the ends. When tensioned with about 500 pounds, this wire will mark the centerline of the hull. Use a spirit level to verify that the centerline wire is level.

To tension the wire, make a 2-foot-long lever from scrap 2 x 4 lumber. It can be made in either a vertical or horizontal plane, depending on the foundation design. Insert a screw into the floor or blocking to use as a pivot. Tie wire around the lever near the pivot. Pull the lever handle and fix it in place, clinching the wire with a screw or nail.

Mark the tops and sides of the long 2 x 12s with ticks to represent the stationlines of the lofting. Use a framing square to determine that

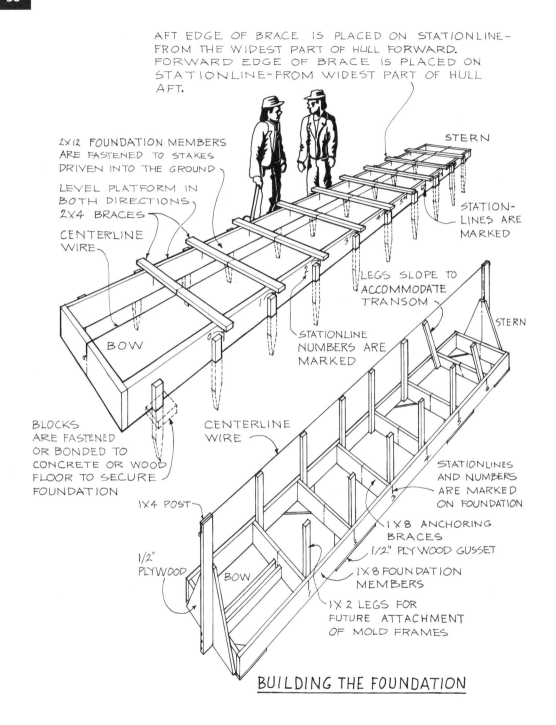

AFT EDGE OF BRACE IS PLACED ON STATIONLINE—
FROM THE WIDEST PART OF HULL FORWARD.
FORWARD EDGE OF BRACE IS PLACED ON
STATIONLINE—FROM WIDEST PART OF HULL
AFT.

STERN

2×12 FOUNDATION MEMBERS
ARE FASTENED TO STAKES
DRIVEN INTO THE GROUND

LEVEL PLATFORM IN
BOTH DIRECTIONS
2×4 BRACES

CENTERLINE
WIRE

STATION-
LINES ARE
MARKED

LEGS SLOPE TO
ACCOMMODATE
TRANSOM

STERN

BOW

STATIONLINE
NUMBERS ARE
MARKED

BLOCKS
ARE FASTENED
OR BONDED TO
CONCRETE OR WOOD
FLOOR TO SECURE
FOUNDATION

CENTERLINE
WIRE

STATIONLINES
AND NUMBERS
ARE MARKED
ON FOUNDATION

1×4 POST

1×8 ANCHORING
BRACES
1/2" PLYWOOD GUSSET

1/2"
PLYWOOD

BOW

1×8 FOUNDATION
MEMBERS

1×2 LEGS FOR
FUTURE ATTACHMENT
OF MOLD FRAMES

BUILDING THE FOUNDATION

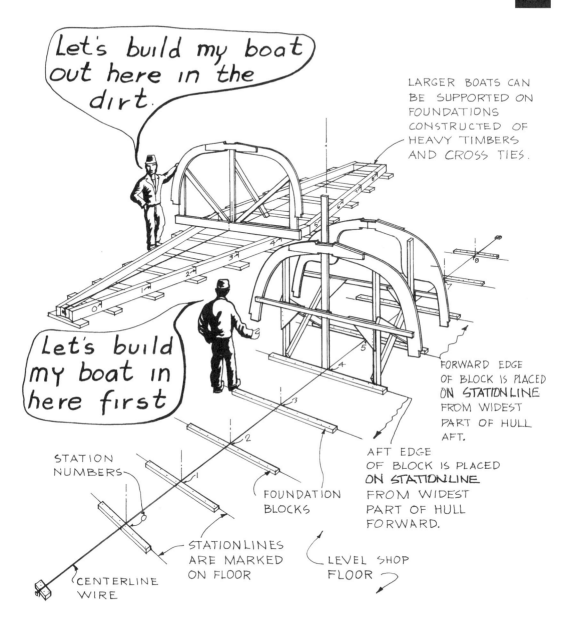

these marks describe an imaginary line that is exactly 90 degrees to the centerline wire and that they are parallel to one another. They must also be spaced exactly as shown on the plan. Cut some 2 x 4s to make anchoring braces that will span the short dimension of the foundation. Place these so that their edges will just touch the station marks. These braces are placed on the forward side of the stationlines from the widest part of the hull toward the bow. Braces aft of the center station will be placed on the after side of the stationlines. Legs holding forms or bulkheads will later be fastened to these braces so that their control edges face the correct direction.

Smaller craft, up to about 16 or 18 feet, can use a lighter foundation constructed of 1 x 8s to resemble a horizontal ladder, with "steps" of 1 x 8s located at the stationlines. The legs that later will support forms or bulkheads can be pre-attached and plumbed to the foundation before molds or bulkheads are made.

Larger craft of, say, 40 or 50 feet in length, require 4 x 10s or even 4 x 12s for the longitudinal foundation members. These are fastened to 2 x 10s or 2 x 12s placed under them like railroad ties. The timbers are marked with stationlines as before, but cross-spalls on the mold frames are placed on them instead of the bracing members. These larger timbers more conveniently approximate the plan shape of the finished hull by converging somewhat toward the ends instead of being parallel. They must, however, remain inside the sheerline as projected on the floor.

Any of these foundations can be placed on a level dirt, wood, or concrete surface. If the surface is dirt, drive stakes alongside the longitudinal timbers and bolt them to the timbers to keep them upright. For heavier hull shells, it helps to place some boards crosswise below the longitudinal timbers for additional support. On wood or concrete floors, fasten or bond wood blocks to the floor; the foundation is secured to these blocks. Shim any voids under the longitudinal timbers to provide support along their entire length. If the floor is level and strong enough, the mold can be set up directly on it by attaching the bracing members to stationlines drawn on the floor.

The size and type of foundation depend more on the final weight of the hull shell than on the length of the boat, so some judgment is called for. Some boatbuilders prefer to string the centerline wire over the mold setup from supports at each end, a method that works best for small boats. If the floor is perfectly level, the centerline can be marked directly on it so that it won't be rubbed off later.

CHAPTER 7

Plugs and Dowels

The beauty of laminated wood construction is its potential to produce a monocoque structure, without reliance on the metal fastenings used in traditional wooden boatbuilding. Because wood is strongest parallel to the grain, planking and framing are run at 90 degrees to each other. The constant give-and-take, working, and wracking as the structure reacts to various stresses places a premium on the strength of the fastenings. Planking and framing pieces are held together by clamping pressure from heads, washers, and the friction of screws, rods, and bolts, and through the mechanical hold of threads, all of which resist the efforts of unbonded joints to separate—as long as the metal fastenings and the surrounding wood retain their strength.

The only give-and-take in a laminated structure is the natural resilience of the wood, unless a glue-line breaks. If the adhesive achieves strength equivalent to the adjacent wood, any structural failure would be just as likely to occur in the wood as in the glue.

While no one would suggest that lead ballast or any metal object should rely solely on adhesive to hold it to the boat, it would seem possible to make most of the wood-to-wood connections without metal fastenings. For wood-to-metal connections, and for any other applications where metal fastenings are necessary, guide holes are drilled for placement of bolts, rods, and screws. Often the heads of these fastenings are countersunk and plugs of wood are inserted in the holes.

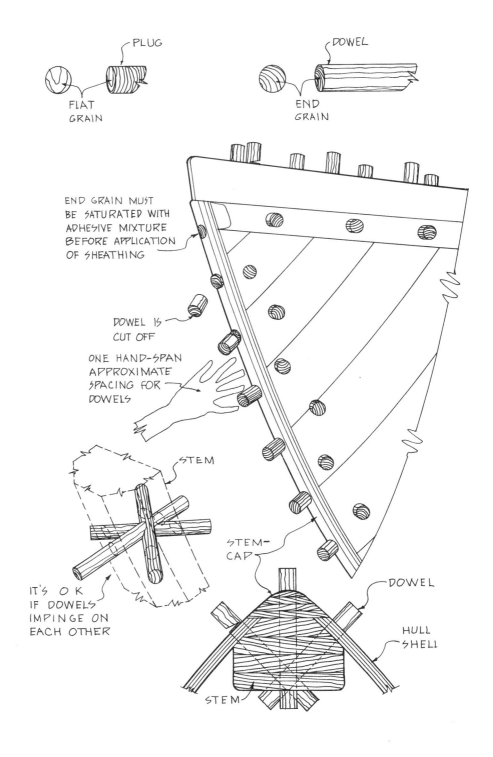

PLUG

FLAT
GRAIN

DOWEL

END
GRAIN

END GRAIN MUST
BE SATURATED WITH
ADHESIVE MIXTURE
BEFORE APPLICATION
OF SHEATHING

DOWEL IS
CUT OFF

ONE HAND-SPAN
APPROXIMATE
SPACING FOR
DOWELS

STEM

IT'S O K
IF DOWELS
IMPINGE ON
EACH OTHER

STEM-
CAP

DOWEL

HULL
SHELL

STEM

For our purposes, a *plug* is a cylindrical piece of wood with grain running across it. When used to fill a hole, it shows parallel lines of grain that can be aligned with the background grain. A *dowel* is a cylindrical piece of wood with grain running parallel to its long axis, showing end grain when in place. In most cases, holes drilled to receive temporary fastenings that hold glued parts together until resin has cured can be enlarged later, and the metal fastenings replaced with dowels. Dowels provide no clamping pressure, but once the cure is achieved, clamping pressure is no longer needed. Besides filling holes, dowels provide some grain at 90 degrees to the grain of the joined pieces.

To take this thinking a step further, it would seem a good idea to drill holes into various joined structural parts and fill the holes with dowels for the sole purpose of supplying some cross grain. Once the dowel is bonded in place, it becomes "unitized" with the structure and does not interrupt the continuity of wood the way a metal fastening does (even if the metal fastening is bonded in). In fact, dowels could impinge on previously placed dowels without disrupting the monocoque effect of the structure. It would simply mean that wood grain is running in various directions.

Wood expands with moisture across the grain rather than along the grain, so it would seem that internal tension could build up as the wood absorbs moisture. Fortunately, the wood will not absorb moisture as long as it has a protective surface coating of resin.

The juncture of stem and keel, for example, could be bonded by a simple scarf joint without the keys required in conventional wood construction. Several dowels could be placed on each side simply to provide some cross grain. Among many examples of where the technique works are connections from stemcap to stem, floor timber to keel, guard to hull, and toerail to deck. It seems pointless to carry around all of the heavy metal fastenings of a carvel-planked hull when their strength would not come into play until it's too late for them to do any good.

CHAPTER 8

Building the Mold: Mold Frame

The next step in the process is building a mold over which the hull shell of laminated wood planks will be laid. First some definitions:

- *Mold* is the shape over which the shell is created, whether or not it is discarded.
- *Mold frame* is a frame that will be discarded.
- *Shell frame* is a frame that becomes a part of the hull structure—a bulkhead, for instance.
- *Ribbands* are longitudinal wood members that will be discarded.
- *Stringers* are longitudinal wood members that become part of the hull structure.

The shapes of mold frames, shell frames, and bulkheads are taken from the lofting; these shapes determine the shape of the completed hull. The shapes are shown on the lofting as "bow view" and "stern view," and are cross sections of the hull at each stationline.

If stringers are shown on the plans, these cross sections correspond with shell frames in the completed boat. In this case, the shell thickness is deducted from the lofting to arrive at their exact shape.

If no stringers are shown on the plans, these cross sections correspond with each mold frame in the mold. In this case, the shell thickness and the ribband thickness are deducted from the lofting to arrive at their exact shape.

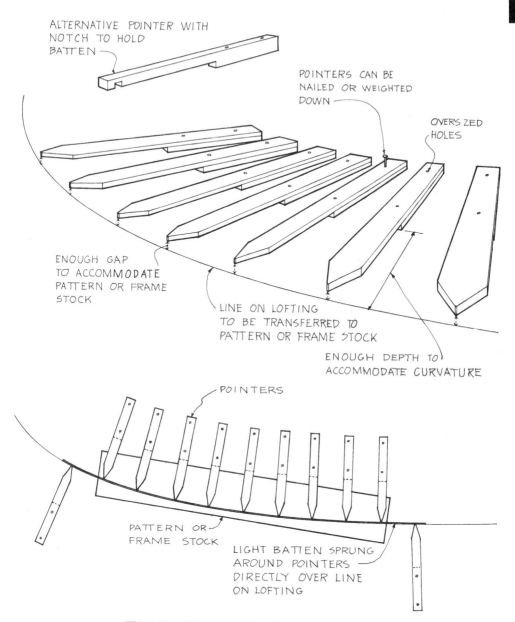

ALTERNATIVE POINTER WITH NOTCH TO HOLD BATTEN

POINTERS CAN BE NAILED OR WEIGHTED DOWN

OVERSIZED HOLES

ENOUGH GAP TO ACCOMMODATE PATTERN OR FRAME STOCK

LINE ON LOFTING TO BE TRANSFERRED TO PATTERN OR FRAME STOCK

ENOUGH DEPTH TO ACCOMMODATE CURVATURE

POINTERS

PATTERN OR FRAME STOCK

LIGHT BATTEN SPRUNG AROUND POINTERS DIRECTLY OVER LINE ON LOFTING

TRANSFERRING LINES

Paper patterns can be made from the lofting and laid over pieces of plywood or solid lumber for marking out shapes. Or, wood templates can be made from the lofting using a series of weighted (or fastened down) wood pointers. Leave gaps between the points and the floor to permit the pattern material to be slid under the points once they are aligned with

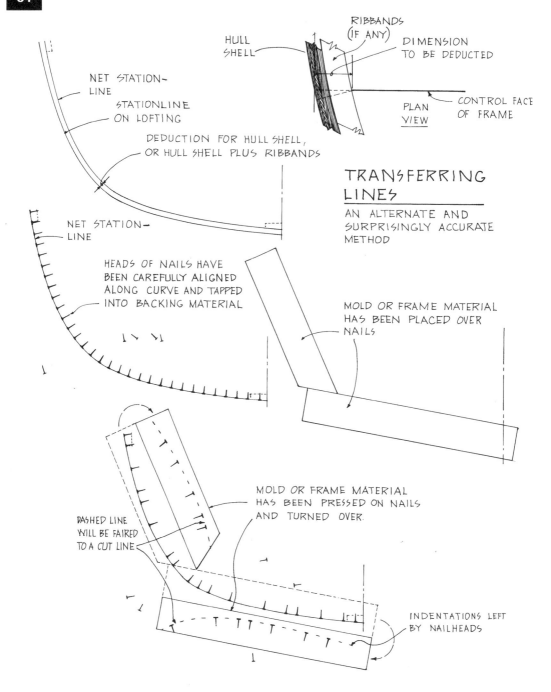

RIBBANDS (IF ANY)

HULL SHELL

DIMENSION TO BE DEDUCTED

PLAN VIEW

CONTROL FACE OF FRAME

NET STATION-LINE

STATIONLINE ON LOFTING

DEDUCTION FOR HULL SHELL, OR HULL SHELL PLUS RIBBANDS

NET STATION-LINE

HEADS OF NAILS HAVE BEEN CAREFULLY ALIGNED ALONG CURVE AND TAPPED INTO BACKING MATERIAL

TRANSFERRING LINES

AN ALTERNATE AND SURPRISINGLY ACCURATE METHOD

MOLD OR FRAME MATERIAL HAS BEEN PLACED OVER NAILS

MOLD OR FRAME MATERIAL HAS BEEN PRESSED ON NAILS AND TURNED OVER.

DASHED LINE WILL BE FAIRED TO A CUT LINE

INDENTATIONS LEFT BY NAILHEADS

the curve shown on the lofting. With the pattern material in place, spring a light batten around the points so the curve can be drawn.

MOLD FRAME CONSTRUCTION

Mold frames are constructed of 1 x 4s or 1 x 6s joined by plywood gussets. Heavier hull shells may require 2 x 6s or 2 x 8s. The lumber must be sufficiently straight and strong to hold its shape during shell lay-up. Particleboard is sometimes used as mold material. It is helpful if the lumber surface is smooth enough to accept accurate markings.

Set up the mold frames on the foundation, plumbing them both fore and aft and across the beam so they are parallel to each other and square with the centerline. The face of the frame that is in contact with the marked stationline becomes the *control face* and carries all markings. The resulting *control edge* must not be cut into, or the hull shape ultimately will be affected. The first frame set up on the foundation, one from the middle of the mold, determines the elevation at which the hull takes shape. Place those frames from the widest beam of the hull toward the bow with their control faces looking aft and all other frames with their control faces looking forward. The markings on the control face consist of a centerline, a reference waterline, and the sheerline. Indicate the waterline all the way across the frame using light wire or a fishing line.

Wood members called *cross-spalls* connect the opposite sides of each frame to hold them steady. Attach these cross-spalls either to the sides of the frame or to the temporary legs extending from them. Mark the centerline on them.

Fasten the legs to braces on the foundation (or to blocks on the floor); these support the weight of the evolving hull shell. Make the legs long enough to allow the stem to be clear of the floor when it is added later. Fasten the legs to the control face with wood screws.

Clamp a spirit level to a straight-edged piece of wood so that the level's edge is flush with the straightedge. Clamp the straightedge to the frame so that its edge is flush with the centerline marks on the frame and cross-spall. The straightedge should be long enough to reach below the centerline wire so it can be used as a height reference. If the centerline is drawn on the floor, then the floor is used as a height reference. When the spirit level indicates that the frame is plumb in the beam direction, fasten the legs to the braces with wood screws.

Attach diagonal struts to the legs with wood screws. The struts angle down in a fore-and-aft direction to support the frame. Plumb the frame in

BUILDING THE MOLD FRAME

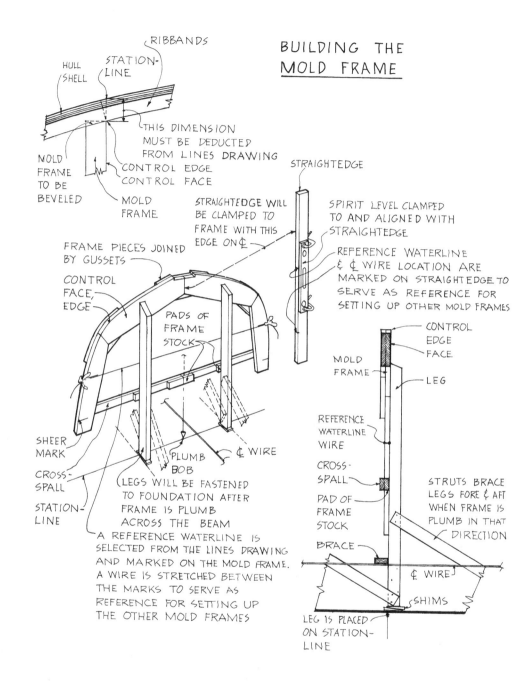

RIBBANDS

HULL SHELL

STATION-LINE

THIS DIMENSION MUST BE DEDUCTED FROM LINES DRAWING

MOLD FRAME TO BE BEVELED

CONTROL EDGE
CONTROL FACE

MOLD FRAME

STRAIGHTEDGE

STRAIGHTEDGE WILL BE CLAMPED TO FRAME WITH THIS EDGE ON ₵

SPIRIT LEVEL CLAMPED TO AND ALIGNED WITH STRAIGHTEDGE

REFERENCE WATERLINE & ₵ WIRE LOCATION ARE MARKED ON STRAIGHTEDGE TO SERVE AS REFERENCE FOR SETTING UP OTHER MOLD FRAMES

FRAME PIECES JOINED BY GUSSETS

CONTROL FACE, EDGE

PADS OF FRAME STOCK

CONTROL EDGE FACE

MOLD FRAME

LEG

REFERENCE WATERLINE WIRE

CROSS-SPALL

PAD OF FRAME STOCK

BRACE

STRUTS BRACE LEGS FORE & AFT WHEN FRAME IS PLUMB IN THAT DIRECTION

SHEER MARK

CROSS-SPALL

STATION-LINE

PLUMB BOB

₵ WIRE

LEGS WILL BE FASTENED TO FOUNDATION AFTER FRAME IS PLUMB ACROSS THE BEAM

A REFERENCE WATERLINE IS SELECTED FROM THE LINES DRAWING AND MARKED ON THE MOLD FRAME. A WIRE IS STRETCHED BETWEEN THE MARKS TO SERVE AS REFERENCE FOR SETTING UP THE OTHER MOLD FRAMES

₵ WIRE

SHIMS

LEG IS PLACED ON STATION-LINE

the fore and aft direction using a plumb bob attached to the top centerline of the frame. If the plumb bob is suspended over the control face of the frame, the bob should point directly at the intersection of the centerline and stationline below. When the frame is plumb in the fore-and-aft direction, attach the struts to the foundation with wood screws.

With the first mold in place, mark the reference waterline and centerline wire locations on the straightedge. If the floor is the reference, then use the bottom of the straightedge for the height reference. The straightedge can now be used to establish the elevation of all successive frames. Set the other frames the same way as the first, and adjust their heights until all the reference waterline marks are at the same elevation.

When all of the frames are on their marks and trued up, add the transom to the setup. It is set at the rake angle shown on the lofting and held by struts. It might be more convenient to add the transom after the hull shell is removed from the mold and set upright. This works well with sailboat hulls, which have relatively small transoms. For power boats with broad transoms, it's usually better to add the transom to the mold already planked.

Bevel the edges of the mold frame to allow fair application of ribbands. To do this, run a long batten over the square edges of the mold frames to serve as a guide. Saw kerfs in the mold frame with a handsaw, being careful not to saw into the control edge. The kerf follows the line indicated by the batten. Saw a kerf on each side of the batten at each mold frame. Remove the batten and chisel out the wood between each kerf. Move the batten and repeat the process every 6 inches or so. This gives a reference bevel periodically along each mold frame to which the completed bevel can be planed. Remember not to plane into the control face because that is what determines the shape of the hull.

When the beveling is done, fair the overall setup by sighting along a long batten to find any humps or flat spots. High places can be planed carefully, but low places may need to have material bonded onto them to bring them up.

FABRICATING THE MOLD STEM

The next step is fabricating the mold stem and bonding it into the setup to provide a place for the ribbands to attach. To find the profile of the stem, go to the profile portion of the lofting. Measure in from the stem a distance equal to the thickness of the stemcap plus the thickness of the stem itself. This information is on the construction plan. This dimension

SETTING UP FIRST
MOLD FRAMES

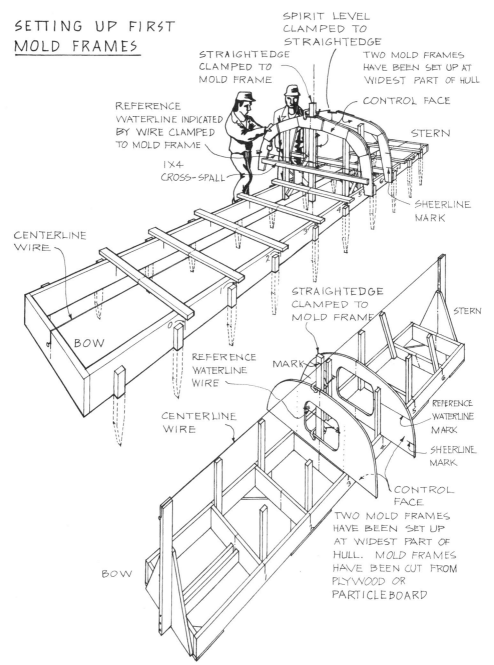

SPIRIT LEVEL
CLAMPED TO
STRAIGHTEDGE

STRAIGHTEDGE
CLAMPED TO
MOLD FRAME

TWO MOLD FRAMES
HAVE BEEN SET UP AT
WIDEST PART OF HULL

CONTROL FACE

STERN

REFERENCE
WATERLINE INDICATED
BY WIRE CLAMPED
TO MOLD FRAME

1X4
CROSS-SPALL

SHEERLINE
MARK

CENTERLINE
WIRE

BOW

REFERENCE
WATERLINE
WIRE

STRAIGHTEDGE
CLAMPED TO
MOLD FRAME

STERN

MARK

CENTERLINE
WIRE

REFERENCE
WATERLINE
MARK

SHEERLINE
MARK

CONTROL
FACE

TWO MOLD FRAMES
HAVE BEEN SET UP
AT WIDEST PART OF
HULL. MOLD FRAMES
HAVE BEEN CUT FROM
PLYWOOD OR
PARTICLEBOARD

BOW

will likely be different at various elevations along the stem, so measure accordingly. The completed line will be the shape for the forward edge of the mold stem. Its width and thickness will be whatever it takes to accommodate the ribbands. When it is set up in the mold, it will be

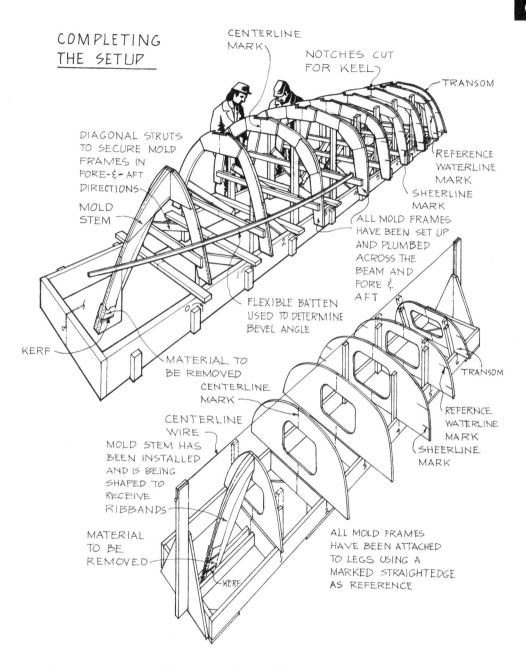

COMPLETING
THE SETUP

CENTERLINE
MARK

NOTCHES CUT
FOR KEEL

TRANSOM

DIAGONAL STRUTS
TO SECURE MOLD
FRAMES IN
FORE-&-AFT
DIRECTIONS

REFERENCE
WATERLINE
MARK

SHEERLINE
MARK

MOLD
STEM

ALL MOLD FRAMES
HAVE BEEN SET UP
AND PLUMBED
ACROSS THE
BEAM AND
FORE &
AFT

FLEXIBLE BATTEN
USED TO DETERMINE
BEVEL ANGLE

KERF

MATERIAL TO
BE REMOVED

CENTERLINE
MARK

TRANSOM

CENTERLINE
WIRE

REFERNCE
WATERLINE
MARK

MOLD STEM HAS
BEEN INSTALLED
AND IS BEING
SHAPED TO
RECEIVE
RIBBANDS

SHEERLINE
MARK

MATERIAL
TO BE
REMOVED

ALL MOLD FRAMES
HAVE BEEN ATTACHED
TO LEGS USING A
MARKED STRAIGHTEDGE
AS REFERENCE

KERF

beveled and faired with the rest of the mold frames.

Alternatively, the mold stem can be laid up of laminates using the back of the stem as a mold. Place a plastic sheet between them to prevent their bonding together.

FABRICATING THE STEM AND KEEL

The stem and keel are fabricated and placed on the mold prior to the application of ribbands. The keel is most likely thicker than the ribbands, so the mold frames must be notched to allow the keel surface to lie flush with the ribbands. The keel and stem shapes are also taken from the lofting, using information given on the construction plan. Templates of the stem profile and forward end of the keel are made. These shapes show the keel/stem juncture. Sometimes these members are laminated, and sometimes they are assembled from solid timber.

Laminated stems are normally made up on the lofting (cover it with sheet plastic to protect it). The laminates are sprung around cleats fastened to the floor and held in place by cleats fastened to the floor on the opposite side of the laminates. Try a dry fit before applying the adhesive mixture. When the laminates are ready for final assembly, apply the adhesive mixture with a foam roller. The inner laminates must be coated on both sides, a potentially messy proposition. Spread some plastic sheeting to keep the laminates from bonding to something they shouldn't. Stem laminates should be longer than required for the hull, reaching the foundation or the floor. They will be cut off later.

Assemble the coated laminates on the form within an hour of the time coating commences. Place clamps across the laminated material at points between the cleats to hold it for curing. Always place pads of wood under the jaws of the clamps so they won't bite into the material. Remove excess adhesive mixture that oozes out before it sets.

After curing, shape the stack of laminates to the profile marked on them, using the template as a guide. If the laminates have been stairstepped so that they approximate the final shape of the stem, the steps can be faired to a smooth curve. Usually it is most convenient to cut out the stem profile on a bandsaw.

The keel can be laminated on the floor using the same process, although the curve, if any, will be much less severe.

To make keels and stems from solid lumber, use templates taken from the lofting to mark the outlines of the keel and stem on the lumber. After they have been cut out, they can be joined on the floor and placed in the form as a unit.

The templates also are used to locate the scarf joint that joins the laminated stem and keel together. The actual joining is done after the keel and stem have been placed in the mold. Dress scarf faces for a perfect fit, coat with adhesive mixture, and use wood screws to hold the pieces

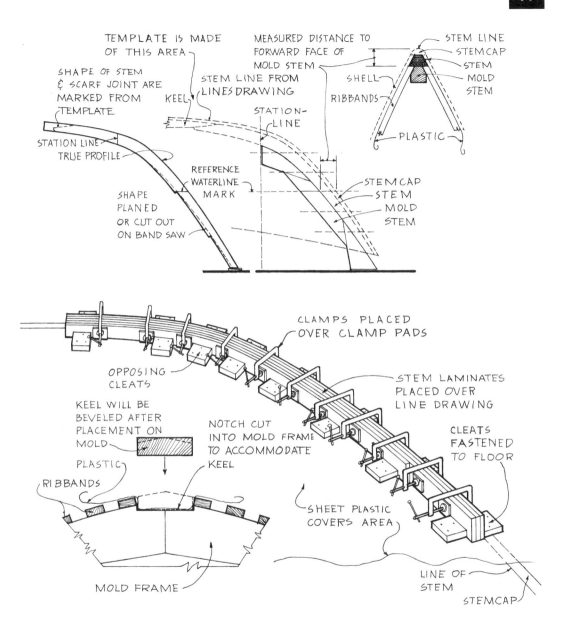

TEMPLATE IS MADE OF THIS AREA

MEASURED DISTANCE TO FORWARD FACE OF MOLD STEM

STEM LINE
STEMCAP
STEM
MOLD STEM

SHAPE OF STEM & SCARF JOINT ARE MARKED FROM TEMPLATE

STEM LINE FROM LINES DRAWING

KEEL

SHELL

RIBBANDS

PLASTIC

STATION LINE TRUE PROFILE

STATION-LINE

REFERENCE WATERLINE MARK

SHAPE PLANED OR CUT OUT ON BAND SAW

STEMCAP
STEM
MOLD STEM

CLAMPS PLACED OVER CLAMP PADS

OPPOSING CLEATS

STEM LAMINATES PLACED OVER LINE DRAWING

KEEL WILL BE BEVELED AFTER PLACEMENT ON MOLD

NOTCH CUT INTO MOLD FRAME TO ACCOMMODATE KEEL

CLEATS FASTENED TO FLOOR

PLASTIC

RIBBANDS

SHEET PLASTIC COVERS AREA

MOLD FRAME

LINE OF STEM

STEMCAP

MOLD STEM AND STEM

together until the resin has cured. After curing, remove wood screws, drill out screw holes, and bond in dowels. The inner face of keel and stem will have been pre-coated with resin but not the outer faces. The outer faces haven't been shaped yet; this process will be described later.

Lay sheet plastic in the keel trough of the mold and over the mold stem so that keel and stem do not bond to the mold during shell lay-up. The stem is long enough to brace it against the foundation or floor. Mark the reference waterline on the stem; this will be used to determine correct elevation in the setup. When the stem is plumb and square with the mold, carefully mark the centerline on it and on the keel. The centerline is used in the final shaping of these members.

ADDING RIBBANDS

When the mold frame and stem have been faired, fasten the ribbands to the molds. Ribbands are usually made up of ¾-inch-thick material. If the first hull laminates are veneers of ⅛-inch thickness or less, use ¾-inch square ribbands, leaving no more than about 2 inches between them. If ¼-inch or heavier plywood is the first laminate, then use ¾-inch by 1½-inch ribbands, with no more than about 6 inches between them. The plywood will span the gap, but if there is any deflection in the ribbands at all, add an additional ribband (or ribbands) in the gap. This is all determined by the span between the mold frames and the sharpness of the hull curve. Test by bending a sample plank around the ribbands to simulate laminating pressure. You may decide at the outset to use thicker ribbands for greater stiffness.

Ribbands must be scarfed end to end for them to reach from stem to stern as a single unit. The scarf angle is one in eight. Fill the end grain with sufficient resin to saturate the wood cells. Coat bonding surfaces with adhesive mixture and clamp for curing. Scarf enough ribbands to complete the mold by the chosen method. Ribband material should be free of any knots or other imperfections that prevent their bending fair over the mold frames.

Place the first ribband over the turn of the bilge, with ends converging slightly toward the sheerline. Make sure the ribband fits flush and does not twist or try to spiral over the frames. When you've achieved a good fit, fix the ribband to the mold frames. Narrow crown staples long enough to grip into the mold frames (say, 1¼ inches long) will work for ribbands up to ¾ inch thick. For thicker material or for tight bends, use wood screws that have been countersunk enough not to interfere with

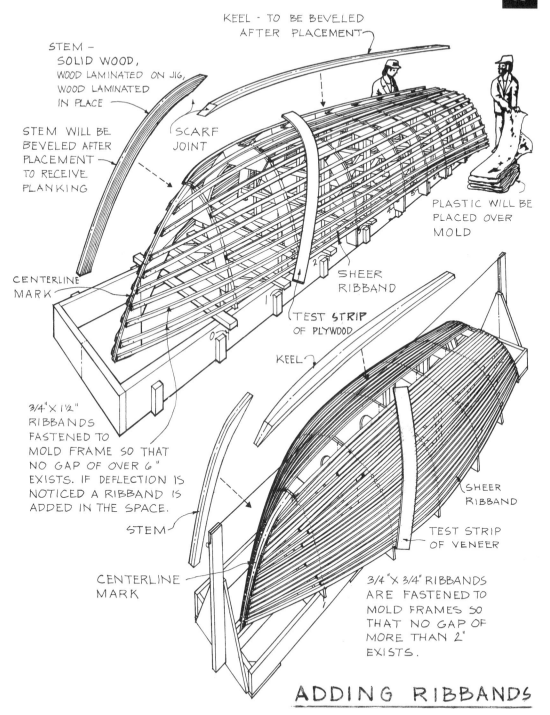

KEEL - TO BE BEVELED AFTER PLACEMENT

STEM –
SOLID WOOD,
WOOD LAMINATED ON JIG,
WOOD LAMINATED IN PLACE

STEM WILL BE BEVELED AFTER PLACEMENT TO RECEIVE PLANKING

SCARF JOINT

PLASTIC WILL BE PLACED OVER MOLD

CENTERLINE MARK

SHEER RIBBAND

TEST STRIP OF PLYWOOD

KEEL

3/4" X 1½" RIBBANDS FASTENED TO MOLD FRAME SO THAT NO GAP OF OVER 6" EXISTS. IF DEFLECTION IS NOTICED A RIBBAND IS ADDED IN THE SPACE.

STEM

CENTERLINE MARK

SHEER RIBBAND

TEST STRIP OF VENEER

3/4" X 3/4" RIBBANDS ARE FASTENED TO MOLD FRAMES SO THAT NO GAP OF MORE THAN 2" EXISTS.

ADDING RIBBANDS

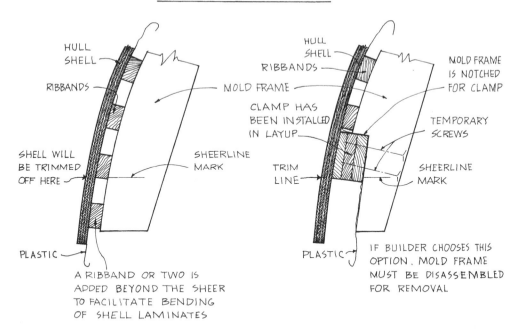

SHEERLINE OPTIONS

HULL SHELL

RIBBANDS

MOLD FRAME

SHELL WILL BE TRIMMED OFF HERE

SHEERLINE MARK

PLASTIC

A RIBBAND OR TWO IS ADDED BEYOND THE SHEER TO FACILITATE BENDING OF SHELL LAMINATES

HULL SHELL

RIBBANDS

MOLD FRAME

CLAMP HAS BEEN INSTALLED IN LAYUP

TRIM LINE

MOLD FRAME IS NOTCHED FOR CLAMP

TEMPORARY SCREWS

SHEERLINE MARK

PLASTIC

IF BUILDER CHOOSES THIS OPTION, MOLD FRAME MUST BE DISASSEMBLED FOR REMOVAL

the shell lamination process.

The other ribbands are added, fanning out from the bow in a fair curve until they converge toward the stern. Where the gap exceeds the maximum allowed amount, add a ribband in the intervening space.

Place a ribband on the mold, following the sheerline (previously marked on each mold frame) exactly, for future reference when trimming off the shell planking. The sheer clamp could be laid up in the mold and fixed with temporary wood screws, driven in from the back of the frame, until the adhesive cures. Separate the clamp from the frame with sheet plastic to prevent their bonding together. Normally, a ribband or two are added beyond the sheerline to facilitate the shell lay-up process. Later, the mold frame will be turned over, along with the hull shell, and disassembled by removing the various screw fastenings.

After the entire mold is covered, check for rigidity. Additional struts may be needed to hold the mold rigid during shell lamination.

SHAPING THE STEM AND KEEL

The stem is now shaped to receive shell planking. Kerf the stem with a handsaw, using an adjacent ribband as a guide. Kerf the stem on the opposite side of the ribband and remove the wood from between the cuts with a chisel. Check fairness with a batten run over the ribband and through the notch. This is the line the shell planking will take. At this point there are substantial flat areas on the front of the keel that will be covered later with the stemcap. Repeat this process until there are enough notches to determine the bonding face of the stem, then plane off the material between the notches. Use the centerline as a reference to determine a fair cut. Using a short batten, find any high or low places. If too much wood has been removed, additional wood can be bonded on and faired.

The keel normally requires some beveling before it will accept the shell planking. This is accomplished by kerfing and planing as described for the stem. The bevel will be faired using a short batten run across the tops of the ribbands. All bonding surfaces on the stem and keel must be sanded to provide the best bonding faces.

Fair the completed mold with a flexible batten to find any high or low areas. Low places are filled with a mixture of resin and filler, and high places are planed carefully. Cover the mold with sheet plastic, leaving exposed only those areas that will bond to the hull shell, including the keel, stem, and clamp (if any).

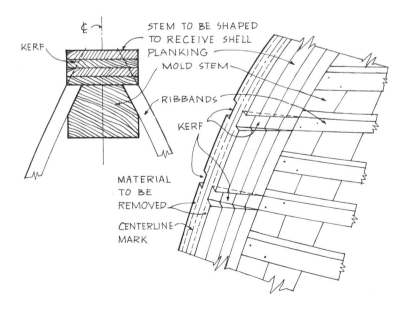

CHAPTER 9

Sandwiches

Certain components of the boat lend themselves to a composite construction consisting of two outer skins of structural material bonded to an inner layer of framing and fill. Sometimes framing is used without a fill material, most often for bulkheads and decks, but berth flats, seat flats, countertops, hatches, and many other parts benefit from this method's strength and lightness. Housetops and decks can be made thinner to conserve headroom, and the overhead becomes a smooth surface. Some fillers, such as rigid foam, have significant thermal insulation value.

The outer skins are commonly plywood, from ⅛ inch to ½ inch thick or more. There are three types of fillers: low-density wood, such as balsa; rigid foam, including Airex and Klegecel; and a manufactured honeycomb of resin-impregnated paper, such as Verticel.

When low-density wood is used as a filler, a choice must be made between running it flat grain or end grain. Cedar or spruce core material can be used with denser outer layers in laminated frames and deck beams. It has sufficient strength across the grain to allow it to be used in flat grain. These lay-ups can be bonded with adhesive mixture in the usual way.

Balsa wood is low in strength across the grain but works well as a filler when used in end-grain blocks. The cost of balsa, however, makes it impractical for use in most laminated wood boatbuilding. Any time balsa, or any wood, is used in end-grain configuration, the end grain must be coated with enough resin to saturate the wood cells. The blocks are coated with resin, using a roller, and bonded to each other as they are placed in the piece being fabricated.

The blocks are then coated with a thickened adhesive mixture spread across the end grain with a toothed plastic squeegee. This mixture fills gaps caused by any slight unevenness in the blocks. When the blocks are bonded in (and to each other), a similar coating is applied across the top of the blocks before receiving the other skin.

Foam core material absorbs resin and must also be saturated prior to coating it with adhesive mixture. A low-density adhesive mixture thickened with microspheres or microballoons will allow the foam to achieve adequate strength, as well as give it gap-filling capability. A toothed plastic squeegee works better than a foam roller for this application.

The resin-impregnated paper honeycomb Verticel is already resin saturated, but bonding the thin edges of the cells to the outer skins may present a problem, and the edges may still need saturation. Apply a very thin coating of resin on the cell edges with a foam roller. Prepare a low-density adhesive mixture for the actual bonding operation. This mixture, applied with a roller, has a tendency to crawl up the surfaces of the honeycomb cells to form tiny fillets between the core material and the skins. It also will span the gaps caused by any small irregularities in the cellular core material.

The strength of the structural sandwich is totally dependent on the quality of the bond between the core and the skins. Any surface that might absorb adhesive mixture from the joint must be pre-saturated with resin. If this saturation is not complete, the bond may break and the part most likely will fail. Be sure that the surfaces of the skins have been coated with resin and allowed to cure before they are used in sandwich structures.

It is a good idea to prepare some trial sandwich-construction panels to develop the best adhesive mixture and the best bonding techniques.

Bulkheads are normally flat and can be built up on a workbench or floor. The skins are cut out in pairs, laying one flat and bonding to it the internal framework specified on the plans. The solid pieces of lumber in the bulkhead become attachment sites for additional construction within the hull. Curved structural members are formed over a mold shaped to the proper camber. Internal framing or beams, as well as any specified blocking, is bonded in. There may be small, thin frames spaced a few

BULKHEAD SANDWICH

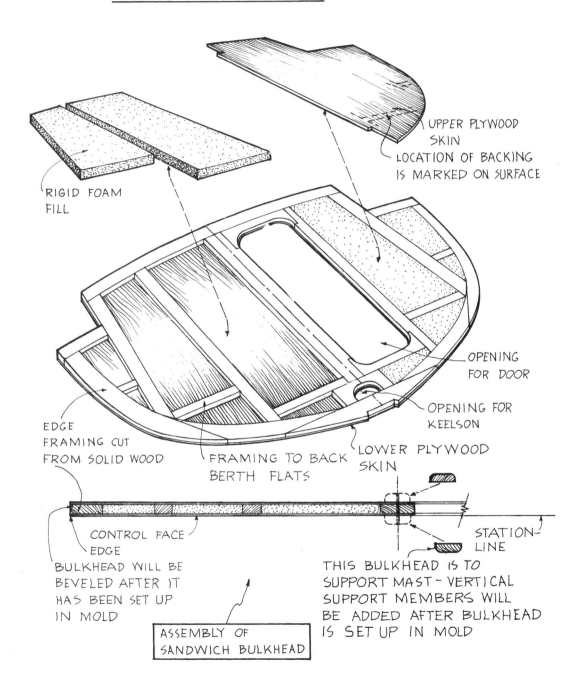

UPPER PLYWOOD
SKIN
LOCATION OF BACKING
IS MARKED ON SURFACE

RIGID FOAM
FILL

OPENING
FOR DOOR

OPENING FOR
KEELSON

EDGE
FRAMING CUT
FROM SOLID WOOD

FRAMING TO BACK
BERTH FLATS

LOWER PLYWOOD
SKIN

CONTROL FACE
EDGE

STATION
LINE

BULKHEAD WILL BE
BEVELED AFTER IT
HAS BEEN SET UP
IN MOLD

THIS BULKHEAD IS TO
SUPPORT MAST — VERTICAL
SUPPORT MEMBERS WILL
BE ADDED AFTER BULKHEAD
IS SET UP IN MOLD

ASSEMBLY OF
SANDWICH BULKHEAD

inches apart, or much larger frames spaced several feet apart. At this point temporary fastenings usually hold the pieces for curing, but weights may be needed to keep things in place.

If core material is cut and fitted into the voids carefully, they should hold themselves for curing. Core materials that will not stay in place will have to be weighted. The top skin relies heavily on weights to assure proper bonding to the framing and core material. Temporary fastenings could be used around the edges or anywhere there is solid framing. The position of any interior framing needed for attachment of joinery should be marked on the exterior of the bulkhead. Weights can be bricks or scraps of iron or rocks, provided they are padded to prevent damage to the surface. A curved sandwich component is easily fixed for cure with padded clamps around its perimeter. Even these components should be weighted, however, if there is any doubt about the completeness of the bond.

SANDWICH DECK CONSTRUCTION

Sandwich deck construction presents special problems. If there is enough floor space in the fabrication shelter, construct the deck outside the hull and install it only after much of the work is done. This is done most easily if the bottom of the deck is to be dead level, with the camber cut into the upper edge of the deck beams. This works best with a relatively flat camber. Cut the entire lower skin out of plywood that has been scarfed together and place it on the floor so the deck beams can be bonded to it. Leave openings for hatches, trunks, and cockpits. Place any blocking that is required for future attachment of hardware now, because it is nearly impossible to change the completed structure. Place any necessary structural solid blocking, including edge blocking around the perimeter of the deck. When this structure is cured, transfer it to the top of the sheer clamps and bond it in place. Insert the core material and carefully fair it (together with all the bridging and blocking) to the varying deck thicknesses as determined by the deck beams.

If the sandwich deck is of uniform thickness and constructed on the floor, a mold must be prepared to create the camber for the bottom of the deck. Make the mold from transverse frames that have the deck camber cut into their upper edges. Run longitudinal 1 x 2 ribbands fore and aft, about 8 inches apart, to support the lower skin. Cover the mold with sheet plastic to prevent it from bonding to the deck structure. Laminate deck beams in place on the lower skin. After placing the blocking and bridging, add the core material. This task is simplified by the fact that the core is all of the same thickness. Lift the deck on top of the sheer clamps for bonding. The sheer clamp is located below the top of the shell planking, at the exact depth of the deck structure, so that the edge of the deck structure can be bonded to it.

Once the deck structure is bonded in place, mark out the upper skin using the edge of the hull shell as a template. The upper skin is then bonded on top, with any required scarfing being done in place.

Clearly the methods just described can be used only on a boat with a nearly flat sheerline. If there is a great deal of hogging or sag to the sheerline, a deck built on a flat floor simply will not fit.

A sandwich deck can be built in place on the boat by constructing a temporary form to support the relatively floppy lower skin of the deck during construction. Begin by laminating an inner sheer clamp to the one already in place. The bottom of the sheer clamp should be flush with the bottom of the eventual deck structure. Laminate the deck beams, and dry fit them into the notches cut in the sheer clamp (as described in the section on decks and superstructure). Cut the notches through the inner sheer clamps and into the original sheer clamps. With the deck beams sitting in place, all of the dimensions can be taken for shaping the lower skin and for determining the elevation of a strongback that will be erected temporarily down the centerline of the hull.

Make the strongback with a top chord consisting of a single 2 x 4 that has a trough 1½ inches wide and ½ inch deep routed out along the center of its bottom side; make some 2 x 4 struts to fit into the trough. Diagonal bracing of 1 x 4s will brace the strongback against the hull shell. Erect the strongback with the deck beams still sitting in place to verify its height. The gap between the top of the strongback and the bottom of the beams must be equal to the thickness of the transverse form boards that will be placed over it. These are usually 1 x 2s, although in larger boats 2 x 2s might be required.

After the strongback is set, number and remove the deck beams. Spring the 1 x 2 form boards over it and tuck their outboard ends under the inner sheer clamps. They will probably hold themselves in place, but it is best to fix the ends with temporary fastenings. If a form board is placed under the clamp at each beam notch, its clamping pressure will ensure a good bond between the deck beam and the skin. Cover the outboard ends of the form boards with pieces of sheet plastic to prevent them from bonding to the sheer clamps. Place the lower skin on the form boards and bond its edge to the inner sheer clamps.

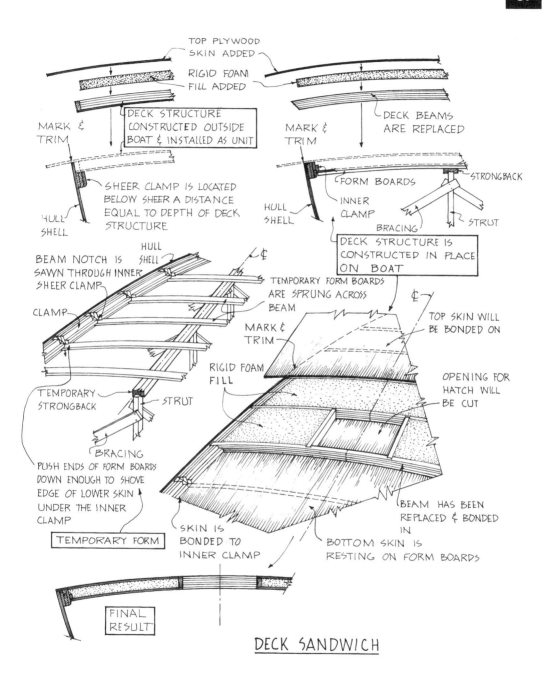

TOP PLYWOOD
SKIN ADDED

RIGID FOAM
FILL ADDED

DECK BEAMS
ARE REPLACED

MARK &
TRIM

DECK STRUCTURE
CONSTRUCTED OUTSIDE
BOAT & INSTALLED AS UNIT

MARK &
TRIM

SHEER CLAMP IS LOCATED
BELOW SHEER A DISTANCE
EQUAL TO DEPTH OF DECK
STRUCTURE

HULL
SHELL

STRONGBACK

FORM BOARDS

INNER
CLAMP

HULL
SHELL

BRACING

STRUT

DECK STRUCTURE IS
CONSTRUCTED IN PLACE
ON BOAT

BEAM NOTCH IS
SAWN THROUGH INNER
SHEER CLAMP

HULL
SHELL

℄

TEMPORARY FORM BOARDS
ARE SPRUNG ACROSS
BEAM

CLAMP

MARK &
TRIM

℄

TOP SKIN WILL
BE BONDED ON

RIGID FOAM
FILL

OPENING FOR
HATCH WILL
BE CUT

TEMPORARY
STRONGBACK

STRUT

BRACING

PUSH ENDS OF FORM BOARDS
DOWN ENOUGH TO SHOVE
EDGE OF LOWER SKIN
UNDER THE INNER
CLAMP

BEAM HAS BEEN
REPLACED & BONDED
IN

TEMPORARY FORM

SKIN IS
BONDED TO
INNER CLAMP

BOTTOM SKIN IS
RESTING ON FORM BOARDS

FINAL
RESULT

DECK SANDWICH

First, replace and bond the laminated deck beams into their notches and to the lower skin. Now place the necessary blocking and bridging. Next, cut the filling and bond it in; do the same with the upper skin, as previously described. The upper skin is always brought out flush with the outer edge of the shell planking. When the deck structure has cured, the strongback with its form boards can be dismantled and removed.

Plans intended for this mode of construction show all shell frames and bulkheads terminating at the lower face of the deck structure to allow continuity of the deck. The shell frames are simply sawn off at that level after the hull has been turned over. A deck beam is located over each bulkhead and solid bridging over each partition. The lower skin is bonded to the top of the bulkhead, and the deck beam, in turn, to the top of the lower skin; then the top skin is bonded on, creating a "unitized" connection all the way through.

Apply a *fillet* (a bead of thickened adhesive mixture) to each side of the bulkhead at the overhead using a low-density adhesive. Use a cake decorator to apply the fillets and form them into a cove shape using a popsicle stick or tongue depressor. Finally, insert dowels downward through the deck and into the bulkhead framing to provide some cross grain.

Place dowels from outside the hull through the shell planking, sheer clamp, and the edge blocking of the deck structure. Dowels can be placed down through the deck edge blocking and into the clamp. When the guard and toerail are added, insert more dowels through them and into the background material. This way, the whole structure is knitted together with an interlocking web of glue lines and grain.

CHAPTER 10

Building the Mold: Shell Frame

For hulls of about 30 feet in length or more, the shell frame method of molding offers advantages over the mold frame method previously described. However, all materials must be of marine quality.

Stringers are distributed over shell frames, both becoming part of the completed hull. It is important that stringers have sufficient depth (measured at 90 degrees to the shell surface) to support the hull shell during lay-up and at sea. Normally, shell frames occur at stationlines on the lofting, so their shapes are easy to determine. This spacing in turn determines the stringer size. Two-inch-deep stringers are good for a spacing of about 3 feet, and 3-inch-deep stringers are good for a spacing of about 4 feet. If the spacing of the shell frames shown on the plans (or stationlines on the lofting) is too great, requiring stringers that are too thick to be practical, add temporary mold frames between the shell frames to support the stringers during shell lay-up.

Shell frames generally are cut from sheets of plywood and occasionally from fitted pieces of solid timber. Transfer the outlines to various pieces of template material, as previously described, but this time deduct only the hull shell thickness. Fit the template pieces together to form an outline of one half-beam of the hull. Trace the outline on the frame material, then saw it out in pairs on a bandsaw. This way both sides of the shell frame are cut out at once. The frame is then joined at the middle and braced with the addition of a cross-spall.

SETTING UP BULKHEADS AND FRAMES

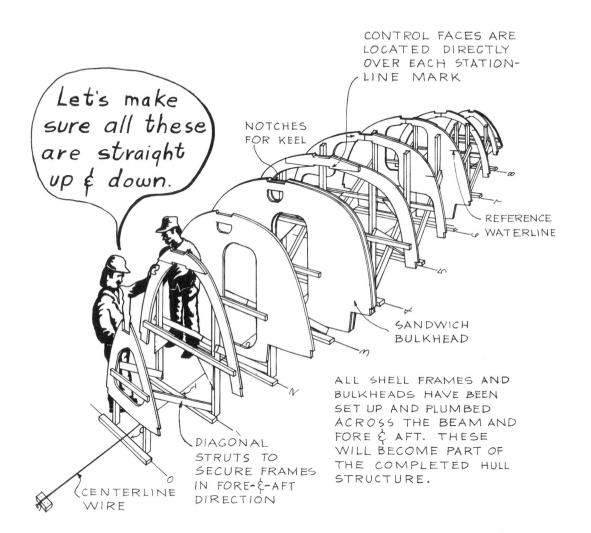

MARKING OUT AND PLACING STRINGERS

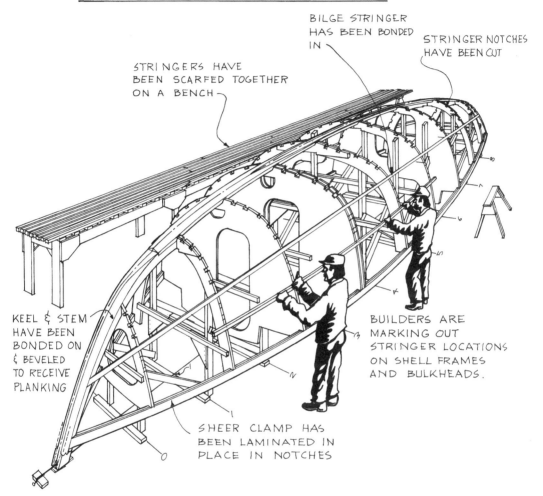

BILGE STRINGER
HAS BEEN BONDED
IN

STRINGER NOTCHES
HAVE BEEN CUT

STRINGERS HAVE
BEEN SCARFED TOGETHER
ON A BENCH

KEEL & STEM
HAVE BEEN
BONDED ON
& BEVELED
TO RECEIVE
PLANKING

BUILDERS ARE
MARKING OUT
STRINGER LOCATIONS
ON SHELL FRAMES
AND BULKHEADS.

SHEER CLAMP HAS
BEEN LAMINATED IN
PLACE IN NOTCHES

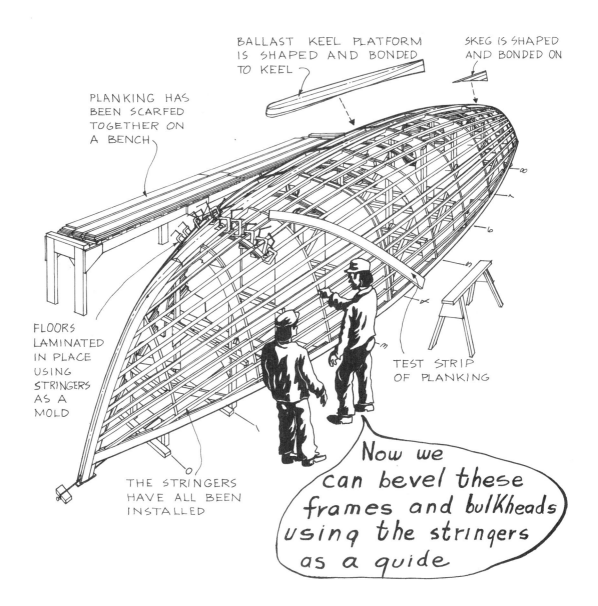

FAIRING FRAME

Plot the reference waterline and sheerline on the frame. Mark the centerline on the frame and on the cross-spall. Verify the beam of each frame by measuring out from the centerline to the sheer on each side and comparing it with the lofting. All the reference marks are used in aligning the frames, using a marked straightedge as previously described. Attach legs to the control edge of each shell frame so that the frames can be set up on the foundation or floor and secured with struts. The edges of the frames need not be beveled at this point.

Bulkheads can be considered shell frames that are solid, or mostly solid, all the way across. They can be made from single-thickness plywood, with or without edges of solid lumber, or they can be made using the sandwich-construction method, with plywood outer surfaces bonded to an internal framework and filled with a rigid foam core.

Shell frames, bulkheads, and partial bulkheads that do not occur on stationlines can be plotted on the lofting as described in Chapter 4. Support partial bulkheads with mold frames during shell lay-up. Set up these frames and bulkheads on the foundation or floor as described before.

Pre-coat all shell frames and bulkheads with resin, allowing the resin to cure before setting these structural members into the mold.

THE KEEL AND STEM

The keel and stem are fabricated as before, but because there are no ribbands to compensate for, the notches at the top of the shell frames are cut deeper so the keel will lie flush with the adjacent shell frame.

If the stem is to be laminated in place, a temporary mold frame is plotted, fabricated, and placed in the setup. It runs from the first shell frame to the foundation or floor and will be removed after the stem has been laid up, bonded, and cured. The centerline is marked on stem and keel.

Shaping the stem to provide a bonding surface for shell planking is complicated somewhat by the absence of ribbands. The shell frames must be relied on, but since they are widely spaced, a long batten will be needed to reach over several of them. Using the batten as a guide, cut notches in the stem close enough to allow shaping of the stem with a plane. When the stem is near its final shape, verify its fairness using a batten placed along as many shell frames as practicable, then sand to final smoothness.

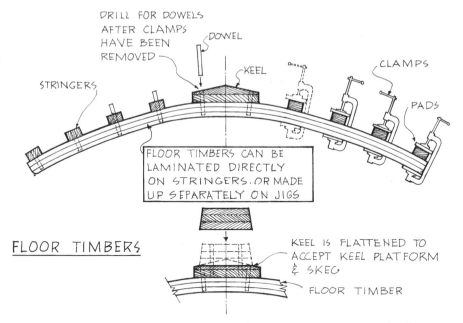

DRILL FOR DOWELS AFTER CLAMPS HAVE BEEN REMOVED

DOWEL

KEEL

CLAMPS

PADS

STRINGERS

FLOOR TIMBERS CAN BE LAMINATED DIRECTLY ON STRINGERS. OR MADE UP SEPARATELY ON JIGS

FLOOR TIMBERS

KEEL IS FLATTENED TO ACCEPT KEEL PLATFORM & SKEG

FLOOR TIMBER

The keel bevel must begin at shell frame locations, using the frame itself as a guide. This leaves long spaces between frames where the keel bevel must be planed. Use a stiff batten placed along the keel bevel to check fairness.

For heavier shell lay-ups, cross-spalls of substantial timber can be used to transfer shell weight to the foundation. Fasten these to shell-frame extensions so that their lower edges are aligned to provide an appropriate working elevation.

MAKING AND INSTALLING STRINGERS

Make stringers the length of the hull shell by scarfing material together end to end. These can be laminated in place, using the shell frames as a form, or fashioned of solid lumber as called for on the plan. A scarfing jig can be made to cut the scarf joint quickly by clamping stringer material together and guiding a power circular saw through it with the help of a fence.

Mark the locations of the stringers, using a long batten as a guide. Place a batten across the shell frames at about the turn of the bilge, with the ends curving toward the sheerline somewhat. When the batten is fair and flat with the frame edges, fix it in place long enough to draw marks on the frame edges. Remove the batten and duplicate the marks for the other side.

SCARFING

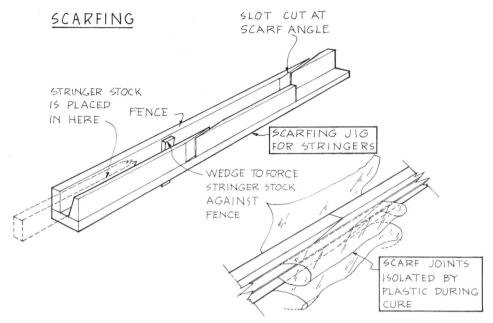

SLOT CUT AT SCARF ANGLE

STRINGER STOCK IS PLACED IN HERE

FENCE

SCARFING JIG FOR STRINGERS

WEDGE TO FORCE STRINGER STOCK AGAINST FENCE

SCARF JOINTS ISOLATED BY PLASTIC DURING CURE

The other stringers cannot be placed simply by dividing the distance along the girth of each shell frame into equal spaces. On most hulls, the stringers would twist and fail to lie fair. With long thin hulls having little compound curve the stringers can run parallel to the sheer at equal spaces. The stringers will then run in to the keel toward the ends. It is important to run the stringers so that their depth is as nearly perpendicular as possible to the shell-frame surface, into which they will be recessed.

Begin locating the stringers on a frame near the boat's maximum beam, measuring out from the first mark a distance equal to the maximum gap permitted by the construction plan. If this area has a sharp curvature, close the gap somewhat and reserve the maximum gap for flatter parts of the curve. Draw tentative location marks to represent all the stringers for that side of the hull. Fix some flexible battens on the marks on the shell frames to see how fair they lie. Move them a little bit if needed. It should be possible to devise a fair run with the lines converging more-or-less uniformly toward the ends. It is best to have closer spacing in areas of sharper curvature because that is where the stringers are most likely to deflect during shell lay-up. Don't terminate stringers at a frame but continue on until they intersect a sheer clamp, keel, stem, or transom. Move the battens to new marks and repeat until a fair run of stringers is marked.

When the location of stringers is marked for the entire hull, draw notches at each mark, using a sawed-off piece of stringer to trace the outline of the cut. Saw along the sides of the outline with a handsaw. Remove the wood between the cuts with a sharp chisel. Alternatively, use a power circular saw with its blade set to notch depth.

Dry fit the stringers in the notches; they should fit snugly. Sight by eye for a fair flow of stringers. The notches of any high stringers can be deepened by filing. Low stringers can be raised slightly with shims.

Cut the stringers so that they butt against the back of the stem where they will be bonded. They are also bonded into triangular notches cut into the transom framing. Stringers are feathered out against clamps and keels for bonding.

When you've finished tentative fairing, remove the dry-fitted stringers. Pre-coat all stringers with resin prior to final installation. With a stiff adhesive mixture, coat the inside surfaces of the line of notches to receive the first stringer. Replace the stringer for setting. If the stringer is laminated, coat the bonding faces of the laminates with adhesive mixture and join them. Before setting begins, place the laminated stringer in the notches. Wrap sheet plastic around the stringer at places where it will be handled. When the fit is reasonably snug, the stringers usually hold themselves in place for curing. If the fit is not snug enough, wood wedges can be inserted to tighten it up. For stringers that pop up, use temporary staples or wood screws to keep them in their notches. Staple or screw them into any convenient adjoining material. Do not bond any mold frames in the setup to the stringers, since the mold frames will be discarded later.

Give the mold a final fairing. Begin by beveling the shell frames, using the bonded stringers as a guide. Bend a flexible batten around the mold in various directions to find any remaining high or flat places that need attention.

CHAPTER 11

Laminating the Shell

Prepare plywood stock for the shell laminates by scarfing 4- by 8-foot panels end to end to accommodate the longest plank required for the hull. This length would be a 45-degree diagonal line reaching from sheer to keel, near the middle of the boat. If the boat is small enough to be accommodated by 8-foot lengths of planking, scarfing won't be necessary, except in the interest of waste reduction.

The scarf bevel is on a one-in-eight slope. The thickest plywood likely to be used in shell lamination is ¼ inch thick, so the scarf line would be 2 inches back from the edge. A stack of plywood panels can be stairstepped with the edge of one panel on the scarf line of the one below. The edge of the lowest panel is flush with the edge of the workbench. Clamp the stack of panels to the workbench and plane them all down at once. Start the planing with a smoothing plane, using a deep-set blade to remove wood as quickly as possible. Finish with a more finely set block plane.

A note of caution: The glue in the plywood will dull the blade quickly. Dull blades remove wood unevenly along the different grain directions, resulting in wavy lines of plys. If this happens, the scarf joints will not mate properly. Avoid this by sharpening the blade often. A power plane can save a lot of time in roughing out a scarf bevel.

Joining a 4-foot scarf joint is more of a challenge than making shorter scarf joints in solid timber. A flat work space large enough to accommodate two panels end to end is needed. This space can be a large

RIPPING AND SPILING

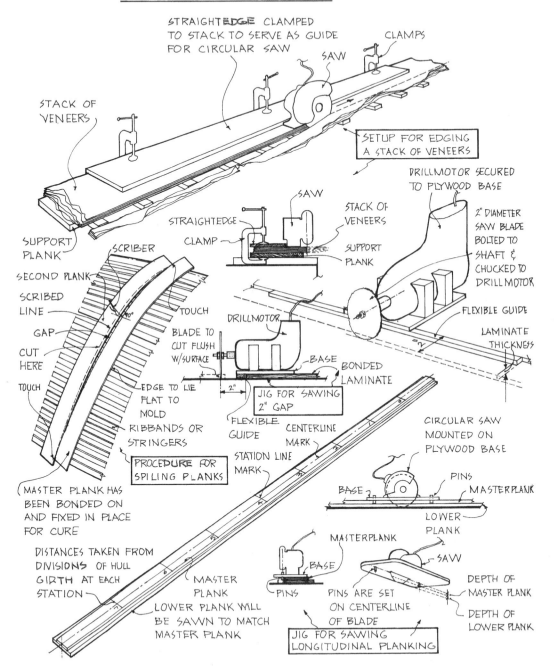

STRAIGHTEDGE CLAMPED TO STACK TO SERVE AS GUIDE FOR CIRCULAR SAW

CLAMPS

SAW

STACK OF VENEERS

SETUP FOR EDGING A STACK OF VENEERS

SUPPORT PLANK

DRILLMOTOR SECURED TO PLYWOOD BASE

2" DIAMETER SAW BLADE BOLTED TO SHAFT & CHUCKED TO DRILLMOTOR

SAW

STRAIGHTEDGE

CLAMP

STACK OF VENEERS

SUPPORT PLANK

SCRIBER

SECOND PLANK

SCRIBED LINE

GAP

CUT HERE

TOUCH

TOUCH

90°

BLADE TO CUT FLUSH W/SURFACE

EDGE TO LIE FLAT TO MOLD RIBBANDS OR STRINGERS

DRILLMOTOR

BASE

BONDED LAMINATE

JIG FOR SAWING 2" GAP

FLEXIBLE GUIDE

FLEXIBLE GUIDE

LAMINATE THICKNESS

2"

CENTERLINE MARK

PROCEDURE FOR SPILING PLANKS

STATION LINE MARK

CIRCULAR SAW MOUNTED ON PLYWOOD BASE

MASTER PLANK HAS BEEN BONDED ON AND FIXED IN PLACE FOR CURE

BASE

PINS

MASTERPLANK

LOWER PLANK

DISTANCES TAKEN FROM DIVISIONS OF HULL GIRTH AT EACH STATION

MASTER PLANK

LOWER PLANK WILL BE SAWN TO MATCH MASTER PLANK

MASTERPLANK

BASE

PINS

MASTERPLANK

SAW

PINS ARE SET ON CENTERLINE OF BLADE

JIG FOR SAWING LONGITUDINAL PLANKING

DEPTH OF MASTER PLANK

DEPTH OF LOWER PLANK

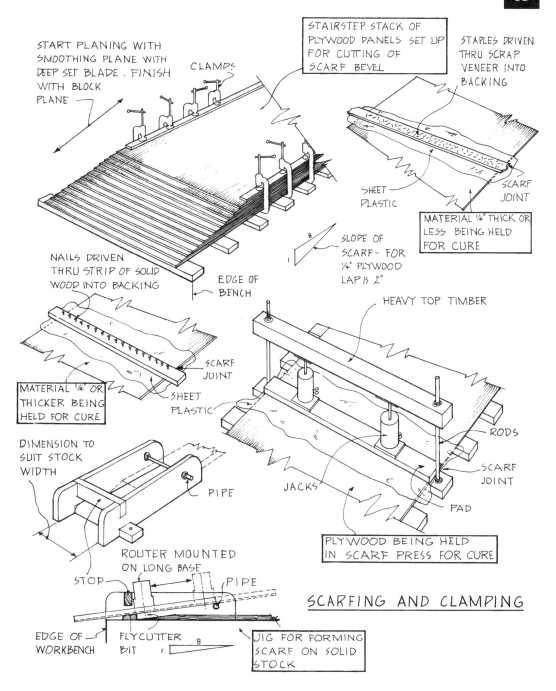

START PLANING WITH SMOOTHING PLANE WITH DEEP SET BLADE. FINISH WITH BLOCK PLANE

CLAMPS

STAIRSTEP STACK OF PLYWOOD PANELS SET UP FOR CUTTING OF SCARF BEVEL

STAPLES DRIVEN THRU SCRAP VENEER INTO BACKING

SHEET PLASTIC

SCARF JOINT

MATERIAL ¼" THICK OR LESS BEING HELD FOR CURE

SLOPE OF SCARF - FOR ¼" PLYWOOD LAP IS 2"

8

1

NAILS DRIVEN THRU STRIP OF SOLID WOOD INTO BACKING

EDGE OF BENCH

HEAVY TOP TIMBER

SCARF JOINT

SHEET PLASTIC

MATERIAL ¼" OR THICKER BEING HELD FOR CURE

RODS

SCARF JOINT

DIMENSION TO SUIT STOCK WIDTH

PIPE

JACKS

PAD

PLYWOOD BEING HELD IN SCARF PRESS FOR CURE

ROUTER MOUNTED ON LONG BASE

STOP

PIPE

SCARFING AND CLAMPING

EDGE OF WORKBENCH

FLYCUTTER BIT

8

1

JIG FOR FORMING SCARF ON SOLID STOCK

workbench or, more likely, the floor. Slide the two panels together so that the scarf faces mate exactly. Check out the fit with a straightedge run across the top of the joint to detect gaps indicating a misfit. If there are any, adjust the panels microscopically until the gaps are gone. Set a staple in the joint near one edge and go to the other side to recheck the fit. When the fit is good, fix that side with a staple. Make several surmarks diagonally across the joint for realignment when bonding. Take apart and coat the bonding surfaces with adhesive mixture, and set them aside long enough for the end grain of the plywood to become saturated. When this has been done, place the reassembled joint over a backing material that will accept staples or nails. When the panels have been aligned exactly, fix each end of the joint with a staple to prevent movement while clamping. Plastic sheeting must be placed above and below the joint to prevent panels from bonding to anything but each other. For plywood up to ¼ inch thick, temporary staples will hold the joint for curing when driven through a strip of scrap veneer or thin plywood, through the scarf joint, and into the backing. For thicker plywood, use nails and a thicker material placed on top. The joined plywood panels are sawn into planking as required for the job.

Solid lumber is also used in laminating hull shells. It is normally dressed on four sides and ranges from ¼-inch to ⅝-inch thickness.

Prepare veneer stock by clamping a stack of veneer between a heavy plank (say a 2 x 12) and a 1 x 8 straightedge. Use the straightedge as a guide for cutting straight edges with a circular saw on the stack of rough veneers. Most commercial veneers are between 5 inches and 12 inches in width after they have been edged, so use the widest veneer that will wrap around the mold without causing humps in the edges of the veneer. There is no reason for all the veneer planking to be the same width, so long as it lies flat on the mold. Tighter bends require narrower planks. Twelve-inch-wide veneer is probably too wide to lie flat; cut it into two 6-inch-wide planks or three 4-inch-wide planks. Use 6-inch-wide planks if they will lie flat.

Cedar veneers can be expected to bend to a 10-inch radius satisfactorily, while ¼-inch okoume plywood will bend to a 24-inch radius if it is applied in the direction of the dominant grain (the usual way).

Normally, veneers are laminated only over a mold with ribbands spaced a maximum of about 2 inches apart or over a shell that has a heavier first lamination of plywood or solid lumber.

Plywood or solid lumber can be laminated over stringers 6 inches to 8 inches apart, depending on the thickness of the laminating material.

Wider spacing than that might be all right for ¼-inch plywood. The laminating material must be stable enough to hold a constant curve, across the gap, for edge evenness during the laminating process. If the gap is too great at 45 degrees for the first lamination, the planks must be run at 90 degrees across the stringers.

Cover the mold with plastic sheeting to prevent bonding of the planking to the mold. Do not cover the stem and keel with the sheeting because these will be bonded to the shell. If the shell planking is laminated over stringers, then plastic sheeting is not used, except where something will not be bonded to the shell.

Veneers are not stable enough to be pre-coated with resin. Their edges become wavy, making edge bonding impossible. Plywood is dimensionally stable for pre-coating with resin, and this should be done on the side facing the interior. Pre-coating does make the plywood stiffer, however, and it may not bend around the tighter curves of the hull. Areas where this would occur should be left dry and coated after the laminate is in place. Solid lumber can be pre-coated, but it is best to test the thinner solid laminates for stability.

In the following discussions about the lamination process, the words *laminate* and *plank* refer to veneers, plywood, or solid lumber. The word *mold* refers to anything that the laminates or planks are built up over, regardless of whether it is a separate mold with ribbands or stringers let into structural bulkheads. In hulls where stringers form the underlying base, it is necessary to outline the location of the stringers on the evolving shell so the builder will know where to place temporary fastenings.

Place one of the planks on the middle of the mold, moving it around a bit to determine a good fit. It should lie about 45 degrees to the horizontal. Each successive layer of laminates lies at about 45 degrees the other way, making them cross the inner layer at 90 degrees. Plan the direction of the first layer and mark the outline of the plank across the mold with a crayon. Duplicate this angle on the opposite side of the hull, producing a mirror image. Replace the plank on its marks after coating all surfaces that the plank will bond to with adhesive mixture. Fix the plank in place for curing by setting staples through the plank and into the mold. The tighter the curve, the more staples will be needed. Planking with a thickness of ¼ inch or more could be clamped to the stringers during the lay-up of the first lamination.

Drive staples through banded strapping tape; they can then be extracted with just a pull on the tape. For planking material that is too

PLASTIC IS PLACED OVER RIBBANDS BUT <u>NOT</u> OVER STEM OR KEEL.

INDICATE WITH PENCIL OUTLINE OF RIBBAND UNDERNEATH

THE FIRST PLANK HAS BEEN BONDED AND TEMPORARILY FASTENED FOR CURE OF ADHESIVE. OTHER PLANKS HAVE BEEN SPILED & BONDED ALONGSIDE, WORKING FORWARD AND AFT FROM THE ORIGINAL PLANK.

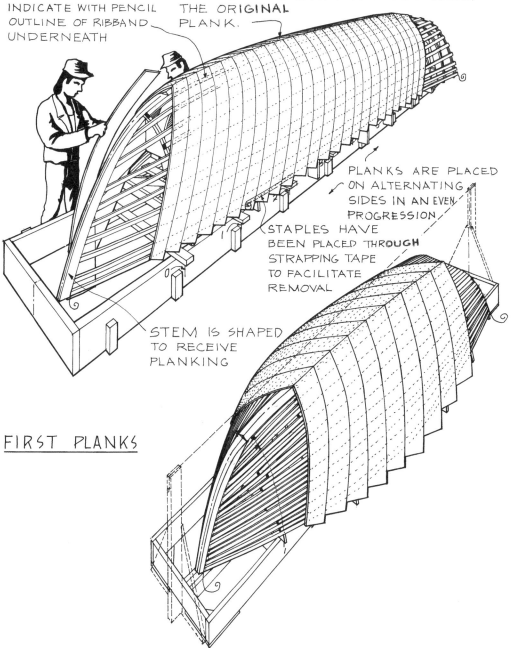

PLANKS ARE PLACED ON ALTERNATING SIDES IN AN EVEN PROGRESSION

STAPLES HAVE BEEN PLACED THROUGH STRAPPING TAPE TO FACILITATE REMOVAL

STEM IS SHAPED TO RECEIVE PLANKING

FIRST PLANKS

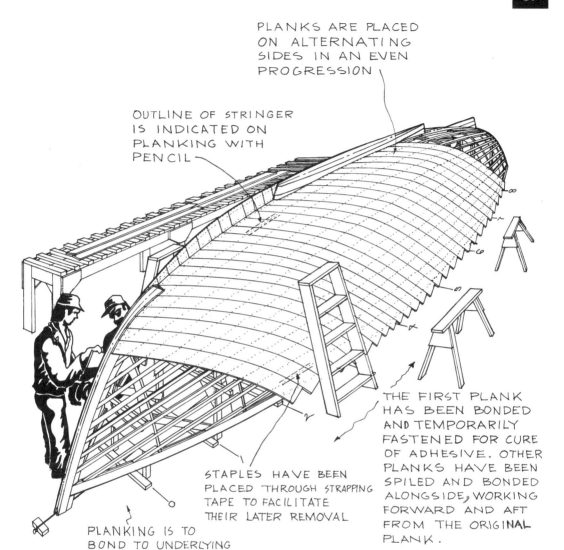

PLANKS ARE PLACED ON ALTERNATING SIDES IN AN EVEN PROGRESSION

OUTLINE OF STRINGER IS INDICATED ON PLANKING WITH PENCIL

THE FIRST PLANK HAS BEEN BONDED AND TEMPORARILY FASTENED FOR CURE OF ADHESIVE. OTHER PLANKS HAVE BEEN SPILED AND BONDED ALONGSIDE, WORKING FORWARD AND AFT FROM THE ORIGINAL PLANK.

STAPLES HAVE BEEN PLACED THROUGH STRAPPING TAPE TO FACILITATE THEIR LATER REMOVAL

PLANKING IS TO BOND TO UNDERLYING STRUCTURE SO NO PLASTIC IS USED

thick for staples, use nails driven through protective wood pads on the surface.

The first plank becomes the master plank because it controls the angle for all the other planks in the lamination. Duplicate it on the opposite side. Planks are added forward and aft of these master planks until the mold is covered. Four teams of plankers can work simultaneously, two teams working forward and two working aft.

When the second plank is placed alongside the master plank, it will become apparent that it won't fit. The top and bottom touch, but the middle will gap open. The art of shaping successive planks to fit is called *spiling.*

Begin the process by placing the second plank alongside the first so that its two edges are equally tight to the mold and it is as close as possible to the first plank. Fix the middle of the plank to the mold with some staples. Verify that the plank lies fair by moving the ends around slightly before fixing the ends temporarily with some staples. You'll need a measuring device that will hold a constant distance (usually a compass) for scribing a line on the temporarily fixed plank using the previously bonded plank as a guide. It is important that the scribed line be parallel to the plank edge being used as a guide; thus the scriber or compass must be kept at 90 degrees to the guide edge.

Rough cut with a bandsaw or sabersaw and finish to the scribed line with a block plane. A power plane can be used on planks thicker than ¼ inch. Planks ⅛ inch thick or less probably can be shaped with a block plane alone. The spiled plank should butt snugly up against the previous plank when dry-fitted for inspection.

When a satisfactory fit has been achieved, coat the surfaces to be bonded with adhesive mixture. Planks placed over a solid mold should be edge-bonded to the preceding plank. Planks placed over stringers or ribbands that have gaps of a couple of inches or more should not be edge-bonded to the previous plank; the second layer of laminates will draw the first layer into line when it is bonded on.

Replace the second plank on the mold, snuggle it up to the preceding plank, and fix it for curing with staples or nails. Spile and bond planks symmetrically right and left as progress is made toward the ends of the hull. If the rake of the planks changes, correct it by installing a tapered plank.

Remove residual adhesive before it can harden and cause havoc during lamination of the next layer. The hardened resin is very difficult to sand when fairing up the hull.

To begin the second lamination layer, start with a master plank in the middle of the hull that crosses the planks of the first lamination at about 90 degrees. Successive veneer planks can be spiled the same way as those of the first lamination. A device can be constructed to fit planks using an alternate method. Mount a 2-inch-diameter saw blade on a drill motor secured to a piece of plywood. Fasten a flexible guide the same thickness as the plank to the plywood base. Now the motor and saw can slide along the first veneer, making a precisely spiled cut on a plank positioned nearby. Rig the saw to make a cut exactly 2 inches away from the edge of the first plank and just deep enough to cut the neighboring plank without cutting into the planks underneath (a router can be rigged to do the same thing). Cover the entire hull with planks that are in no place more than 2 inches apart. Then, with one of these handy gadgets, zip out spaces exactly 2 inches wide between all the bonded planks. Bond between each pair of planks a bunch of 2-inch-wide planks you've previously prepared, and spiling can be avoided altogether. This process normally is used for the inner laminations. The exposed inner and outer laminations of the hull are usually spiled just because this looks better.

As successive planks are marked out and placed in the second layer of laminates, remove the staples or nails used to fix the first layer during curing from the space to be occupied by the next plank. Thicken the adhesive mixture with enough filler so it can fill any gaps that develop between the laminations. Take care to ensure even distribution of adhesive mixture over the bonding surfaces. Some builders prefer to apply adhesive with a standard foam roller. Others prefer a notched plastic spreader, which is probably best for evenly coating the bonding surface.

Clean the surface area where the next plank will be bonded. Apply adhesive mixture to it and to the underside of the plank. Fix the plank with enough fastenings to hold it in place. Staples driven into a solid backing should be about 2 inches apart. Nails can be spaced farther apart, but they must be driven into the underlying stringers, the locations of which should be marked on the planking.

Remove any excess adhesive oozing out along the edges of the plank beyond that needed to coat the edge of the plank (okay for this and later layers). Adhesive buildup under the planking can cause a hump that is difficult to fair. When the second lamination layer is underway, allow several hours for previously bonded planks to cure, then pull up the staples or nails. The first couple of laminations will require staples long enough to penetrate into the mold. Successive laminations require

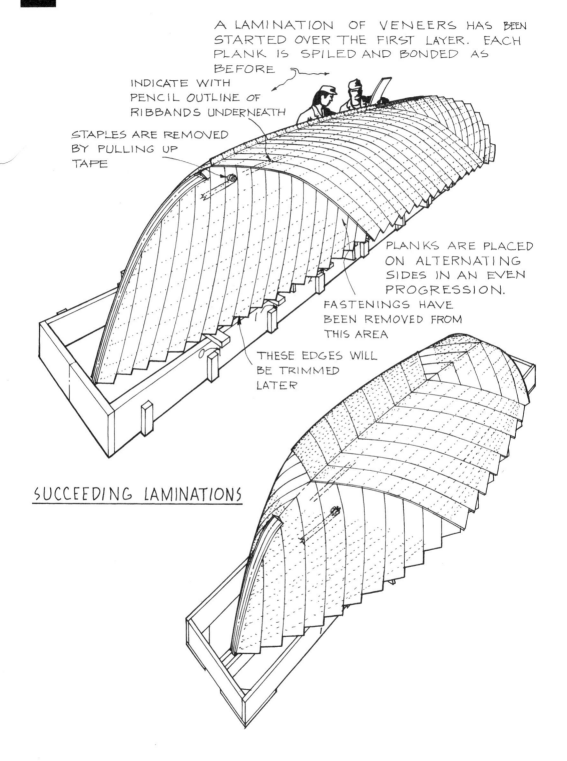

A LAMINATION OF VENEERS HAS BEEN STARTED OVER THE FIRST LAYER. EACH PLANK IS SPILED AND BONDED AS BEFORE

INDICATE WITH PENCIL OUTLINE OF RIBBANDS UNDERNEATH

STAPLES ARE REMOVED BY PULLING UP TAPE

PLANKS ARE PLACED ON ALTERNATING SIDES IN AN EVEN PROGRESSION.

FASTENINGS HAVE BEEN REMOVED FROM THIS AREA

THESE EDGES WILL BE TRIMMED LATER

SUCCEEDING LAMINATIONS

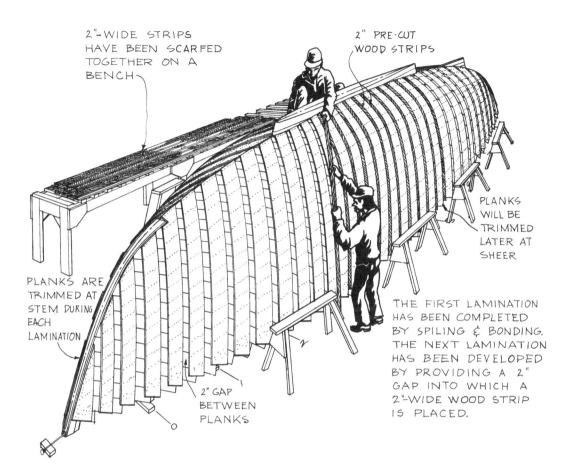

2"-WIDE STRIPS HAVE BEEN SCARFED TOGETHER ON A BENCH

2" PRE-CUT WOOD STRIPS

PLANKS WILL BE TRIMMED LATER AT SHEER

PLANKS ARE TRIMMED AT STEM DURING EACH LAMINATION

2" GAP BETWEEN PLANKS

THE FIRST LAMINATION HAS BEEN COMPLETED BY SPILING & BONDING. THE NEXT LAMINATION HAS BEEN DEVELOPED BY PROVIDING A 2" GAP INTO WHICH A 2"-WIDE WOOD STRIP IS PLACED.

staples short enough to grip into the previous layers, but not so long that they penetrate the shell.

The lower the temperature in the work space, the longer the adhesive takes to cure, and the longer the time until it is safe to extract the temporary fastenings. If a lump of excess adhesive feels firm when poked with your finger but will still dent, the time is right to remove the fastenings.

After completing the second layer of laminates and removing all the fastenings, lightly sand the entire surface to remove any beads of adhesive and to fair the edges of any planks that have not been pulled completely flush. The object is to provide a smooth and fair surface for a completely uniform coating of adhesive for the next lamination. Apply successive laminations as previously described. If the hull is to be varnished, the final lamination can be run horizontally for the sake of appearance. This is strictly an aesthetic decision, however, and diagonal planking is seen frequently.

To prepare planking for horizontal lamination, wood must be cut and scarfed together so each plank is long enough to cover the hull from end to end. The width of these planks is determined by the curvature of the hull. The narrowest radius will control plank width; a 3- to 5-inch width seems to work best for most round-bilge boats. Test these roughed-out planks to see how they lie against the previously laid-up planking, then taper them toward the ends so they fit fairly over the hull. This can be done without spiling by shaping a master plank to be used as a pattern for all the other planks. Usually a couple of these master planks are used per side, since the topsides will have a plank shaped slightly differently from the bottom planks.

To begin the process, temporarily fix one of the roughed-out planks along the middle of the bilge. This should be positioned by eye so that the ends curve slightly toward the sheerline. The two edges of the plank should be uniformly tight to the shell surface. If it has not been done previously, the line of the sheer should be marked out or indicated with a batten fixed to the shell. Measure from sheerline to plank at the widest girth of the hull, and divide that dimension evenly into divisions narrower than the roughed-out planks. Remember, tighter turns require narrower planks. Repeat this measurement at points all along the hull from end to end, and divide all these dimensions into the number of divisions that was chosen for the first measurement. Mark where these measurements were taken on the master plank. Remove the master plank and strike a centerline on it from end to end.

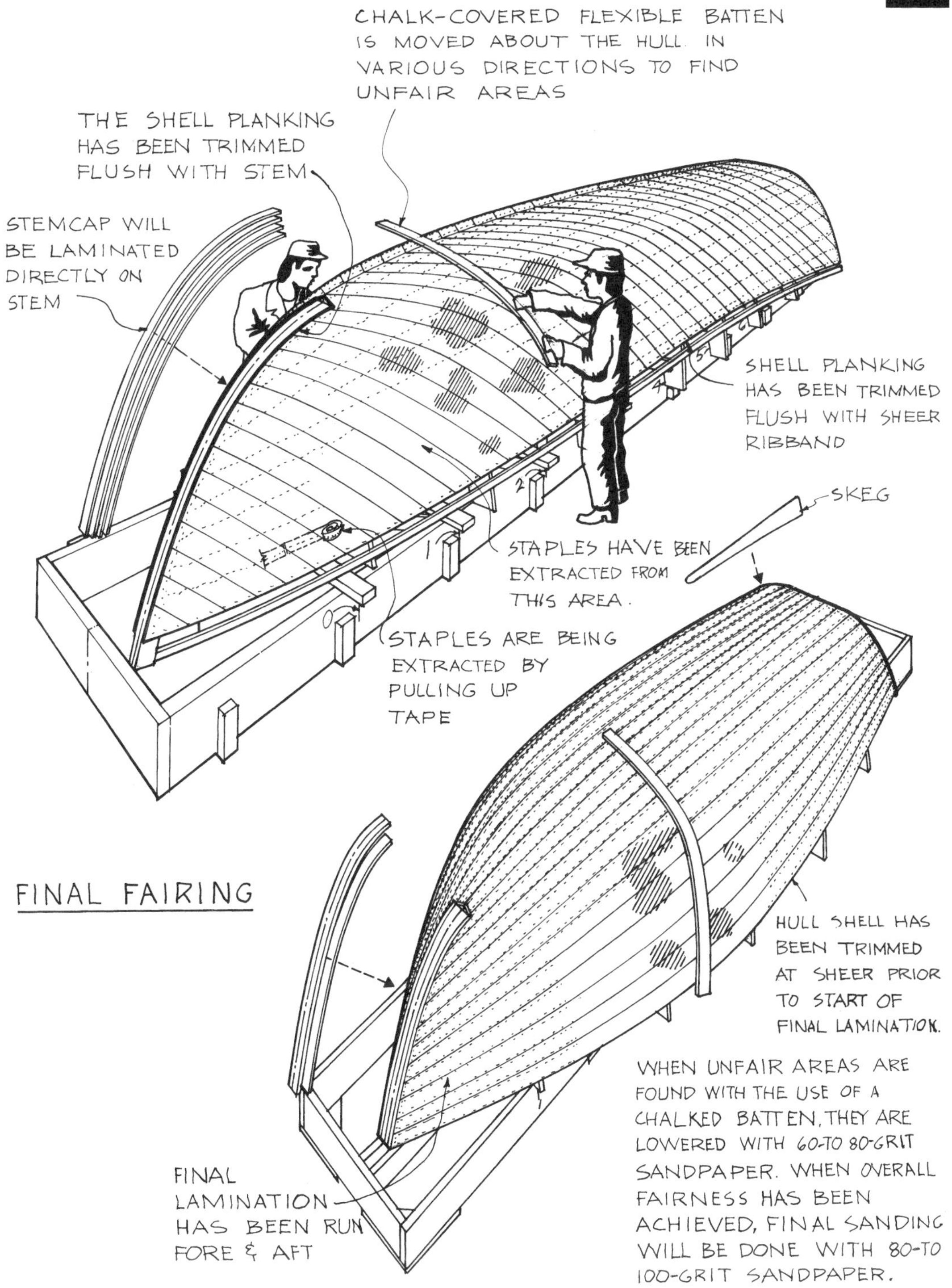

CHALK-COVERED FLEXIBLE BATTEN IS MOVED ABOUT THE HULL IN VARIOUS DIRECTIONS TO FIND UNFAIR AREAS

THE SHELL PLANKING HAS BEEN TRIMMED FLUSH WITH STEM

STEMCAP WILL BE LAMINATED DIRECTLY ON STEM

SHELL PLANKING HAS BEEN TRIMMED FLUSH WITH SHEER RIBBAND

SKEG

STAPLES HAVE BEEN EXTRACTED FROM THIS AREA.

STAPLES ARE BEING EXTRACTED BY PULLING UP TAPE

FINAL FAIRING

HULL SHELL HAS BEEN TRIMMED AT SHEER PRIOR TO START OF FINAL LAMINATION.

WHEN UNFAIR AREAS ARE FOUND WITH THE USE OF A CHALKED BATTEN, THEY ARE LOWERED WITH 60-TO 80-GRIT SANDPAPER. WHEN OVERALL FAIRNESS HAS BEEN ACHIEVED, FINAL SANDING WILL BE DONE WITH 80-TO 100-GRIT SANDPAPER.

FINAL LAMINATION HAS BEEN RUN FORE & AFT

FINAL FAIRING

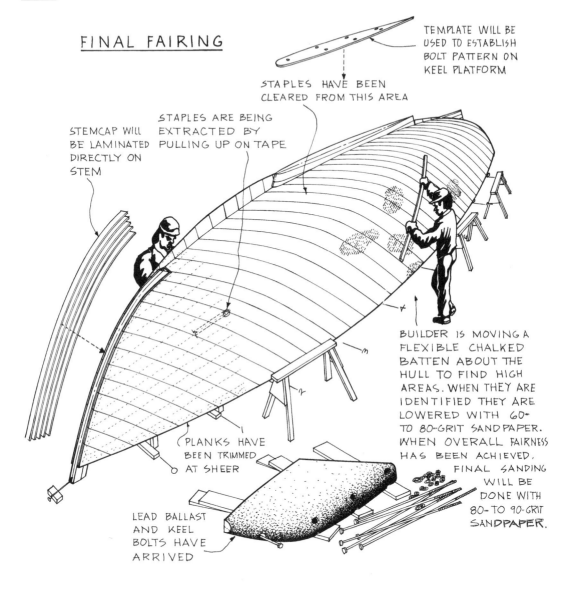

TEMPLATE WILL BE USED TO ESTABLISH BOLT PATTERN ON KEEL PLATFORM

STAPLES HAVE BEEN CLEARED FROM THIS AREA

STEMCAP WILL BE LAMINATED DIRECTLY ON STEM

STAPLES ARE BEING EXTRACTED BY PULLING UP ON TAPE

BUILDER IS MOVING A FLEXIBLE CHALKED BATTEN ABOUT THE HULL TO FIND HIGH AREAS. WHEN THEY ARE IDENTIFIED THEY ARE LOWERED WITH 60- TO 80-GRIT SANDPAPER. WHEN OVERALL FAIRNESS HAS BEEN ACHIEVED, FINAL SANDING WILL BE DONE WITH 80- TO 90-GRIT SANDPAPER.

PLANKS HAVE BEEN TRIMMED AT SHEER

LEAD BALLAST AND KEEL BOLTS HAVE ARRIVED

The plank width is now known at each place where the girth measurement was taken. Mark the corresponding plank width at each point along the master plank, using the centerline as a reference. The resulting line of dots can be joined, using a long, flexible batten, to show the outline of the master plank.

Cut out the plank using a portable power saw and shape it to the line with a plane. Using this master plank as a pattern, cut and shape a sufficient number of other planks to cover each side to the level where the master plank was originally fixed. A guide can be prepared for a portable power saw that will enable the boatbuilder to cut out the other planks without having to mark the shape on them. Cut and shape thin planks with hand tools.

Start bonding the planks at the sheer, and continue the bonding process on alternate sides until all the shaped planks have been used up. Divide the balance of the shell into plank widths by taking girth measurements from the last horizontal plank bonded to the keel. Use these widths to generate a master plank for the remaining planks.

Cut completed shell planking off flush at the stem and at the transom where it has been bonded over the edge of the transom structure. Cut the planking also at the centerline or shoe line of the keel, and trim it off at the sheer. Laminate the stemcap directly over the forward end of the shell to cover the end grain of the shell laminates. Before starting the stemcap lamination, coat the end grain of the shell laminates with sufficient resin to saturate the wood cells. Before the shell cap has been shaped and is still square, it can be drilled and doweled as called for on the plans. The shaping of the completed stemcap lay-up is done using the same process as previously described for the stem.

Once the final shell lamination is complete, sand the hull with 60- to 80-grit sandpaper to remove any lumps of adhesive and obvious high spots. Finish fairing with a block or smoothing plane and 80- to 100-grit sandpaper, concentrating on local areas. A chalked, flexible batten can aid overall fairing. Slide the chalked batten about the hull in various directions until high areas begin to show up. When the entire hull is completely fair and smooth, it is ready for sheathing.

CHAPTER 12

Applying Sheathing

Fiberglass cloth is suitable for sheathing a laminated wood hull because such a hull is dimensionally stable and does not require an elastic sheathing material. Other woven fabrics used in boatbuilding can stretch almost 30 percent, compared with 3 percent for fiberglass. This stretching ability is useful for some applications, but a laminated wood hull would break before the advantages of these materials came into play. Fiberglass cloth adds strength and stiffness to the hull, as well as much-needed abrasion and impact resistance.

To prepare the hull for sheathing, saturate the bare wood with an even coating of resin. If the weather is cold, heat the work space, or at least heat the resin so that it is thin enough for the air in the wood fiber to bubble out through it. The resin must thoroughly penetrate the wood to gain the strength of the wood grain itself. Begin by rolling a coating of resin over the entire hull, then wait a few minutes to see if any dry spots appear; re-roll any dry areas. Now is the time to fill dings and staple holes with a slightly thickened adhesive mixture.

Cut out and drape a dry panel of fiberglass cloth over the middle of the hull from sheer to sheer. Drape a second one next to it, with about a ½-inch overlap. Continue until the entire hull is covered. At the bow it will be necessary to tape across the stem and at the forefoot temporarily. Once the epoxy is combined, the resin will allow at most one hour of work time before it starts to set up, so plan accordingly. Wearing rubber gloves, roll on resin starting at the middle panel and work toward the ends. Start to squeegee at the centerline and work toward the sheer, then do the same thing to the other side.

Apply fiberglass to the transom using the "wet" method. Lightly coat the transom with resin and place a panel of fiberglass cloth in the wet resin. Begin squeegeeing, ensuring that the fabric is properly wet out, with no epoxy buildup causing the fabric to float off the surface. Air trapped in the cloth–resin matrix must be forced out. Just as important, dry spots, which appear as dull, whitish areas, should be re-coated as soon as possible. When the hull is properly coated, the weave in the cloth should be about two-thirds filled.

The fabric is easiest to trim using a sharp, clean blade, after curing for two or three hours. If your timing is right, the fabric overlap can be sliced down the middle in a straight line. Remove the extra strips of cloth from each side, then smooth the fabric back down on the hull surface for a perfect butt joint. If the cloth has become too hard to cut and lift, the overlap will have to be sanded fair.

Use the wet method to apply strips of fiberglass cloth over the stem, forefoot, and transom junctions, lapping the cloth over the hull from 4 to 6 inches. The edges will be sanded fair later with the hull.

If the hull will be varnished, use glass cloth with a weight of no more than 4 ounces; otherwise, the weave will show through the finish.

If the boat will have a different bottom color than topside color, a thin string of nylon or some other synthetic material can be bonded to the hull at the separation, or waterline. With the hull upside down it is relatively easy to locate this separation line from the plans. Set up a horizontal straightedge at each end of the hull in the plane of the separation. Stretch a string between the straightedges around the hull to mark the location of the line. On long hulls it is helpful to have straightedges set up in the middle as well. Alternatively, a movable device could be set up that locates the line by means of a cantilevered arm with an indicator at the end, positioned at the appropriate distance above the floor. The series of points marked can by joined using a flexible batten.

Normally, however, the separation line sweeps toward the sheer in the forward half of the hull. Mark the inverted hull on the stem below the waterline mark. The separation fairs into the horizontal line at about the middle of the hull. This can be done by eye, using a long, flexible batten. Once the line is faired in on one side, it can be copied on the other side using the horizontal waterline as a reference.

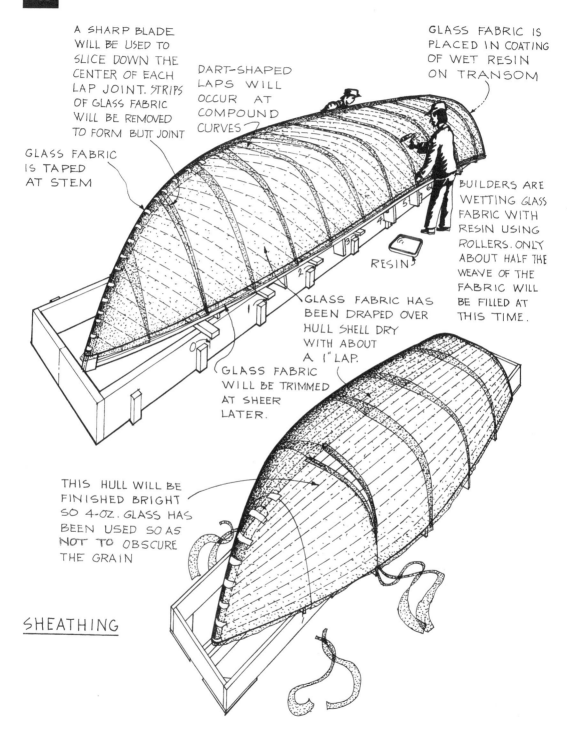

A SHARP BLADE WILL BE USED TO SLICE DOWN THE CENTER OF EACH LAP JOINT. STRIPS OF GLASS FABRIC WILL BE REMOVED TO FORM BUTT JOINT

DART-SHAPED LAPS WILL OCCUR AT COMPOUND CURVES

GLASS FABRIC IS PLACED IN COATING OF WET RESIN ON TRANSOM

GLASS FABRIC IS TAPED AT STEM

BUILDERS ARE WETTING GLASS FABRIC WITH RESIN USING ROLLERS. ONLY ABOUT HALF THE WEAVE OF THE FABRIC WILL BE FILLED AT THIS TIME.

RESIN

GLASS FABRIC HAS BEEN DRAPED OVER HULL SHELL DRY WITH ABOUT A 1" LAP.

GLASS FABRIC WILL BE TRIMMED AT SHEER LATER.

THIS HULL WILL BE FINISHED BRIGHT SO 4-OZ. GLASS HAS BEEN USED SO AS NOT TO OBSCURE THE GRAIN

SHEATHING

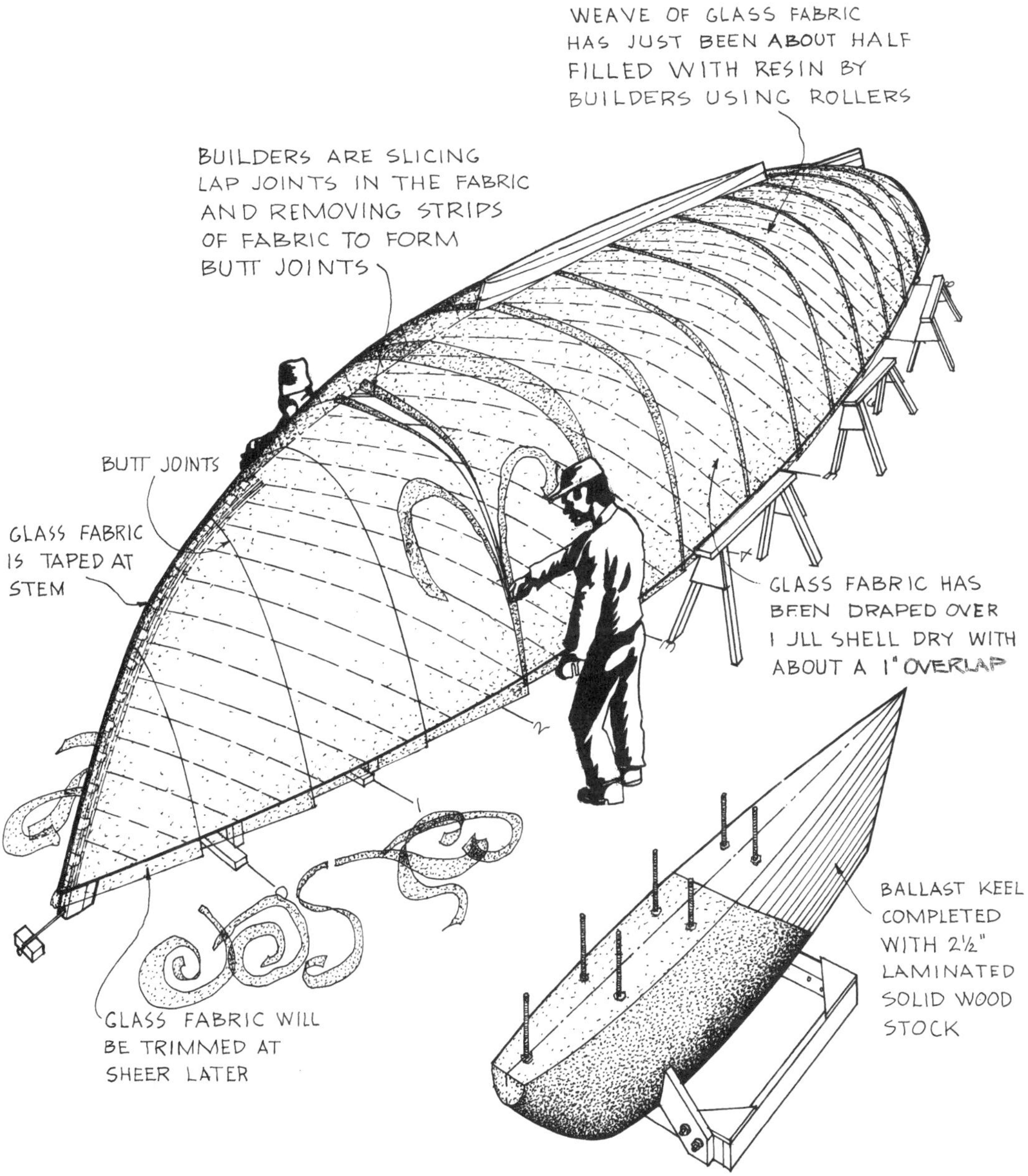

WEAVE OF GLASS FABRIC
HAS JUST BEEN ABOUT HALF
FILLED WITH RESIN BY
BUILDERS USING ROLLERS

BUILDERS ARE SLICING
LAP JOINTS IN THE FABRIC
AND REMOVING STRIPS
OF FABRIC TO FORM
BUTT JOINTS

BUTT JOINTS

GLASS FABRIC
IS TAPED AT
STEM

GLASS FABRIC HAS
BEEN DRAPED OVER
HULL SHELL DRY WITH
ABOUT A 1" OVERLAP

BALLAST KEEL
COMPLETED
WITH 2½"
LAMINATED
SOLID WOOD
STOCK

GLASS FABRIC WILL
BE TRIMMED AT
SHEER LATER

FORMING SEPARATION

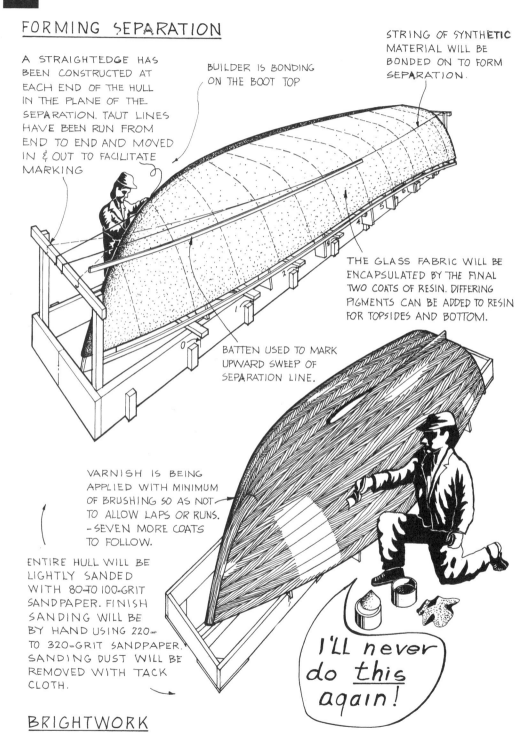

A STRAIGHTEDGE HAS BEEN CONSTRUCTED AT EACH END OF THE HULL IN THE PLANE OF THE SEPARATION. TAUT LINES HAVE BEEN RUN FROM END TO END AND MOVED IN & OUT TO FACILITATE MARKING

BUILDER IS BONDING ON THE BOOT TOP

STRING OF SYNTHETIC MATERIAL WILL BE BONDED ON TO FORM SEPARATION.

THE GLASS FABRIC WILL BE ENCAPSULATED BY THE FINAL TWO COATS OF RESIN. DIFFERING PIGMENTS CAN BE ADDED TO RESIN FOR TOPSIDES AND BOTTOM.

BATTEN USED TO MARK UPWARD SWEEP OF SEPARATION LINE.

VARNISH IS BEING APPLIED WITH MINIMUM OF BRUSHING SO AS NOT TO ALLOW LAPS OR RUNS. — SEVEN MORE COATS TO FOLLOW.

ENTIRE HULL WILL BE LIGHTLY SANDED WITH 80 TO 100 GRIT SANDPAPER. FINISH SANDING WILL BE BY HAND USING 220 TO 320 GRIT SANDPAPER. SANDING DUST WILL BE REMOVED WITH TACK CLOTH.

I'LL never do this again!

BRIGHTWORK

WHEN WEAVE OF GLASS CLOTH HAS
BEEN ENCAPSULATED, THE ENTIRE
HULL WILL BE LIGHTLY SANDED
WITH 80-TO 100-GRIT SANDPAPER.
FINISH SANDING WILL BE BY
HAND USING 220-TO 320-GRIT
SANDPAPER. SANDING DUST WILL
BE REMOVED WITH TACK CLOTH.

BUILDER IS TAPING STRING
OF SYNTHETIC MATERIAL
ALONG SEPARATION
LINE FOR LATER BONDING.

BATTEN USED TO MARK
UPWARD SWEEP OF
SEPARATION LINE

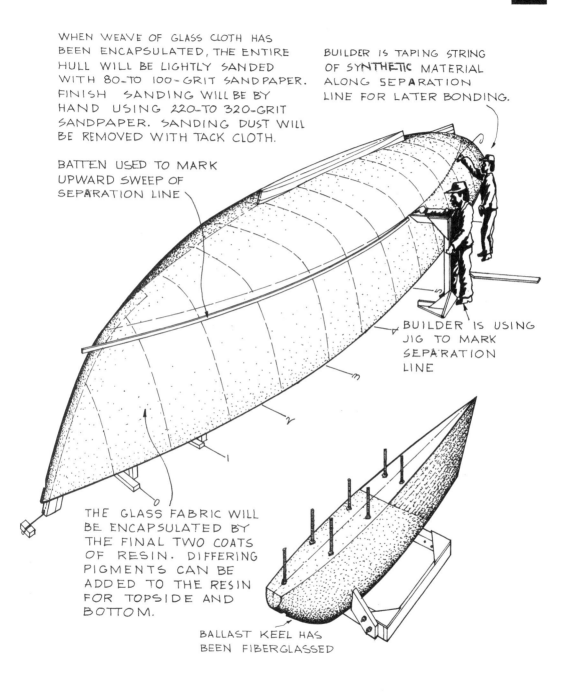

BUILDER IS USING
JIG TO MARK
SEPARATION
LINE

THE GLASS FABRIC WILL
BE ENCAPSULATED BY
THE FINAL TWO COATS
OF RESIN. DIFFERING
PIGMENTS CAN BE
ADDED TO THE RESIN
FOR TOPSIDE AND
BOTTOM.

BALLAST KEEL HAS
BEEN FIBERGLASSED

Run two strips of masking tape, leaving about a ½-inch gap between them, from stem to stern along the path the string will follow. The string itself can be held in place by short pieces of masking tape at close intervals, as you apply the resin with a small brush. After curing begins, remove the tape and re-coat the entire string with resin.

Pigment can be added to the final coats of resin. If the bottom color differs from the topside color, use pigments of contrasting colors, with the string as a demarcation line. Coat topsides that will be varnished with clear resin.

Re-coat the entire hull with two additional coats of resin, beginning the second coat after the preceding coat has begun curing. Be sure the glass cloth's weave is entirely encapsulated in resin. Lightly sand the entire hull with 80- to 100-grit paper. Finish sanding by hand, using 220- to 320-grit paper. Remove sanding dust completely with a tack cloth.

CHAPTER 13

Turning Over the Hull

Because it is easier to build the hull upside down, eventually one faces the prospect of turning it over. Some preparation is in order. For example, for small hulls that don't have projecting keels, cradles to support the rightside-up hull can be laminated, using the hull as a mold. Place plastic sheeting over the hull to prevent the laminates bonding to it. Larger hulls, and ones with projecting keels, will require shoring and chocks. The original foundation for the mold frames can be utilized in the support structure. If the overhead structure will be used, be sure that it is strong enough to hold the hull's weight.

When the hull shell is set up on its cradle or chocks, it must be leveled in each direction. The centerline should be re-rigged overhead for use in making measurements.

One approach for hulls that have been laid up on a mold is simply to line up enough people on each side of the inverted hull to lift it straight up, high enough to clear the mold. They then can carry the hull clear forward or aft and set it down, still inverted, on some blocking.

Dismantle the mold, leaving only the strongback. Attach the laminated cradles to the foundation at the points where they were molded. The hull shell will require some bracing across the beam to preserve its shape. Have everyone lift and rotate the hull by hand, using mattresses or other padding as required. Bring the rightside-up hull back and set it on the padded cradles.

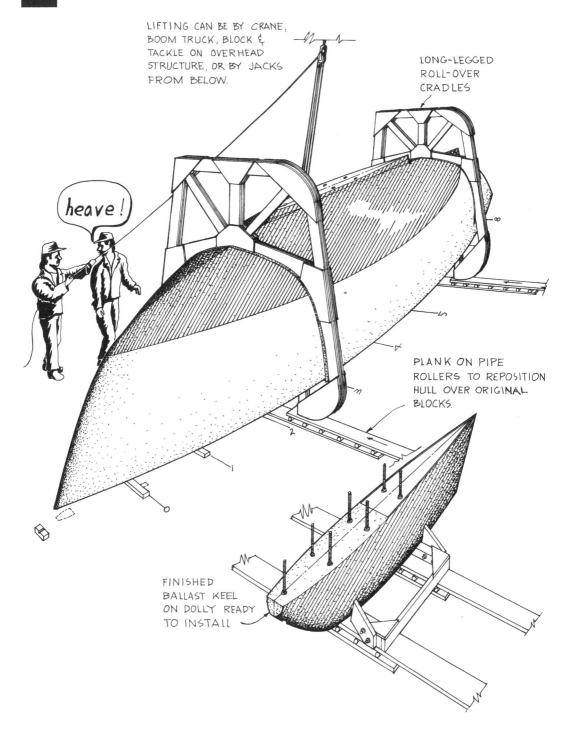

LIFTING CAN BE BY CRANE, BOOM TRUCK, BLOCK & TACKLE ON OVERHEAD STRUCTURE, OR BY JACKS FROM BELOW.

LONG-LEGGED ROLL-OVER CRADLES

heave!

PLANK ON PIPE ROLLERS TO REPOSITION HULL OVER ORIGINAL BLOCKS.

FINISHED BALLAST KEEL ON DOLLY READY TO INSTALL

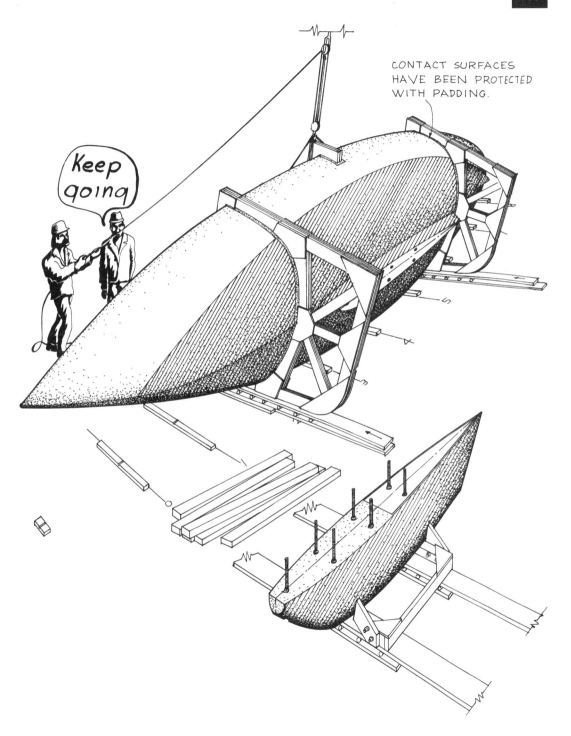

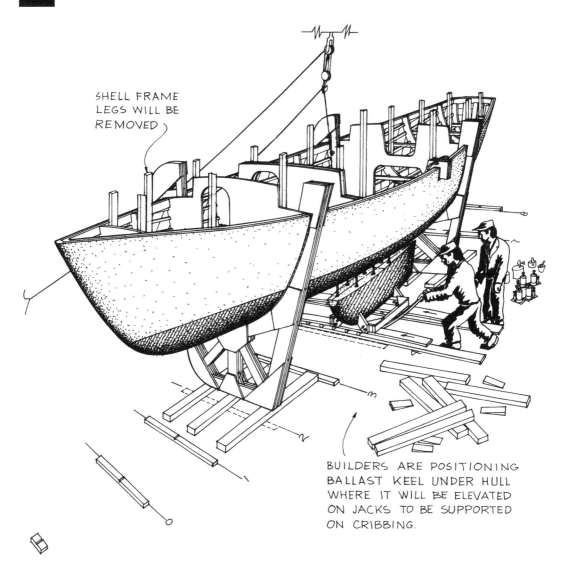

SHELL FRAME
LEGS WILL BE
REMOVED

BUILDERS ARE POSITIONING
BALLAST KEEL UNDER HULL
WHERE IT WILL BE ELEVATED
ON JACKS TO BE SUPPORTED
ON CRIBBING.

Another possibility is to rotate the hull and mold (the mold holds the hull shape as it is rotated) right on the spot. To do this, support the hull on some temporary blocking placed on the foundation or floor. Saw off the mold frames' legs and diagonal struts and remove them. As soon as possible, install the padded cradles to the strongback. Secure the mold to the hull with temporary fastenings or clamps so that the mold does not fall out of the hull as it is turned over. Now, with people on both sides, lift the hull-with-mold enough to walk it to one side. Lift one sheer while bracing the opposite sheer on the padded cradles. Secure lines to the high-side mold frames. Rotate hull to the beam-ends position on the cradles. Carefully lower the hull with lines and with people at the opposite bilge. Finally, center the hull on the cradles and dismantle the mold.

Hulls laminated over stringers and integral bulkheads can be turned over without worrying about the mold falling out of the hull. Hulls up to 36 feet long have been turned over entirely by muscle power. Nevertheless, larger hulls will be turned more easily with the aid of come-a-longs or blocks and tackle secured to adequate structures. This is usually done with a pair of tackles lashed to opposite sheers in such a way that the load is distributed over several mold frames or bulkheads. Another tackle is secured to a temporary fastening in the keel. By means of these tackles, the hull can be lifted and turned and then placed on its cradles or shores. Larger hulls may require two sets of tackles.

Another method is to construct a pair of rings from rough lumber that conform to the curve of one hull side. These half-rings are hooked over one sheer and reach to the keel. Using jacks and cribbing, raise one sheer until the hull is at beam ends. Then use the jacks under the pair of half-rings to lower the hull to the upright position.

Various other methods have been employed to turn hulls—especially larger ones—rightside up. Some have been launched upside down and turned over in the water, while others have been turned over so that they fall into a waterway alongside. The largest hulls may need to be turned over with the aid of building cranes.

CHAPTER 14

Interior Structure

Hulls laid up on disposable molds will present an unobstructed and smooth interior surface. Hulls built over stringers will have the complexity of those stringers and, perhaps, some bulkheads, clamps, and other objects bonded in. These items will have been pre-coated with resin but not the interior of the hull shell. In either case, the preparation of the hull for the addition of interior structure requires the same cleaning process used for the exterior of the hull (see Chapter 19). Coat the previously uncoated surfaces with resin, making sure all dry areas are re-coated. Touch up pre-coated surfaces where required, so that the wood is evenly coated with resin to prevent water from soaking in and allowing rot fungus to form.

If sheer clamps have not been placed in the mold, they can be laminated directly into the hull at this time, using the hull itself as a mold. The clamps will be run along the sheerline, either as a single piece of lumber or as several laminates.

Pre-coat the portion of sheer-clamp material that will be exposed to the atmosphere with resin and allow curing to start. When you are ready to begin the lamination procedure, coat both bonding surfaces with adhesive mixture and install the clamp in the boat, using C-clamps to fix it in position for curing. Lots of C-clamps are required, each with clamp pads to protect the finish material (or use a continuous clamp pad). Apply successive laminates one at a time, using the above procedure.

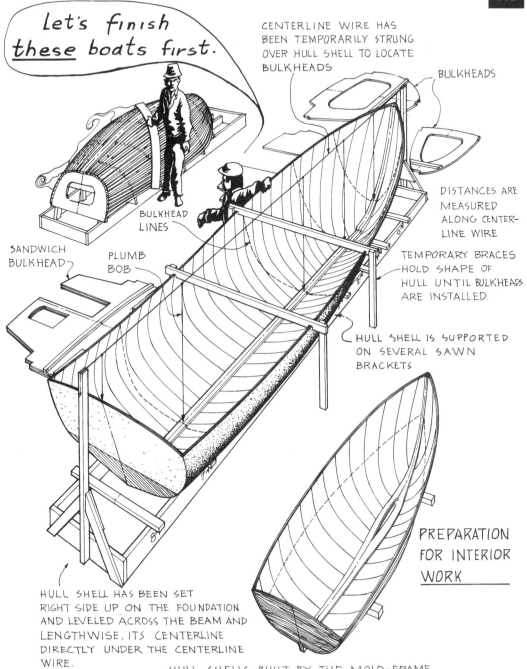

let's finish **these** boats first.

CENTERLINE WIRE HAS BEEN TEMPORARILY STRUNG OVER HULL SHELL TO LOCATE BULKHEADS

BULKHEADS

BULKHEAD LINES

SANDWICH BULKHEAD

PLUMB BOB

DISTANCES ARE MEASURED ALONG CENTER-LINE WIRE

TEMPORARY BRACES HOLD SHAPE OF HULL UNTIL BULKHEADS ARE INSTALLED.

HULL SHELL IS SUPPORTED ON SEVERAL SAWN BRACKETS

HULL SHELL HAS BEEN SET RIGHT SIDE UP ON THE FOUNDATION AND LEVELED ACROSS THE BEAM AND LENGTHWISE, ITS CENTERLINE DIRECTLY UNDER THE CENTERLINE WIRE.

PREPARATION FOR INTERIOR WORK

HULL SHELLS BUILT BY THE MOLD-FRAME METHOD PRESENT AN UNOBSTRUCTED INTERIOR FOR INSTALLATION OF LONGITUDINAL AS WELL AS LATERAL BULKHEADS.

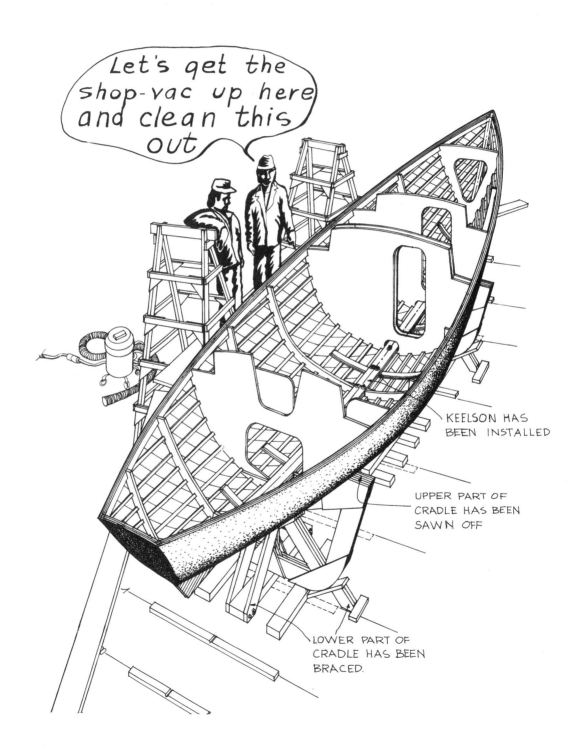

After all of the laminates are applied, bevel the inner surface of the sheer clamp to the required rake angle to accept coamings, house, and trunk sides.

SPILING AND INSTALLING BULKHEADS

Measure and mark the locations for bulkheads and floors in the hull using the centerline wire stretched over the hull and plumb bobs. The shape of the bulkheads to be installed at this time can be taken from the lofting, after deducting for hull-shell thickness, or from patterns previously made. It is also practical to spile certain parts to the boat's curved surfaces. Bulkheads occurring on stationlines can be taken easily from the lofting, but the shape of bulkheads and partitions occurring at other places, particularly longitudinal ones, are less easily obtained from the lofting (although it can be done). Begin the spiling procedure by making a template on scrap veneer, plywood, or fiberboard of some kind that has been cut out to the rough shape of the finished part.

It is easy to modify this template if it won't fit in or on the hull. Place the template against the hull on the mark. Open a compass to some distance and mark a sample arc on the template. Now, using that distance, place the point of the compass against the hull and swing an arc on the template. Move the point of the compass and swing another arc. Keep doing this every few inches until the entire curve is covered. Remove the template and place it on the material that will become the fitted part. Using the same compass gap used on the template, mark arcs on the part. Then move the point of the compass to the other end of that same arc on the template and mark a second arc on the part. The two arcs on the part cross, defining a point. Repeat this process for each of the arcs on the template. Using a pencil and a flexible batten, scribe the line described by the resulting series of points. If this line is carefully scribed with a thin point, it will show any bumps on the hull surface, such as the keel or stringers.

Carefully follow the lines while cutting out the shape, and it will fit the chosen place in or on the boat. The side of the part that has the scribed marks is the control side. Any dressing or beveling of the part must preserve these marks or the part will cease to fit. Carefully dress the bonding edges of all parts with a block plane, achieving just enough bevel to fit flush with the hull.

Test the fit of each part by placing it in the hull. Remove and sand the bonding edges to final smoothness. When you've achieved a

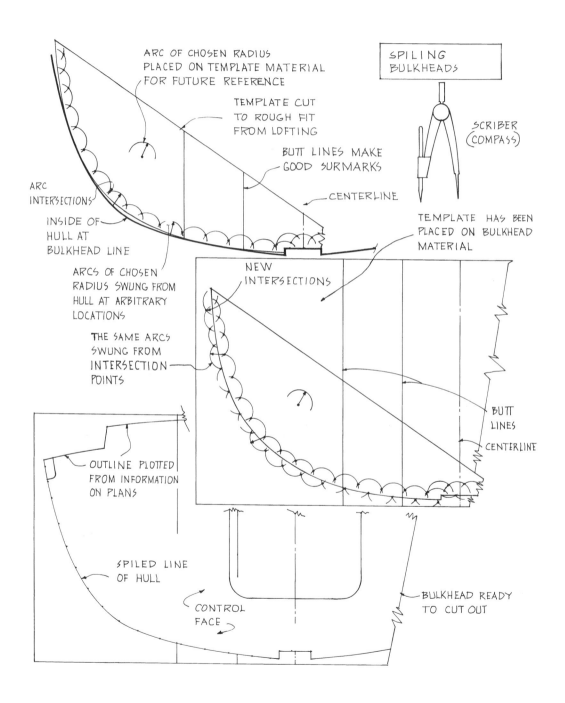

ARC OF CHOSEN RADIUS
PLACED ON TEMPLATE MATERIAL
FOR FUTURE REFERENCE

TEMPLATE CUT
TO ROUGH FIT
FROM LOFTING

BUTT LINES MAKE
GOOD SURMARKS

CENTERLINE

SPILING
BULKHEADS

SCRIBER
(COMPASS)

TEMPLATE HAS BEEN
PLACED ON BULKHEAD
MATERIAL

ARC
INTERSECTIONS

INSIDE OF
HULL AT
BULKHEAD LINE

ARCS OF CHOSEN
RADIUS SWUNG FROM
HULL AT ARBITRARY
LOCATIONS

THE SAME ARCS
SWUNG FROM
INTERSECTION
POINTS

NEW
INTERSECTIONS

BUTT
LINES

CENTERLINE

OUTLINE PLOTTED
FROM INFORMATION
ON PLANS

SPILED LINE
OF HULL

CONTROL
FACE

BULKHEAD READY
TO CUT OUT

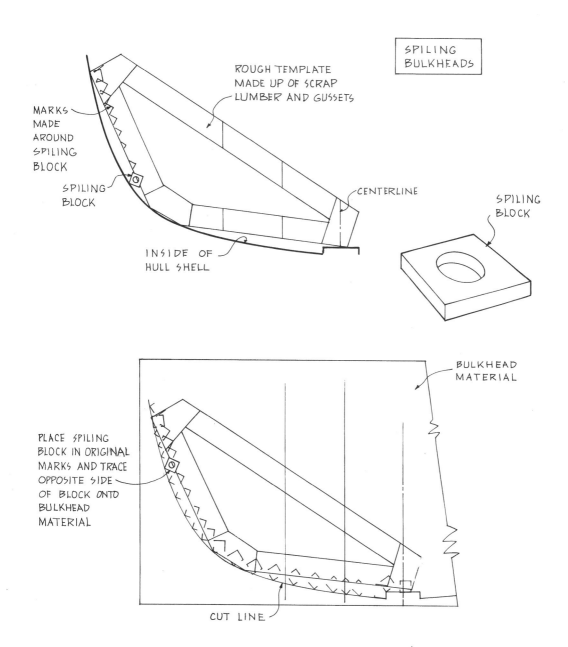

SPILING BULKHEADS

ROUGH TEMPLATE MADE UP OF SCRAP LUMBER AND GUSSETS

MARKS MADE AROUND SPILING BLOCK

SPILING BLOCK

INSIDE OF HULL SHELL

CENTERLINE

SPILING BLOCK

BULKHEAD MATERIAL

PLACE SPILING BLOCK IN ORIGINAL MARKS AND TRACE OPPOSITE SIDE OF BLOCK ONTO BULKHEAD MATERIAL

CUT LINE

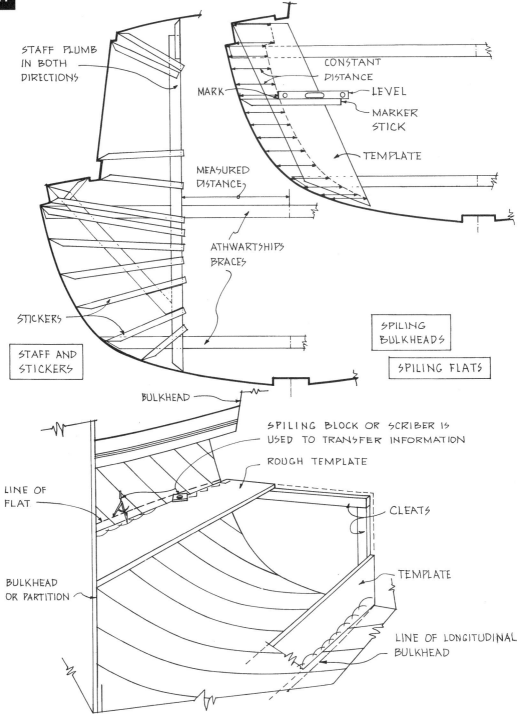

STAFF PLUMB
IN BOTH
DIRECTIONS

CONSTANT
DISTANCE

MARK

LEVEL

MARKER
STICK

TEMPLATE

MEASURED
DISTANCE

ATHWARTSHIPS
BRACES

STICKERS

STAFF AND
STICKERS

SPILING
BULKHEADS

SPILING FLATS

BULKHEAD

SPILING BLOCK OR SCRIBER IS
USED TO TRANSFER INFORMATION

ROUGH TEMPLATE

LINE OF
FLAT

CLEATS

TEMPLATE

BULKHEAD
OR PARTITION

LINE OF LONGITUDINAL
BULKHEAD

satisfactory fit, place surmarks from the part to the hull in several locations to ensure proper placement of the part when bonding.

Pre-coat with resin all surfaces of parts that will be exposed in the boat. Coat bonding edges with a thick adhesive mixture, and install the part in or on the hull by realigning the surmarks. Hold the part in place temporarily with staples or small nails. Quickly remove any adhesive mixture that oozes out.

Place bulkheads in the hull with their control edge on the location line. This means that the aft face of the bulkhead will be placed on the location line where the hull narrows toward the bow, and the forward face of the bulkhead will be placed on the location line where the hull narrows toward the stern. This is done so that beveled edges can be made to fit the hull without losing the overall dimensions of the bulkhead. Bulkheads and partitions are held in place using fillets applied with a disposable syringe or cake decorator filled with a thick adhesive mixture. Place a bead of this mixture wherever shown on the plan. Cut the end of a stick in a semicircular curve to the same diameter as the fillet shown on the plan. This stick, which looks something like a tongue depressor, is drawn along the bead to form a smooth fillet. Quickly clean away all excess mixture; it will be very hard to remove later.

Any full frames that need to be laminated are best laminated outside the hull, taking the shape from the lofting and deducting for the hull-shell thickness. Laminating them directly in the hull will be messy. Bond the completed frame into the hull as a unit, right on its marks, removing excess adhesive mixture right away.

INSTALLING FLOOR TIMBERS AND KEELSON

Laminated floor timbers will be laid up directly in the boat, using the hull as a form. Chocks of solid wood are required under the first floor laminate to elevate it over the keel. Leave space on either side of the keel to serve as limber holes. Pre-coat with resin all surfaces of frames and floors that will be exposed within the hull. Bond chocks to the hull with adhesive mixture, and apply weights until the cure sets in. Staple each successive floor laminate to secure it until its adhesive mixture sets. Remove the staples and fill the staple holes with a stiff adhesive mixture.

If the plan calls for a keelson or bonded sole plank over the keel, prepare for it by cutting solid blocking to fit on top of the keel between floors so that they are exactly flush with the tops of the floors. Pre-coat with resin all surfaces of blocking that will be exposed within the hull.

INSTALLATION OF BULKHEADS
LAMINATING THE SHEER CLAMPS

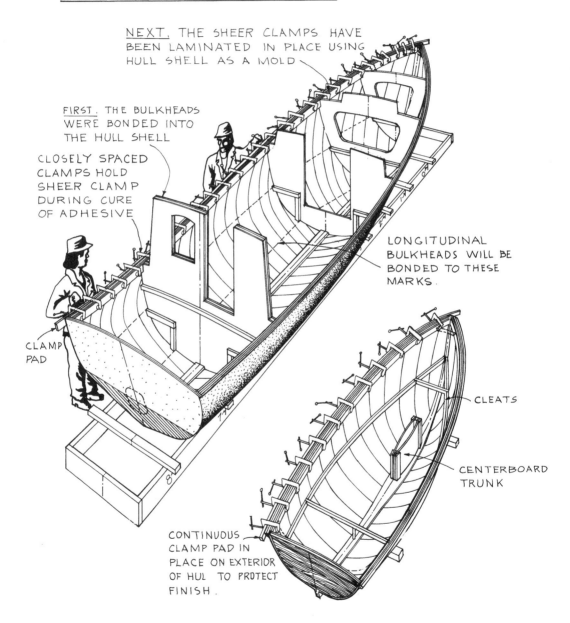

NEXT, THE SHEER CLAMPS HAVE BEEN LAMINATED IN PLACE USING HULL SHELL AS A MOLD

FIRST, THE BULKHEADS WERE BONDED INTO THE HULL SHELL

CLOSELY SPACED CLAMPS HOLD SHEER CLAMP DURING CURE OF ADHESIVE

CLAMP PAD

LONGITUDINAL BULKHEADS WILL BE BONDED TO THESE MARKS.

CLEATS

CENTERBOARD TRUNK

CONTINUOUS CLAMP PAD IN PLACE ON EXTERIOR OF HULL TO PROTECT FINISH.

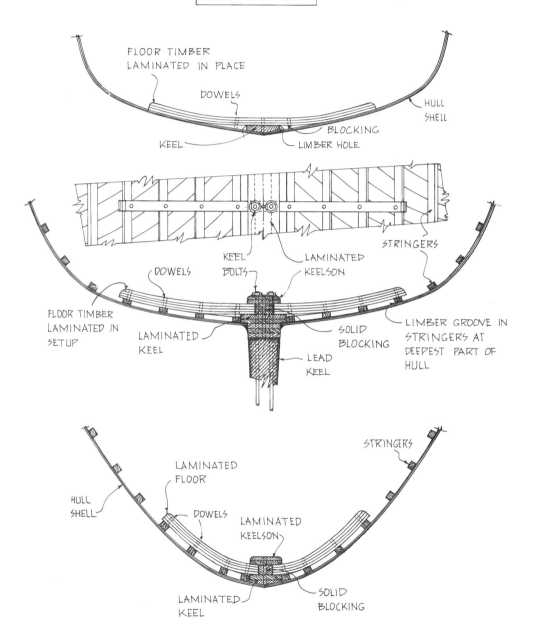

FLOOR TIMBERS

FLOOR TIMBER LAMINATED IN PLACE

DOWELS

HULL SHELL

BLOCKING

KEEL

LIMBER HOLE

STRINGERS

KEEL BOLTS

DOWELS

LAMINATED KEELSON

FLOOR TIMBER LAMINATED IN SETUP

LAMINATED KEEL

SOLID BLOCKING

LIMBER GROOVE IN STRINGERS AT DEEPEST PART OF HULL

LEAD KEEL

STRINGERS

LAMINATED FLOOR

HULL SHELL

DOWELS

LAMINATED KEELSON

LAMINATED KEEL

SOLID BLOCKING

Tightly bond blocking to each floor timber on the centerline of the keel with adhesive mixture. Prepare the keelson or sole plank by cutting it to shape, easing the upper corners to a radius, and sanding. Bond pre-coated keelson or sole plank to the floors and blocking with adhesive mixture, and fix it in place with a temporary wood screw at each floor. When the adhesive has cured, remove the screws and drill out the screw holes to receive wood dowels. Make the holes about ⅛ inch larger than the diameter of the dowels called for; for instance, drill ⅝-inch-diameter holes for ½-inch-diameter dowels. If you inadvertently drill a hole through the bottom of the boat, simply run a dowel clear through and finish the bottom as though the dowel were a plug. It will save work, however, if the dowels terminate within the keel.

Coat interiors of drilled holes with adhesive mixture, using a pipe cleaner or stick. Coat the dowels with adhesive mixture, allow them to sit for 10 minutes or so, and install them just before the adhesive begins to set. If the dowels have not been cut to length, cut them off now and sand flush. Saturate the end grain of the dowels with resin, and clean off the excess resin and adhesive mixture that oozes out. It is important that there be no voids in the adhesive mixture around the dowels, or at their ends at the bottom of the holes.

SHAFTLOG DRILLING

Long holes for propeller shafts will be needed for some boats. These must pass through the shaftlog, keel, and often a considerable amount of deadwood. The deadwood, keel, and log structure must be built exactly as shown on the plans for correct alignment. The shaftlog is made in two parts (usually top and bottom), with the centerline of the shaft scribed on its inner faces. If the keel interrupts the shaftlog, its lower part is positioned on the keel to show the location and angle of the required guide hole. If there is outside deadwood, the shaftlog will be part of its structure. Cut a groove along the scribed lines on the shaftlog's inner faces.

When the hull has been completed and turned over, there will be a guide hole passing through the structure very close to the centerline of the future propeller shaft. Stretch a taut line through the guide hole and secure it to solidly constructed staging at each end to verify the accuracy of the hole's location and its relationship to the engine beds. Corrections can be made by slight adjustments at the ends of the line. Mark the new location clearly on the staging.

SHAFTLOG DRILLING

BORING FOR PROPELLER SHAFT

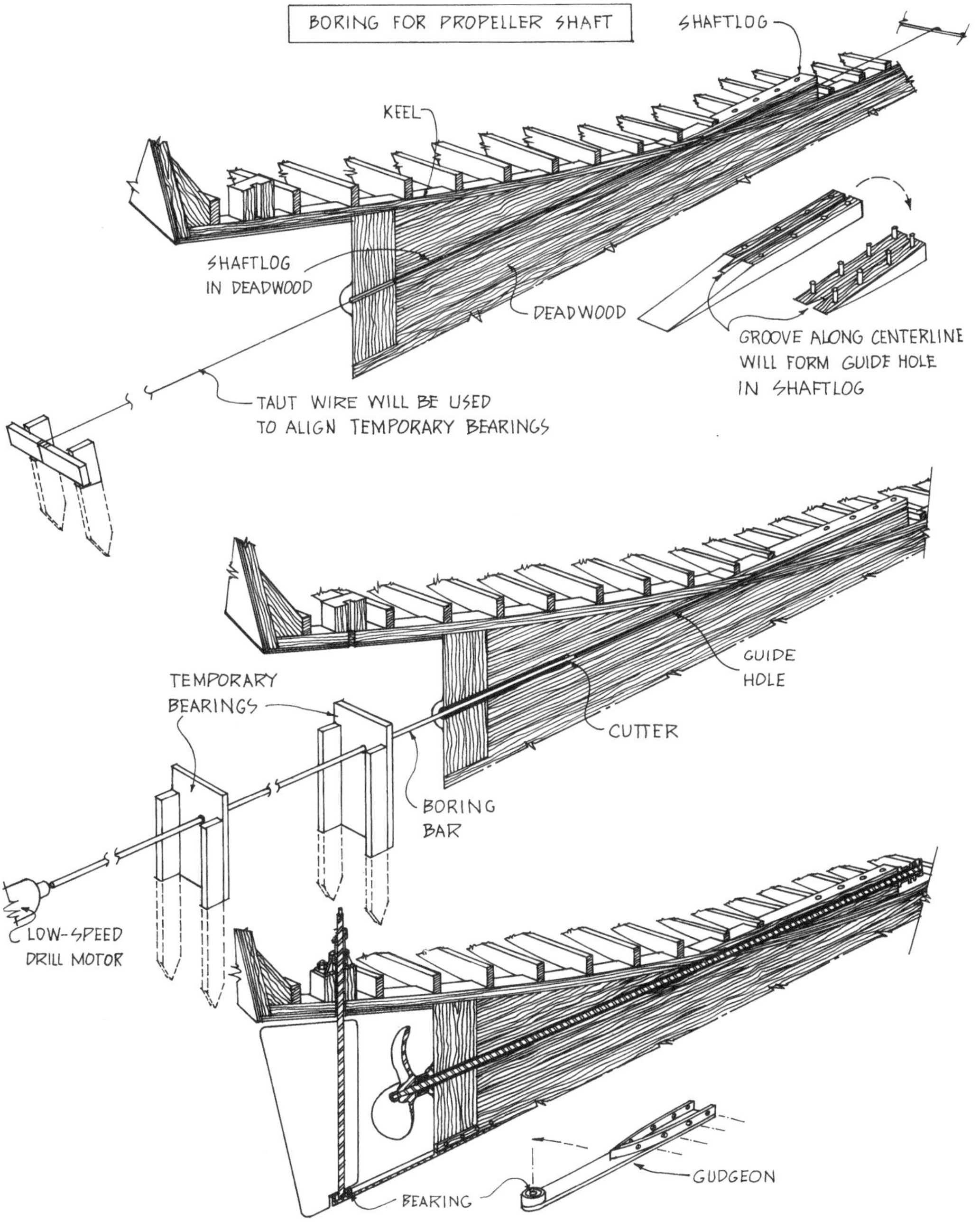

SHAFTLOG

KEEL

SHAFTLOG
IN DEADWOOD

DEADWOOD

GROOVE ALONG CENTERLINE
WILL FORM GUIDE HOLE
IN SHAFTLOG

TAUT WIRE WILL BE USED
TO ALIGN TEMPORARY BEARINGS

GUIDE
HOLE

TEMPORARY
BEARINGS

CUTTER

BORING
BAR

LOW-SPEED
DRILL MOTOR

BEARING

GUDGEON

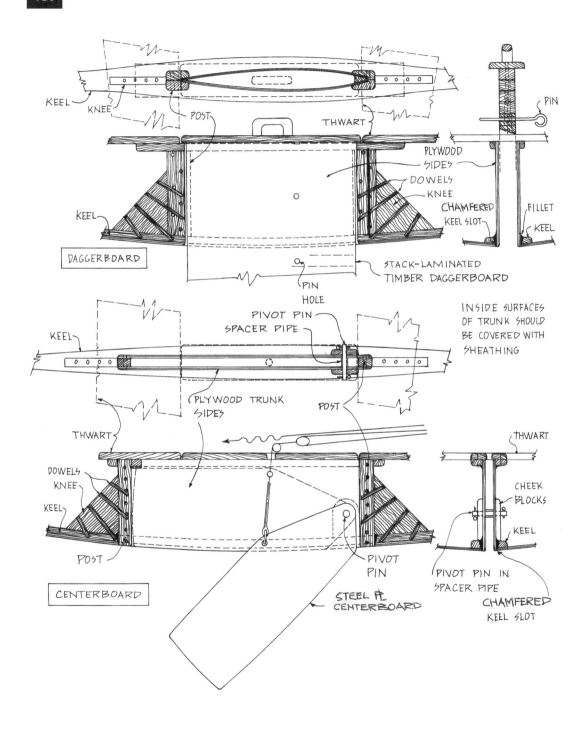

KEEL

KNEE

POST

THWART

PLYWOOD
SIDES

DOWELS

KNEE

KEEL

CHAMFERED
KEEL SLOT

PIN

FILLET

KEEL

DAGGERBOARD

STACK-LAMINATED
TIMBER DAGGERBOARD

PIN
HOLE

KEEL

PIVOT PIN
SPACER PIPE

INSIDE SURFACES
OF TRUNK SHOULD
BE COVERED WITH
SHEATHING

PLYWOOD TRUNK
SIDES

POST

THWART

DOWELS
KNEE

KEEL

POST

CENTERBOARD

PIVOT
PIN

STEEL ₵
CENTERBOARD

THWART

CHEEK
BLOCKS

KEEL

PIVOT PIN IN
SPACER PIPE

CHAMFERED
KEEL SLOT

Fabricate a boring bar that will chuck into a low-speed drill motor. It should be long enough to get through the material and have a cutter of appropriate diameter near its working end. Make some temporary bearings out of hardwood planks and drill holes through them to carry the boring bar. Position these holes so that when the line is re-stretched and attached exactly to the marks on the staging, it will pass through the center of each hole. These temporary bearings now will align exactly and support the boring bar for the entire drilling event.

OTHER INTERIOR STRUCTURES

If the boat has a daggerboard, the keel will be wide enough to have a cut-out for the trunk, which is built up of plywood bonded to vertical members of solid wood. Sheathe the interior surface of the trunk with glass cloth, as described for hull sheathing. Pre-coat all other wood surfaces with resin. Cut out the opening through the keel so that the hole is wider at the top than at the bottom; there will be a wedge-shaped trench all around the base of the trunk after it is installed. Block up a piece of scrap veneer or plywood under the opening to prevent adhesive mixture from running out, placing plastic sheeting over the blocking to prevent its bonding to the hull. Install the trunk structure in the opening so that its bottom is flush with the bottom of the boat. Press adhesive mixture into the trench and form a fillet on top.

It is more convenient to build any berth and settee flats, counter-tops, and platforms outside the boat and install them after they are complete. Scribe the locations of these flats on the hull shell as previously described. Bevel all edges that will bond to the hull shell for a tight fit, plane and sand to final smoothness, but do not cut into the scribed marks on the top of the flats or the parts will not fit. A fillet may be called for at the joints and a good bond must be achieved because these flats become part of the structure of the hull. After a satisfactory fit has been achieved for each flat, make several surmarks between each flat and the hull shell and from the flat to the bulkhead. Remove the flats, coat all bonding surfaces with adhesive mixture, and replace them by aligning the surmarks. Be sure all wood surfaces that will be exposed to the atmosphere are pre-coated with resin.

Secure the flats for curing with temporary staples or small nails. Run beads of stiff adhesive mixture where they are called for on the plan. Clean up all excess resin and adhesive mixture. Make up items of interior

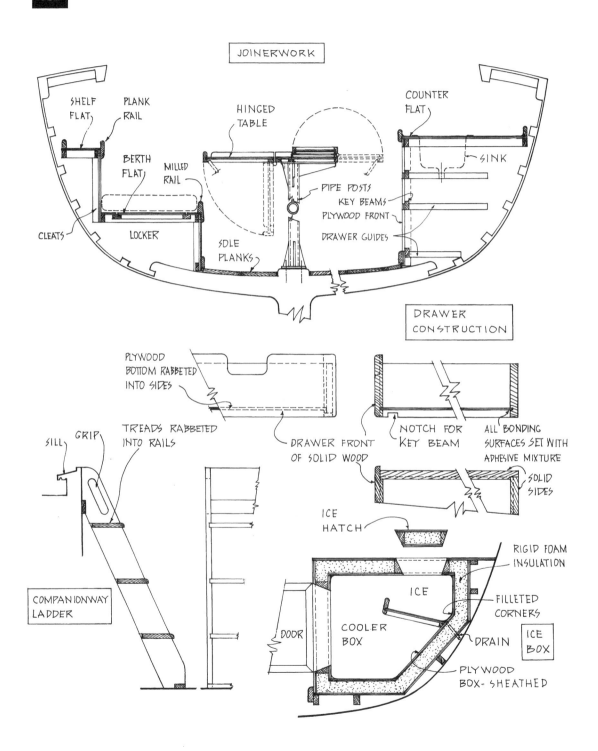

JOINERWORK

SHELF FLAT

PLANK RAIL

HINGED TABLE

COUNTER FLAT

BERTH FLAT

MILLED RAIL

SINK

PIPE POSTS
KEY BEAMS
PLYWOOD FRONT
DRAWER GUIDES

CLEATS

LOCKER

SOLE PLANKS

DRAWER CONSTRUCTION

PLYWOOD BOTTOM RABBETED INTO SIDES

TREADS RABBETED INTO RAILS

SILL

GRIP

DRAWER FRONT OF SOLID WOOD

NOTCH FOR KEY BEAM

ALL BONDING SURFACES SET WITH ADHESIVE MIXTURE

SOLID SIDES

ICE HATCH

RIGID FOAM INSULATION

ICE

FILLETED CORNERS

ICE BOX

COMPANIONWAY LADDER

DOOR

COOLER BOX

DRAIN

PLYWOOD BOX-SHEATHED

joinerwork such as hanging lockers, dressers, galley joinery, and chests of drawers. Install these items complete, including all fronts and sides.

ENGINE BEDS

Engine beds, if any, are laminated from solid stock bonded together and cut to shape. They are then bonded and fastened to floor timbers. Sometimes laminated solid stock for the top and bottom of the engine bed is specified. These parts are held apart by plywood sides, like hollow box girders. Engine stringers are sometimes solid wood parts running across a series of floor timbers, and sometimes they are longitudinal plywood bulkheads.

If there are any other structures that will to be bonded into the hull structure and that can be fabricated outside the hull, it is more convenient to do so before the decks are built.

Thoroughly clean the interior of the hull, watching for any areas where bare wood is showing. Coat any suspect areas using a brush lightly loaded with epoxy.

Additional drawings on interior construction follow.

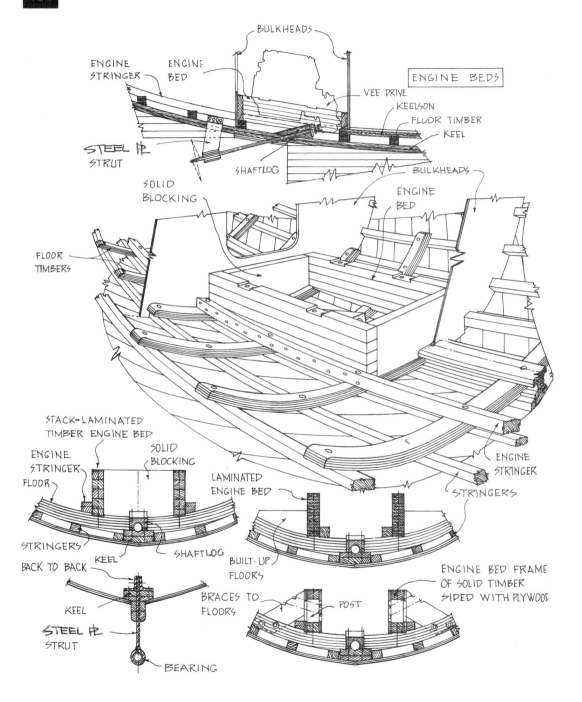

ENGINE BEDS

BULKHEADS

ENGINE STRINGER

ENGINE BED

VEE DRIVE
KEELSON
FLOOR TIMBER
KEEL

STEEL PL
STRUT

SHAFTLOG

BULKHEADS

ENGINE BED

SOLID BLOCKING

FLOOR TIMBERS

STACK-LAMINATED TIMBER ENGINE BED

ENGINE STRINGER
FLOOR

SOLID BLOCKING

LAMINATED ENGINE BED

ENGINE STRINGER

STRINGERS

STRINGERS
KEEL
BACK TO BACK

SHAFTLOG

BUILT-UP FLOORS

KEEL

STEEL PL
STRUT

BEARING

BRACES TO FLOORS

POST

ENGINE BED FRAME OF SOLID TIMBER SIDED WITH PLYWOOD

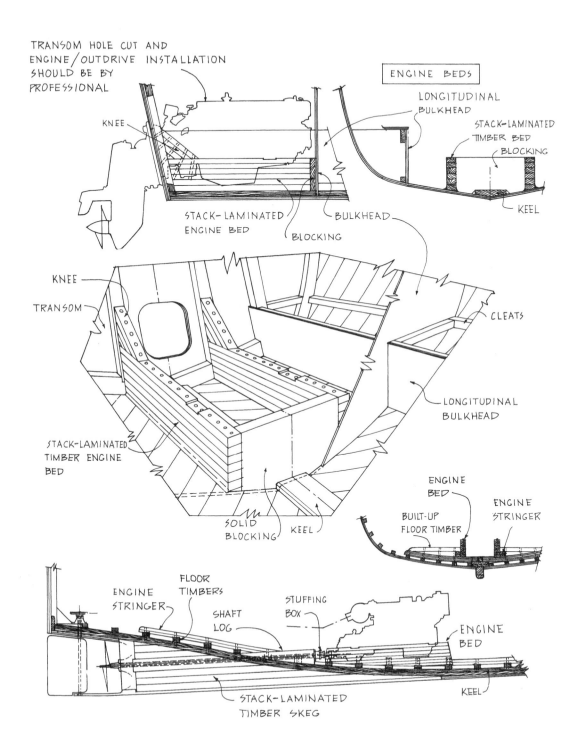

TRANSOM HOLE CUT AND
ENGINE/OUTDRIVE INSTALLATION
SHOULD BE BY
PROFESSIONAL

KNEE

STACK-LAMINATED
ENGINE BED

BLOCKING

BULKHEAD

ENGINE BEDS

LONGITUDINAL
BULKHEAD

STACK-LAMINATED
TIMBER BED

BLOCKING

KEEL

KNEE

TRANSOM

STACK-LAMINATED
TIMBER ENGINE
BED

SOLID
BLOCKING

KEEL

CLEATS

LONGITUDINAL
BULKHEAD

ENGINE
BED

BUILT-UP
FLOOR TIMBER

ENGINE
STRINGER

ENGINE
STRINGER

FLOOR
TIMBERS

SHAFT
LOG

STUFFING
BOX

ENGINE
BED

KEEL

STACK-LAMINATED
TIMBER SKEG

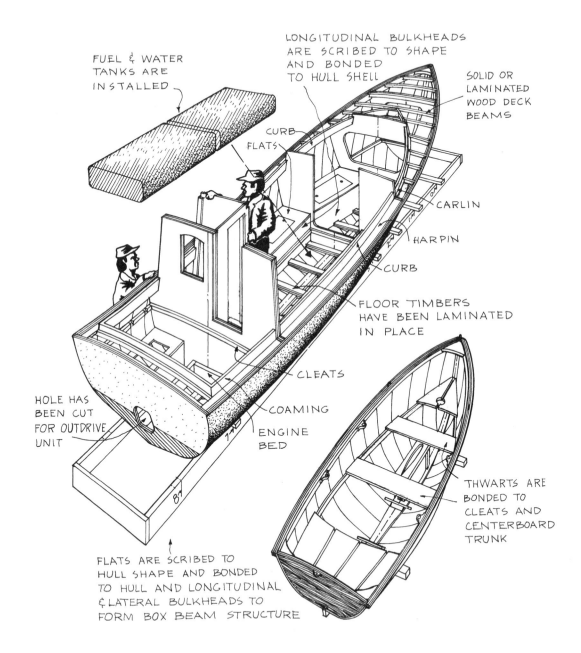

FUEL & WATER
TANKS ARE
INSTALLED

LONGITUDINAL BULKHEADS
ARE SCRIBED TO SHAPE
AND BONDED
TO HULL SHELL

SOLID OR
LAMINATED
WOOD DECK
BEAMS

CURB
FLATS

CARLIN

HARPIN

CURB

FLOOR TIMBERS
HAVE BEEN LAMINATED
IN PLACE

HOLE HAS
BEEN CUT
FOR OUTDRIVE
UNIT

CLEATS

COAMING

ENGINE
BED

THWARTS ARE
BONDED TO
CLEATS AND
CENTERBOARD
TRUNK

FLATS ARE SCRIBED TO
HULL SHAPE AND BONDED
TO HULL AND LONGITUDINAL
& LATERAL BULKHEADS TO
FORM BOX BEAM STRUCTURE

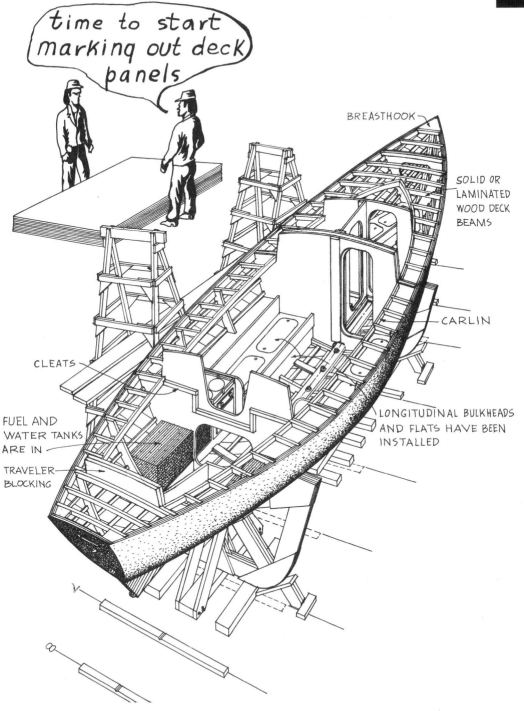

CHAPTER 15

Deck and Superstructure

I f the boat will have a deck, it is important that the clamp and hull-shell upper edge be beveled to receive the decking. To do this, cut a template from scrap plywood or veneer to the camber of the deck, as shown on the plan. The camber can be plotted from the information given there.

An alternative method uses two battens as follows: Mark a straight line on scrap plywood or veneer that is exactly the same length as the widest beam of the hull, and place a nail at each end. Find the middle of the line and mark the centerline at 90 degrees across it. On the centerline, mark the high point of the deck camber, as taken from the plans. Now fasten the two battens together with a gusset to fix them in relation to each other. The legs of the battens should be placed against the two nails; the inside apex of the battens should coincide with the mark on the centerline, and the battens should be free to slide back and forth along the two nails. Place a pencil at the inner apex of the battens and slide the battens across the nails so that the pencil traces the outline of the deck camber on the plywood or veneer. Cut carefully along the line and the camber template will emerge. If the boat has a housetop, its camber may be different from the deck camber and will require a separate template.

Place the deck-camber template across the hull at any point along the sheer where decking will occur, and kerf the clamp and hull shell with a handsaw to the bevel indicated by the template. Make enough of

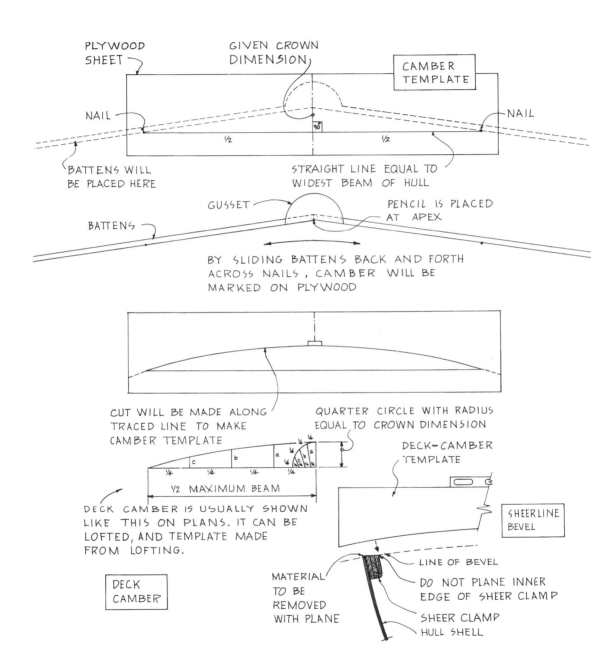

PLYWOOD SHEET

GIVEN CROWN DIMENSION

CAMBER TEMPLATE

NAIL

NAIL

BATTENS WILL BE PLACED HERE

½   90   ½

STRAIGHT LINE EQUAL TO WIDEST BEAM OF HULL

GUSSET

PENCIL IS PLACED AT APEX

BATTENS

BY SLIDING BATTENS BACK AND FORTH ACROSS NAILS, CAMBER WILL BE MARKED ON PLYWOOD

CUT WILL BE MADE ALONG TRACED LINE TO MAKE CAMBER TEMPLATE

QUARTER CIRCLE WITH RADIUS EQUAL TO CROWN DIMENSION

DECK-CAMBER TEMPLATE

SHEERLINE BEVEL

c   b   a

¼   ¼   ¼   ¼

½ MAXIMUM BEAM

DECK CAMBER IS USUALLY SHOWN LIKE THIS ON PLANS. IT CAN BE LOFTED, AND TEMPLATE MADE FROM LOFTING.

DECK CAMBER

LINE OF BEVEL

DO NOT PLANE INNER EDGE OF SHEER CLAMP

MATERIAL TO BE REMOVED WITH PLANE

SHEER CLAMP

HULL SHELL

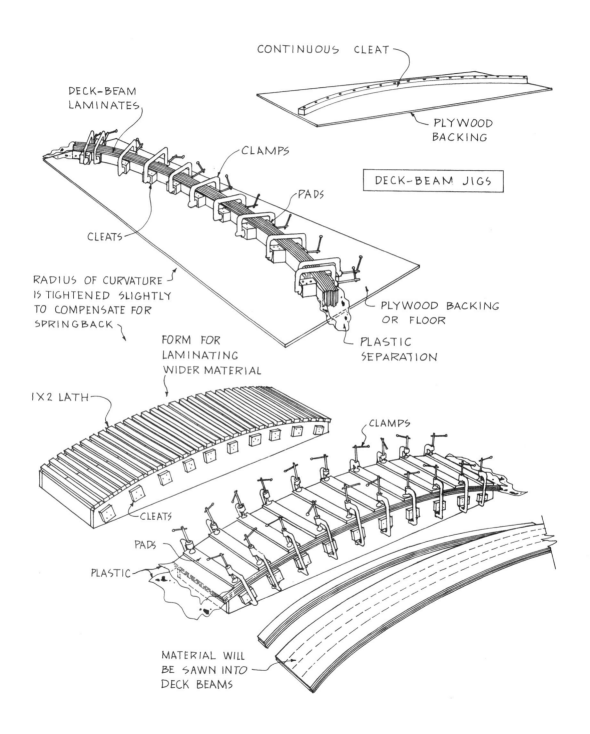

CONTINUOUS CLEAT

PLYWOOD BACKING

DECK-BEAM LAMINATES

CLAMPS

PADS

CLEATS

DECK-BEAM JIGS

RADIUS OF CURVATURE IS TIGHTENED SLIGHTLY TO COMPENSATE FOR SPRINGBACK

PLYWOOD BACKING OR FLOOR

PLASTIC SEPARATION

FORM FOR LAMINATING WIDER MATERIAL

1X2 LATH

CLAMPS

CLEATS

PADS

PLASTIC

MATERIAL WILL BE SAWN INTO DECK BEAMS

these kerf marks so that they can be joined by planing with a long-bed plane. Do not cut into the inner face of the clamp or the sheerline will be affected. Plane and sand the bevel smooth from stem to transom.

The template is now used in laminating the deck beams from layers of thinner material. Prepare a jig for laminating individual beams by nailing cleats to a piece of plywood backing. Alternatively, build a form of scrap solid wood with plywood sides, and laminate the beams from wider material, which is then sawn up into individual beams, like so many pork ribs. Use the template to mark out the shape of the jig or form.

INSTALLING DECK BEAMS

The deck beams are fitted into triangular notches cut into the sheer clamps. Start by carefully marking the location of all the beam ends on the top surface of the sheer clamp. Make two parallel marks for each beam the same distance apart as the width of the beam. Extend these two parallel marks vertically down the inside face of the sheer clamp. Mark the bottom of the notch at a point equal to the depth of the beam at its deepest side. Connect this point horizontally to the other line. This describes the section of the beam as it intersects the sheer clamp. Repeat for each beam.

If the sheerline slopes at the point at which the beam intersects the sheer clamp, the upper face of the beam will protrude from the top of the sheer clamp at the shallow side of the notch, and it will have to be beveled to accept the deck. If the beam were cut into the sloping sheer clamp at 90 degrees, the beam would lean to one side, causing problems at the juncture with the bulkheads, partitions, and, possibly, with the house and trunk fronts. Naturally, if the sheerline is dead level, none of this matters.

Mark the deck-beam notch on top of the sheer clamp with parallel lines extending to a point near, but not quite to, the planking. Cut straight into the sheer clamp with a handsaw to these limit marks. Use a chisel to remove the material between the cuts, and clean up the notch with a file. Take some laminated material, long enough to become the longest deck beam, and place it upside down over the notches. Mark the length required on the beam. Next, measure the bevel of the notch with a bevel gauge and transfer it to the beam. Cut the beam ends along the bevel marks, and dry fit the beam into the notches. It is important that the fit be snug and that the beam does not protrude above the clamp and planking. For this reason, the protruding upper face of any beam must

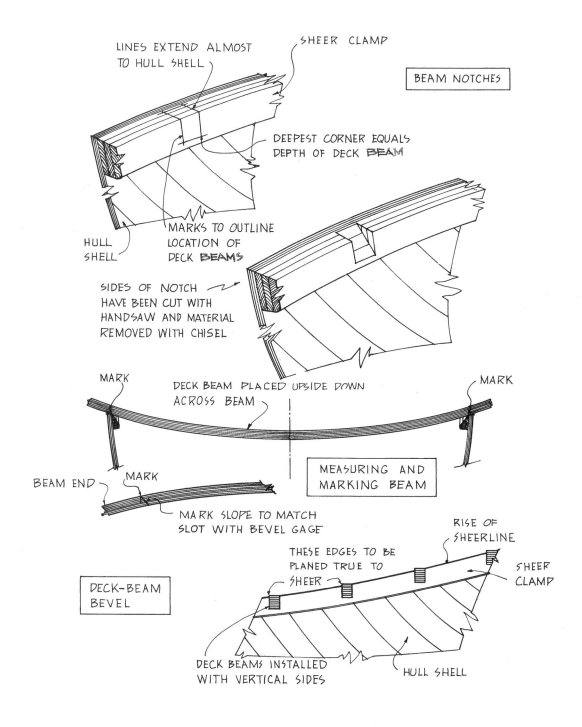

LINES EXTEND ALMOST TO HULL SHELL

SHEER CLAMP

BEAM NOTCHES

DEEPEST CORNER EQUALS DEPTH OF DECK BEAM

MARKS TO OUTLINE LOCATION OF DECK BEAMS

HULL SHELL

SIDES OF NOTCH HAVE BEEN CUT WITH HANDSAW AND MATERIAL REMOVED WITH CHISEL

MARK

DECK BEAM PLACED UPSIDE DOWN ACROSS BEAM

MARK

BEAM END

MARK

MEASURING AND MARKING BEAM

MARK SLOPE TO MATCH SLOT WITH BEVEL GAGE

RISE OF SHEERLINE

THESE EDGES TO BE PLANED TRUE TO SHEER

SHEER CLAMP

DECK-BEAM BEVEL

DECK BEAMS INSTALLED WITH VERTICAL SIDES

HULL SHELL

be planed to the angle of the deck and checked for fairness with a batten across several beams. Cut and dry fit all of the deck beams and check for fairness before bonding. Remember, deck beams, clamps, and planking should be as flush as possible because the decking must bond uniformly to them.

Coat all surfaces with resin before finally bonding the deck beams into the hull; be sure to saturate the end grain. Bond all deck beams to notches in the sheer clamp, using a stiff adhesive mixture, and fasten them temporarily with small nails until the adhesive cures. Bond solid blocking for any hardware called for on the plan to the deck beams at this time. The top of the blocking must be flush with the deck beams to ensure later bonding to the decking. Use a strip of plywood several inches wide as a fairing batten to detect any remaining high or low areas in the overall deck framing. Make any corrections with a long-bed hand plane and sandpaper.

APPLYING DECKING

When the deck has been faired, it's time to apply the plywood decking panels. Many deck areas can be gotten out of a single sheet of 4 x 8 plywood. Other areas, such as a housetop, will require several pieces scarfed together. To scarf plywood, clamp the sheet down on a workbench, aligning plywood edge with workbench edge. Mark a line on the surface of the plywood parallel to the edge and eight times the thickness of the plywood back from it. This will be the edge of the bevel, easily shaped with a power plane. If a power plane is not available, begin with a very sharp smoothing plane with a deep-set blade to remove material as fast as possible; continue with a more finely set block plane. The trick is to keep the bevel cut flat, because the cross grain of plywood will try to cut away at different rates. Keep blades as sharp as possible and use extra caution when sanding bevel cuts.

It may be convenient to bevel several sheets at once by stairstepping the plywood panels back, aligning them with the marked lines, and planing them down all at once. Match up pairs of bevels to see how they fit. As the panels are aligned, make sure that a complete contact has been achieved in all cases. Plan the panel sizing so that scarf joints will occur over beams or some other support.

Rough out a panel the approximate shape of the deck to be covered (the foredeck, for example). Place the panel over the area to be covered and trace the outline of the deck on it from below. Draw the outline of the

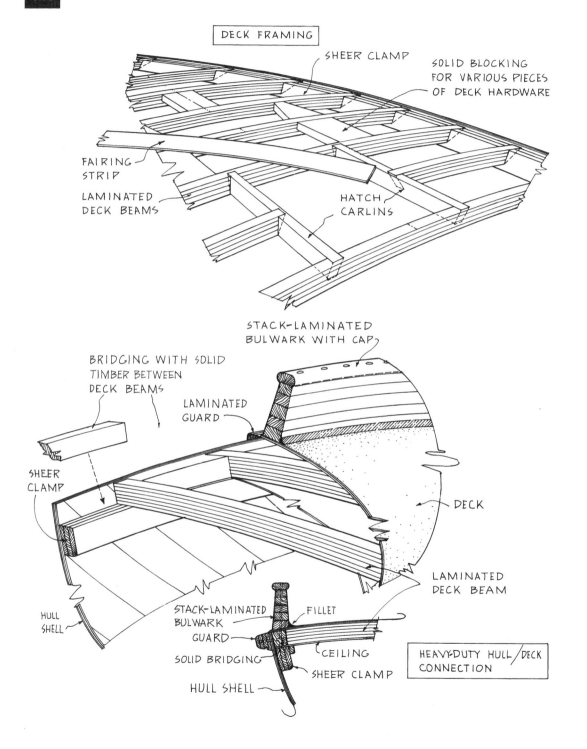

DECK FRAMING

SHEER CLAMP

SOLID BLOCKING
FOR VARIOUS PIECES
OF DECK HARDWARE

FAIRING
STRIP

LAMINATED
DECK BEAMS

HATCH
CARLINS

STACK-LAMINATED
BULWARK WITH CAP

BRIDGING WITH SOLID
TIMBER BETWEEN
DECK BEAMS

LAMINATED
GUARD

SHEER
CLAMP

DECK

HULL
SHELL

LAMINATED
DECK BEAM

STACK-LAMINATED
BULWARK

FILLET

GUARD

CEILING

SOLID BRIDGING

SHEER CLAMP

HULL SHELL

HEAVY-DUTY HULL/DECK
CONNECTION

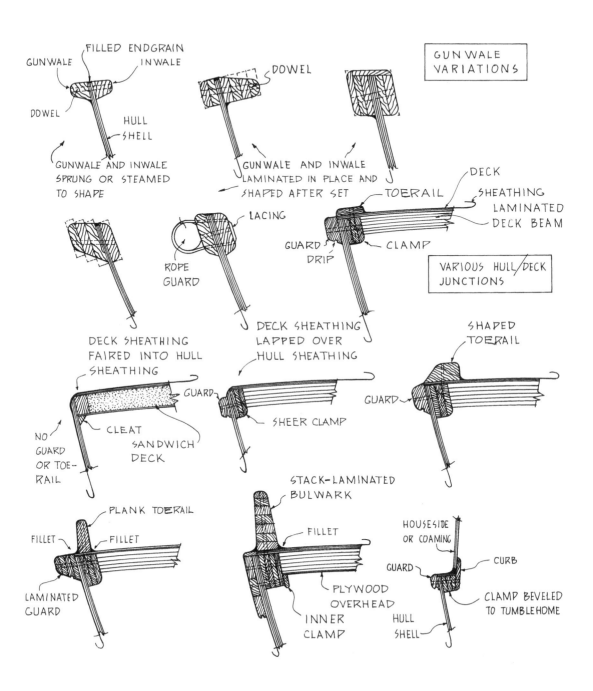

GUNWALE
VARIATIONS

GUNWALE
FILLED ENDGRAIN
INWALE
DOWEL
HULL
SHELL
GUNWALE AND INWALE
SPRUNG OR STEAMED
TO SHAPE

DOWEL
GUNWALE AND INWALE
LAMINATED IN PLACE AND
SHAPED AFTER SET

DECK
TOERAIL
SHEATHING
LAMINATED
DECK BEAM
GUARD
DRIP
CLAMP

VARIOUS HULL/DECK
JUNCTIONS

LACING
ROPE
GUARD

DECK SHEATHING
LAPPED OVER
HULL SHEATHING

SHAPED
TOERAIL

DECK SHEATHING
FAIRED INTO HULL
SHEATHING
GUARD
NO
GUARD
OR TOE-
RAIL
CLEAT
SANDWICH
DECK

GUARD
SHEER CLAMP

GUARD

STACK-LAMINATED
BULWARK

PLANK TOERAIL
FILLET
FILLET
LAMINATED
GUARD

FILLET
PLYWOOD
OVERHEAD
INNER
CLAMP

HOUSESIDE
OR COAMING
GUARD
CURB
CLAMP BEVELED
TO TUMBLEHOME
HULL
SHELL

deck beams lightly on the top of the plywood to assist in stapling later on.

Cut and dry fit the panel to the deck beams, and draw surmarks to assist in replacing the panel. Remove the panel and pre-coat all surfaces with resin. Apply adhesive mixture to the bonding surface of the deck beams and replace the panel. After final adjustments are made, begin stapling in the center of the panel, with staples going through the plywood and into a deck beam. Continue stapling toward the outer perimeter until the panel is completely secured. Follow the same procedure with any second and successive layers.

Scarf joints normally are formed in place on decks and housetops. Because of the curvature of the deck, it takes more clamping pressure on the joint than would be necessary if it were flat. Place a batten of scrap plywood or veneer over the scarf joint and drill pilot holes for temporary screws. When bonding the joint, place sheet plastic between the plywood and the batten, and drive screws (use washers with the screws) through the batten joint and into the beam.

If you're laminating several layers of plywood, the layers will have to be pulled together while the adhesive mixture cures. It is best to draw a grid with about 9-inch squares on the deck and drill a guide hole for a temporary wood screw at each intersection. Stagger the scarf joints of these successive layers on beams or supports other than those used for the first layer. Before beginning other work, clean away all adhesive mixture that oozed from the deck beams' edges.

The guard can be made from solid wood or from pieces laminated directly onto the hull. On boats with decks, the guard covers—or partially covers—the edge grain of the decking. Pieces of solid stock will have to be scarfed together in lengths that reach from stem to stern. Secure solid timber for curing with temporary screws. Laminated guards can be held with staples until the adhesive sets, then shaped with a plane, sanded, and coated carefully with resin. At this point, dowels can be placed in holes drilled through the guard, hull shell, and right through the clamps. Coat the end grain of the dowels with enough resin to saturate the wood fibers. Clean away residue before it sets. A similar process can be followed to secure any trim around the trunk or housetops.

Plot the superstructure shape directly on the construction material. Sometimes the superstructure is made up of shapes cut from solid timber and fitted together. More often it is fashioned from plywood sheets that have been scarfed together prior to plotting its shape. Some dimensions may be given on the plans, but other dimensions may be taken more easily from the completed hull. Where the houseside curves, the dimensions can be taken from the completed work and used in making a pattern for scribing the houseside to the hull. The height is usually shown on the plans and represents the slant dimension up the rake or tumblehome of the houseside. Once the overall shape of the houseside is drawn on the plywood, it is an easy matter to follow the plans in plotting out the shapes of windows and other openings. If the houseside is built up of several layers, it is best to complete the lamination process before plotting the openings and cutting them out.

A considerable range of possibilities exists for good design and construction of the house or trunk. Some have internal framing of studs or posts, while others rely on the strength of the surface material. A good method for attaching housesides to the deck is to bond it to a curb or sill that is part of hull or deck structure, and incorporates the rake or tumblehome of the housesides. The cut-out housesides can be dry-fitted and shored in place before measuring for the house ends. The entire house can be preassembled and installed as a unit once the house ends are determined. Sometimes low trunks and coamings are constructed in place and other superstructure is added later. Houses constructed entirely on top of the deck can be framed up and sheathed with plywood in a manner more like house building ashore.

Bond houses, trunks, and coamings to the curb or sill with adhesive mixture and hold them in place for curing with temporary screws. When these screws are removed, drill the holes out to install wood dowels. For heavy-duty use, glass-cloth sheathing on housesides and tops may be called for. All wood surfaces in the superstructure must be coated with an even coat of resin and cleaned of residue prior to painting or varnishing.

Additional drawings on deck and superstructure follow.

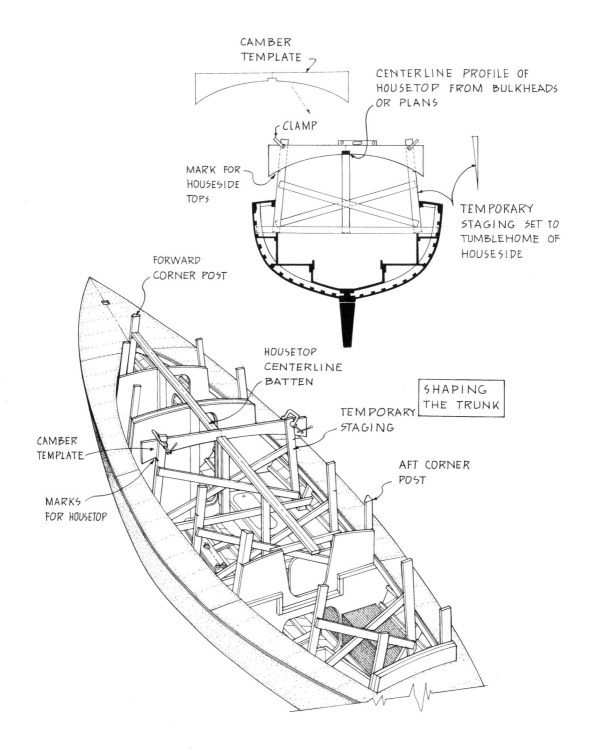

CAMBER
TEMPLATE

CENTERLINE PROFILE OF
HOUSETOP FROM BULKHEADS
OR PLANS

CLAMP

MARK FOR
HOUSESIDE
TOPS

TEMPORARY
STAGING SET TO
TUMBLEHOME OF
HOUSESIDE

FORWARD
CORNER POST

HOUSETOP
CENTERLINE
BATTEN

TEMPORARY
STAGING

SHAPING
THE TRUNK

CAMBER
TEMPLATE

AFT CORNER
POST

MARKS
FOR HOUSETOP

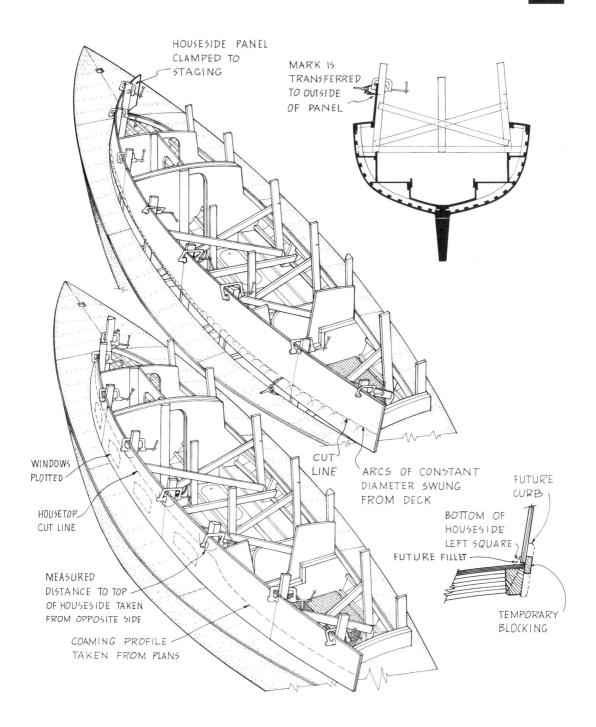

HOUSESIDE PANEL CLAMPED TO STAGING

MARK IS TRANSFERRED TO OUTSIDE OF PANEL

WINDOWS PLOTTED

HOUSETOP CUT LINE

CUT LINE

ARCS OF CONSTANT DIAMETER SWUNG FROM DECK

MEASURED DISTANCE TO TOP OF HOUSESIDE TAKEN FROM OPPOSITE SIDE

COAMING PROFILE TAKEN FROM PLANS

FUTURE CURB

BOTTOM OF HOUSESIDE LEFT SQUARE

FUTURE FILLET

TEMPORARY BLOCKING

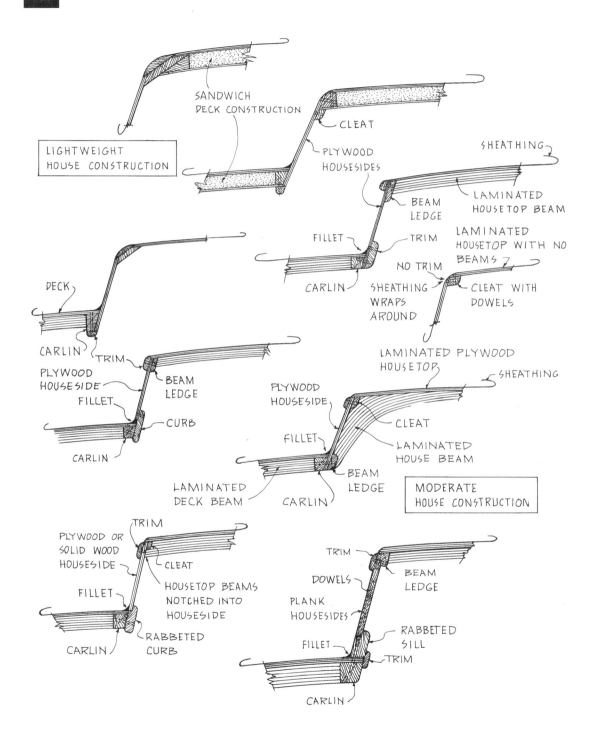

SANDWICH
DECK CONSTRUCTION

LIGHTWEIGHT
HOUSE CONSTRUCTION

CLEAT

PLYWOOD
HOUSESIDES

SHEATHING

BEAM
LEDGE

LAMINATED
HOUSETOP BEAM

FILLET

TRIM

LAMINATED
HOUSETOP WITH NO
BEAMS

CARLIN

NO TRIM

SHEATHING
WRAPS
AROUND

CLEAT WITH
DOWELS

DECK

CARLIN

TRIM

PLYWOOD
HOUSESIDE

BEAM
LEDGE

FILLET

CURB

CARLIN

LAMINATED
DECK BEAM

PLYWOOD
HOUSESIDE

FILLET

CARLIN

BEAM
LEDGE

LAMINATED PLYWOOD
HOUSETOP

SHEATHING

CLEAT

LAMINATED
HOUSE BEAM

MODERATE
HOUSE CONSTRUCTION

TRIM

PLYWOOD OR
SOLID WOOD
HOUSESIDE

CLEAT

FILLET

HOUSETOP BEAMS
NOTCHED INTO
HOUSESIDE

CARLIN

RABBETED
CURB

TRIM

DOWELS

PLANK
HOUSESIDES

FILLET

BEAM
LEDGE

RABBETED
SILL

TRIM

CARLIN

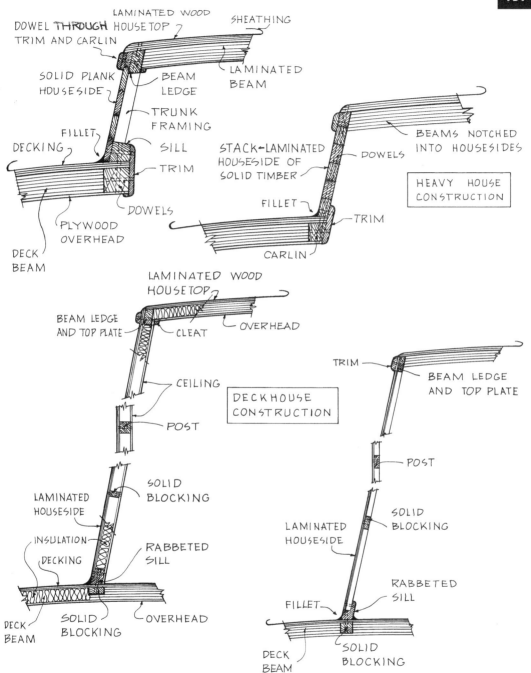

DOWEL **THROUGH** LAMINATED WOOD HOUSE TOP
TRIM AND CARLIN
SHEATHING

SOLID PLANK HOUSE SIDE
BEAM LEDGE
LAMINATED BEAM

TRUNK FRAMING

FILLET
SILL

DECKING
TRIM

STACK-LAMINATED HOUSESIDE OF SOLID TIMBER
DOWELS
BEAMS NOTCHED INTO HOUSESIDES

HEAVY HOUSE CONSTRUCTION

DOWELS

FILLET
TRIM

PLYWOOD OVERHEAD

DECK BEAM
CARLIN

LAMINATED WOOD HOUSE TOP

BEAM LEDGE AND TOP PLATE
CLEAT
OVERHEAD

TRIM

BEAM LEDGE AND TOP PLATE

CEILING

DECKHOUSE CONSTRUCTION

POST

POST

SOLID BLOCKING

LAMINATED HOUSESIDE

SOLID BLOCKING

INSULATION

LAMINATED HOUSESIDE

DECKING
RABBETED SILL

RABBETED SILL

FILLET

DECK BEAM
SOLID BLOCKING
OVERHEAD

DECK BEAM
SOLID BLOCKING

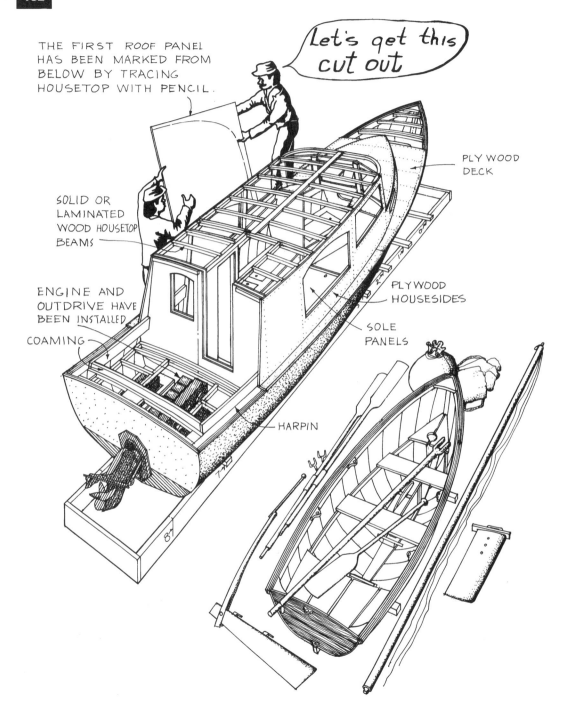

THE FIRST ROOF PANEL
HAS BEEN MARKED FROM
BELOW BY TRACING
HOUSETOP WITH PENCIL.

Let's get this cut out

SOLID OR
LAMINATED
WOOD HOUSETOP
BEAMS

PLYWOOD
DECK

ENGINE AND
OUTDRIVE HAVE
BEEN INSTALLED

PLYWOOD
HOUSESIDES

COAMING

SOLE
PANELS

HARPIN

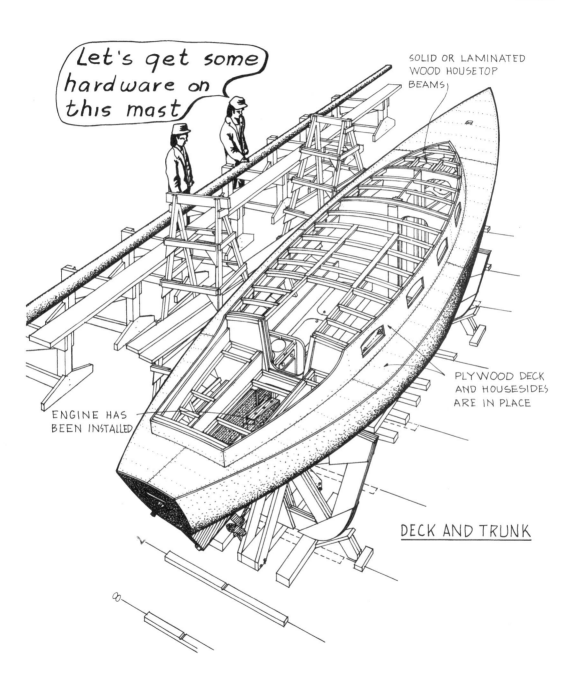

DECK AND TRUNK

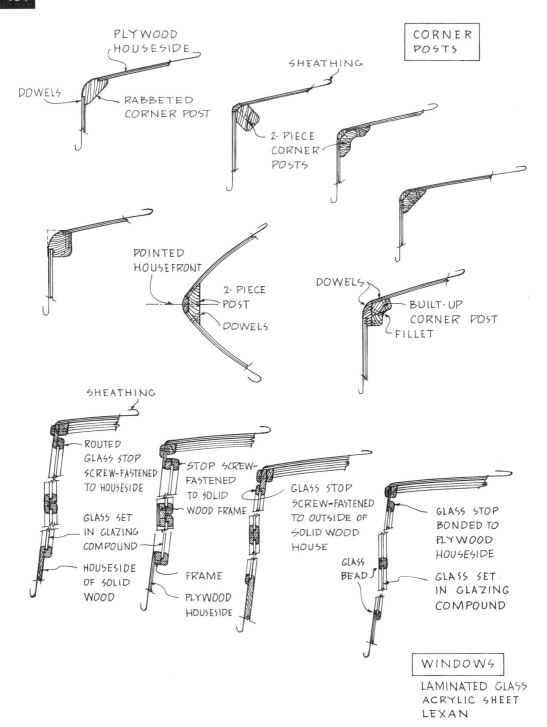

PLYWOOD HOUSESIDE

DOWELS

RABBETED CORNER POST

SHEATHING

2-PIECE CORNER POSTS

CORNER POSTS

POINTED HOUSEFRONT

2-PIECE POST

DOWELS

DOWELS

BUILT-UP CORNER POST

FILLET

SHEATHING

ROUTED GLASS STOP SCREW-FASTENED TO HOUSESIDE

GLASS SET IN GLAZING COMPOUND

HOUSESIDE OF SOLID WOOD

STOP SCREW-FASTENED TO SOLID WOOD FRAME

FRAME

PLYWOOD HOUSESIDE

GLASS STOP SCREW-FASTENED TO OUTSIDE OF SOLID WOOD HOUSE

GLASS BEAD

GLASS STOP BONDED TO PLYWOOD HOUSESIDE

GLASS SET IN GLAZING COMPOUND

WINDOWS

LAMINATED GLASS
ACRYLIC SHEET
LEXAN

155

WINDOWS

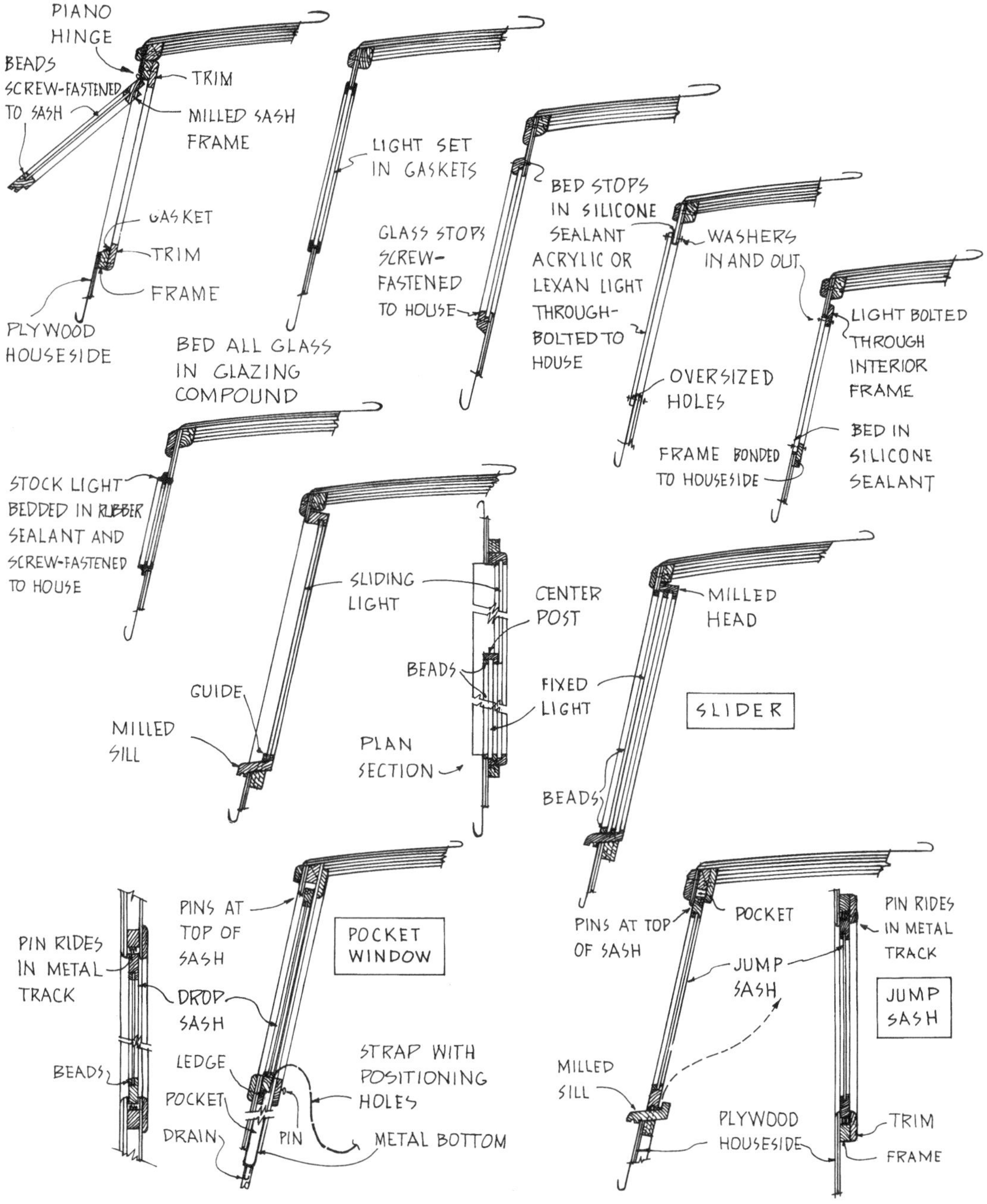

PIANO HINGE

BEADS SCREW-FASTENED TO SASH

TRIM

MILLED SASH FRAME

GASKET

TRIM

FRAME

PLYWOOD HOUSESIDE

BED ALL GLASS IN GLAZING COMPOUND

LIGHT SET IN GASKETS

GLASS STOPS SCREW-FASTENED TO HOUSE

BED STOPS IN SILICONE SEALANT ACRYLIC OR LEXAN LIGHT THROUGH-BOLTED TO HOUSE

OVERSIZED HOLES

FRAME BONDED TO HOUSESIDE

WASHERS IN AND OUT

LIGHT BOLTED THROUGH INTERIOR FRAME

BED IN SILICONE SEALANT

STOCK LIGHT BEDDED IN RUBBER SEALANT AND SCREW-FASTENED TO HOUSE

SLIDING LIGHT

GUIDE

MILLED SILL

PLAN SECTION

CENTER POST

BEADS

FIXED LIGHT

BEADS

MILLED HEAD

SLIDER

PIN RIDES IN METAL TRACK

BEADS

PINS AT TOP OF SASH

DROP SASH

LEDGE

POCKET

DRAIN

PIN

POCKET WINDOW

STRAP WITH POSITIONING HOLES

METAL BOTTOM

PINS AT TOP OF SASH

MILLED SILL

POCKET

JUMP SASH

PLYWOOD HOUSESIDE

PIN RIDES IN METAL TRACK

JUMP SASH

TRIM

FRAME

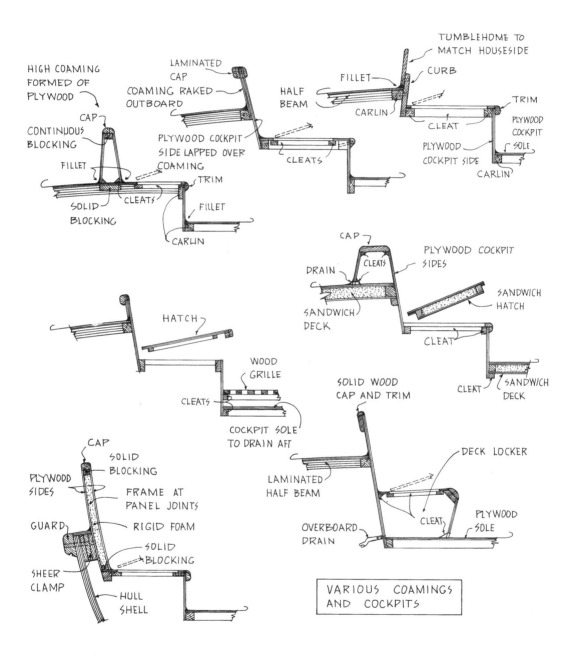

HIGH COAMING FORMED OF PLYWOOD

CAP

CONTINUOUS BLOCKING

FILLET

SOLID BLOCKING

CLEATS

TRIM

FILLET

CARLIN

LAMINATED CAP

COAMING RAKED OUTBOARD

PLYWOOD COCKPIT SIDE LAPPED OVER COAMING

HALF BEAM

CLEATS

FILLET

CARLIN

TUMBLEHOME TO MATCH HOUSESIDE

CURB

TRIM

CLEAT

PLYWOOD COCKPIT

PLYWOOD COCKPIT SIDE

SOLE

CARLIN

CAP

CLEATS

DRAIN

SANDWICH DECK

PLYWOOD COCKPIT SIDES

SANDWICH HATCH

CLEAT

CLEAT

SANDWICH DECK

HATCH

WOOD GRILLE

CLEATS

COCKPIT SOLE TO DRAIN AFT

CAP

SOLID BLOCKING

PLYWOOD SIDES

FRAME AT PANEL JOINTS

GUARD

RIGID FOAM

SOLID BLOCKING

SHEER CLAMP

HULL SHELL

SOLID WOOD CAP AND TRIM

DECK LOCKER

LAMINATED HALF BEAM

OVERBOARD DRAIN

CLEAT

PLYWOOD SOLE

VARIOUS COAMINGS AND COCKPITS

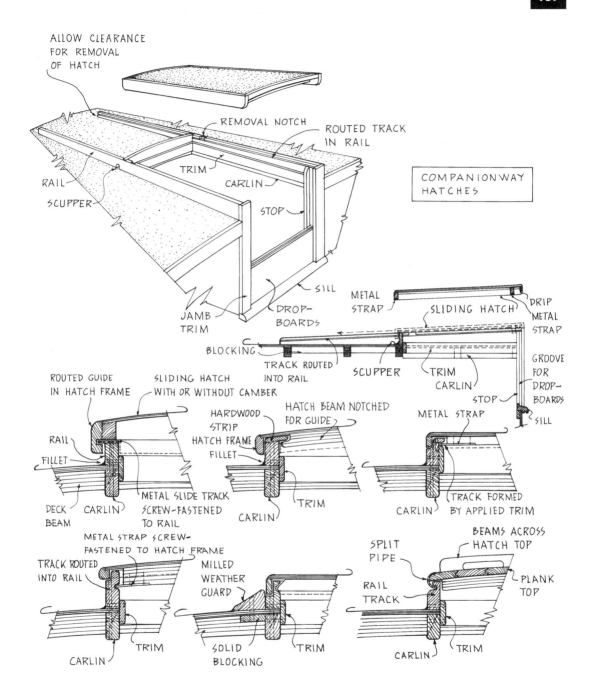

ALLOW CLEARANCE FOR REMOVAL OF HATCH

REMOVAL NOTCH

ROUTED TRACK IN RAIL

TRIM

CARLIN

RAIL

SCUPPER

STOP

COMPANIONWAY HATCHES

SILL

JAMB TRIM

DROP-BOARDS

METAL STRAP

SLIDING HATCH

DRIP METAL STRAP

BLOCKING

TRACK ROUTED INTO RAIL

SCUPPER

TRIM CARLIN

STOP

GROOVE FOR DROP-BOARDS

SILL

ROUTED GUIDE IN HATCH FRAME

SLIDING HATCH WITH OR WITHOUT CAMBER

HATCH BEAM NOTCHED FOR GUIDE

METAL STRAP

RAIL

FILLET

HARDWOOD STRIP HATCH FRAME

FILLET

DECK BEAM

CARLIN

METAL SLIDE TRACK SCREW-FASTENED TO RAIL

TRIM

CARLIN

TRACK FORMED BY APPLIED TRIM

CARLIN

METAL STRAP SCREW-FASTENED TO HATCH FRAME

TRACK ROUTED INTO RAIL

MILLED WEATHER GUARD

SPLIT PIPE

BEAMS ACROSS HATCH TOP

RAIL TRACK

PLANK TOP

CARLIN

TRIM

SOLID BLOCKING

TRIM

CARLIN

TRIM

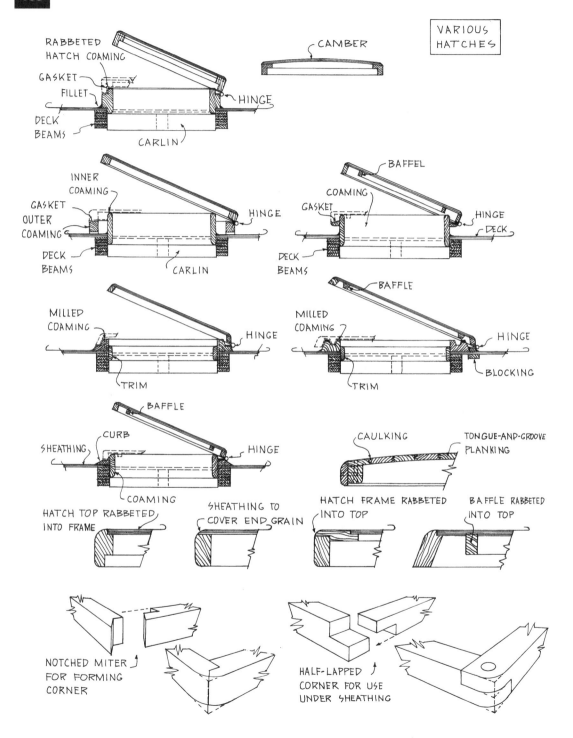

VARIOUS HATCHES

RABBETED HATCH COAMING
GASKET
FILLET
DECK BEAMS
HINGE
CARLIN

CAMBER

INNER COAMING
GASKET
OUTER COAMING
DECK BEAMS
HINGE
CARLIN

BAFFEL
COAMING
GASKET
HINGE
DECK
DECK BEAMS

MILLED COAMING
HINGE
TRIM

MILLED COAMING
BAFFLE
HINGE
BLOCKING
TRIM

BAFFLE
CURB
SHEATHING
HINGE
COAMING

CAULKING
TONGUE-AND-GROOVE PLANKING

HATCH TOP RABBETED INTO FRAME

SHEATHING TO COVER END GRAIN

HATCH FRAME RABBETED INTO TOP

BAFFLE RABBETED INTO TOP

NOTCHED MITER FOR FORMING CORNER

HALF-LAPPED CORNER FOR USE UNDER SHEATHING

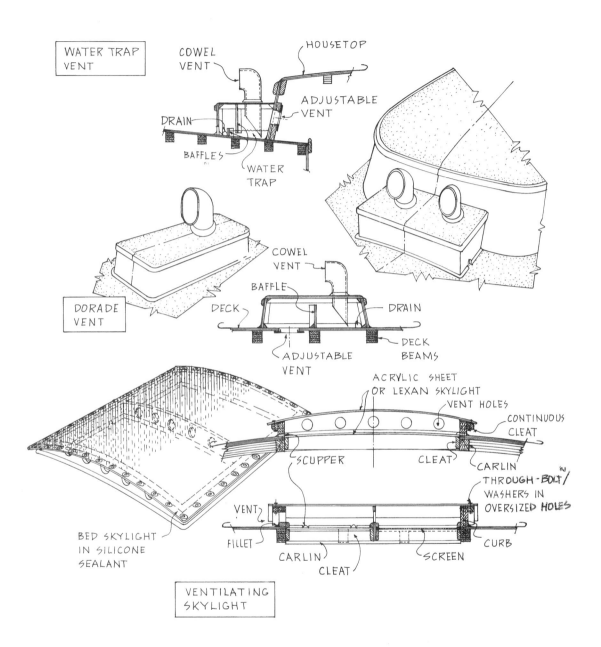

WATER TRAP VENT

COWEL VENT

HOUSETOP

ADJUSTABLE VENT

DRAIN

BAFFLES

WATER TRAP

COWEL VENT

DORADE VENT

DECK

BAFFLE

DRAIN

DECK BEAMS

ADJUSTABLE VENT

ACRYLIC SHEET OR LEXAN SKYLIGHT

VENT HOLES

CONTINUOUS CLEAT

SCUPPER

CLEAT

CARLIN

THROUGH-BOLT/ WASHERS IN OVERSIZED HOLES

BED SKYLIGHT IN SILICONE SEALANT

VENT

FILLET

CARLIN

CLEAT

SCREEN

CURB

VENTILATING SKYLIGHT

CHAPTER 16

Rudders
and Boards

Make rudders and boards of stack-laminated solid timber covered with glass fabric sheathing. The cores can also be covered with one or more layers of veneer or plywood before being sheathed.

Centerboards are usually flat plates that fit in centerboard trunks having parallel sides. Centerboards themselves could be made in airfoil shapes, but the trunks could not accommodate them snugly since they are pulled back and up into the boat. Daggerboards easily could be made in a streamlined shape, since they slide straight up and down. The trunks of boats with streamlined daggerboards have curved walls to accommodate them. Rudders made of wood always are shaped to approximate a laminar flow curve.

Rudders and boards can be laminated from vertical timbers that have been bonded and cured on a perfectly flat surface. Lay a full-size pattern over this platform of boards so the outline of the finished object can be traced. After carefully cutting out the rudder or board, mark a centerline along each edge. Use a power plane to shape the surface, either working by eye or matching a template that has been prepared. When shaping with the power plane, take care not to cut into the centerline mark, which determines the shape of the piece.

Alternatively, rudders and boards can be stack-laminated from horizontal timber sawn to the shape given in the plans. When these cake layers are bonded, the final object emerges without having to be shaped.

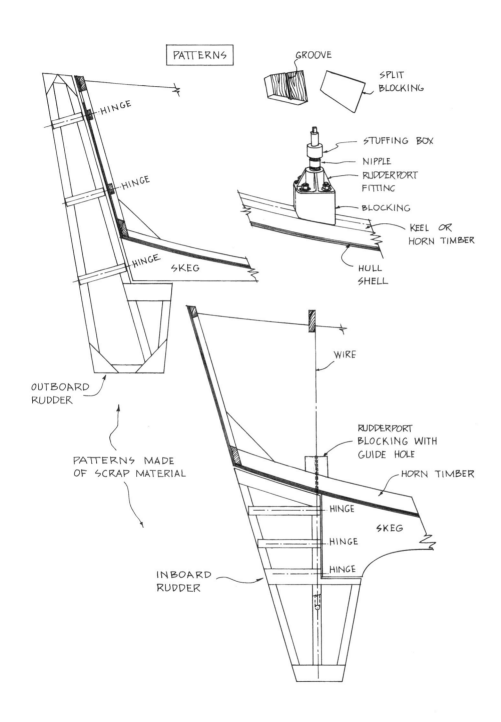

PATTERNS

GROOVE

SPLIT BLOCKING

HINGE

HINGE

HINGE

SKEG

STUFFING BOX

NIPPLE

RUDDERPORT FITTING

BLOCKING

KEEL OR HORN TIMBER

HULL SHELL

OUTBOARD RUDDER

PATTERNS MADE OF SCRAP MATERIAL

WIRE

RUDDERPORT BLOCKING WITH GUIDE HOLE

HORN TIMBER

HINGE

SKEG

HINGE

HINGE

INBOARD RUDDER

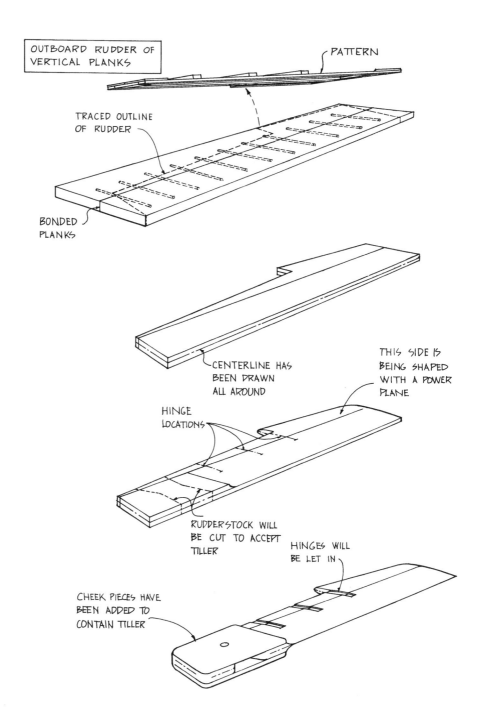

OUTBOARD RUDDER OF VERTICAL PLANKS

PATTERN

TRACED OUTLINE OF RUDDER

BONDED PLANKS

CENTERLINE HAS BEEN DRAWN ALL AROUND

THIS SIDE IS BEING SHAPED WITH A POWER PLANE

HINGE LOCATIONS

RUDDERSTOCK WILL BE CUT TO ACCEPT TILLER

HINGES WILL BE LET IN

CHEEK PIECES HAVE BEEN ADDED TO CONTAIN TILLER

In either case, it is a good idea to make a full-size pattern from scrap material, and work out the angles that will be used and the location of hardware. If the pattern is for a core that will have more wood laminated to it, the thickness of those laminates must be deducted from the pattern before it is used to trace outlines.

Rudders can be hung inboard or outboard. In either case, the twisting force required for steering must be transferred to the rudder surface by a stock that rises within or behind the boat to an elevation where it can be manipulated by a tiller or wheel. In the simplest case, an outboard rudder consists of a vertical plank or two that become a rudderstock at its upper extremity. Outboard rudders constructed of several pieces of wood may rely on sheathing or surface lamination to keep them true. With large transom-hung rudders with long horizontal dimensions, it is better to have a heavy timber stock into which the rudder material is morticed.

Inboard rudders must have a stock capable of passing through the bottom of the boat. A stainless steel or bronze shaft is normally used and must somehow transfer its torque to the rudder surface. This can be done by means of plates welded or brazed to the rudderstock and let into the rudder material. Another way is to bore and tap the rudderstock, so that rods can be threaded into it. These rods can then be used as bolts to hold the rudder together. Sometimes the rudderstock is bored for bolts that are run into the rudder material.

Drill holes through the horn timber, keel, and blocking to accommodate the rudderstock. Blocking for supporting the rudder port fitting can be made in right- and left-hand parts. Scribe a line on the inner faces as shown on the plans. Cut a groove along these lines, bond the blocking together, and position it on the keel or horn timber precisely as indicated on the drawings. The groove serves as a guide for drilling a ¼-inch-diameter hole clear through the horn timber, keel, and hull shell. This hole in turn serves as a sight line to the gudgeon or the lowest hinge to determine if any slight adjustments need to be made when boring the full-size hole.

Saturate all wood surfaces within the bore with resin before installing the rudder parts. A good way to do this is to tape the bottom of the hole, filling it up so that the mixture soaks in.

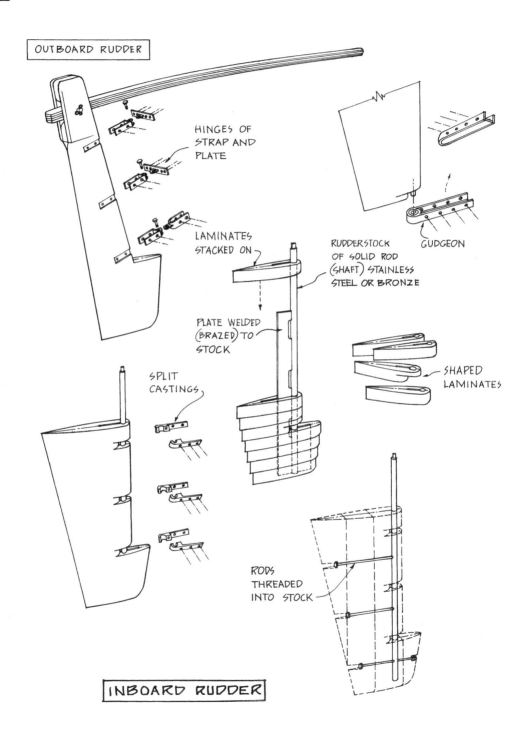

OUTBOARD RUDDER

HINGES OF
STRAP AND
PLATE

GUDGEON

LAMINATES
STACKED ON

RUDDERSTOCK
OF SOLID ROD
(SHAFT) STAINLESS
STEEL OR BRONZE

PLATE WELDED
(BRAZED) TO
STOCK

SHAPED
LAMINATES

SPLIT
CASTINGS

RODS
THREADED
INTO STOCK

INBOARD RUDDER

CHAPTER 17

Installing Fastenings and Hardware

Tests and procedures developed by the Gougeon Brothers of Bay City, Michigan, have demonstrated that fastenings set in resin and placed in oversized holes resist extraction better than fastenings relying solely on a mechanical bite into untreated wood. This has great significance when applied to laminated wood boatbuilding.

PREPARATION

In a laminated wood boat, the greatest areas of concern in the structure are where fastenings penetrate the protective resin and sheathing, creating possible avenues of entry for moisture and oxygen to the wood underneath. Consequently, nuts, washers, and bolt ends should be encapsulated wherever they are exposed to the atmosphere. The usual way is to countersink the hardware and plug the holes. A simpler way is to use a threaded rod that has been bonded into an oversized hole. Any exposed ends of the rod in the hole are then covered when the holes are filled with a thickened adhesive mixture.

When a connection needs to be undone readily, a stud (a length of threaded rod, or a machine screw with the head cut off) can be bonded into the structure as described above. The piece to be fastened on can then be held to the structure with a nut and a lock washer.

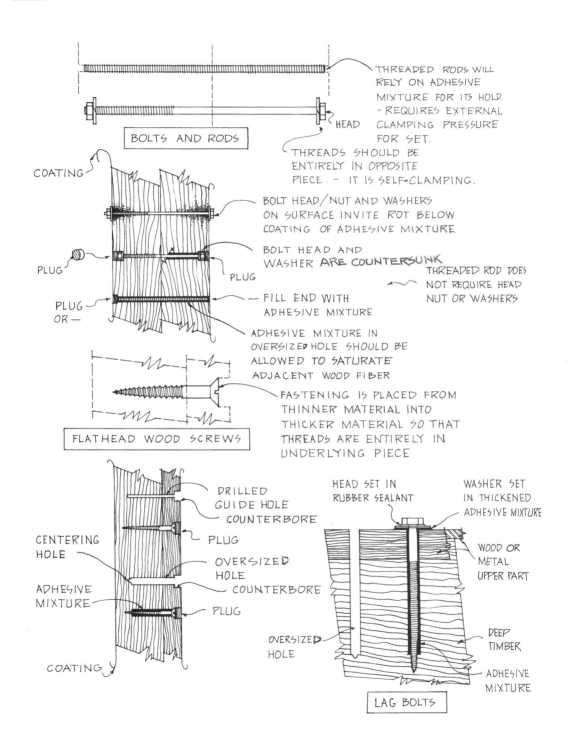

BOLTS AND RODS

THREADED RODS WILL RELY ON ADHESIVE MIXTURE FOR ITS HOLD - REQUIRES EXTERNAL CLAMPING PRESSURE FOR SET.

HEAD

THREADS SHOULD BE ENTIRELY IN OPPOSITE PIECE. - IT IS SELF-CLAMPING.

COATING

BOLT HEAD/NUT AND WASHERS ON SURFACE INVITE ROT BELOW COATING OF ADHESIVE MIXTURE.

BOLT HEAD AND WASHER ARE COUNTERSUNK

THREADED ROD DOES NOT REQUIRE HEAD NUT OR WASHERS

PLUG

PLUG

PLUG OR —

FILL END WITH ADHESIVE MIXTURE

ADHESIVE MIXTURE IN OVERSIZED HOLE SHOULD BE ALLOWED TO SATURATE ADJACENT WOOD FIBER

FASTENING IS PLACED FROM THINNER MATERIAL INTO THICKER MATERIAL SO THAT THREADS ARE ENTIRELY IN UNDERLYING PIECE

FLATHEAD WOOD SCREWS

DRILLED GUIDE HOLE COUNTERBORE

HEAD SET IN RUBBER SEALANT

WASHER SET IN THICKENED ADHESIVE MIXTURE

CENTERING HOLE

PLUG

OVERSIZED HOLE

COUNTERBORE

WOOD OR METAL UPPER PART

ADHESIVE MIXTURE

PLUG

OVERSIZED HOLE

DEEP TIMBER

COATING

ADHESIVE MIXTURE

LAG BOLTS

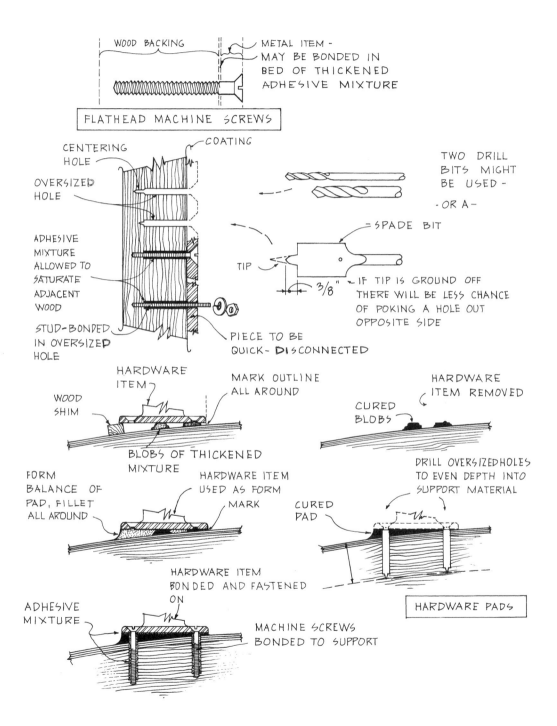

WOOD BACKING

METAL ITEM —
MAY BE BONDED IN
BED OF THICKENED
ADHESIVE MIXTURE

FLATHEAD MACHINE SCREWS

CENTERING
HOLE

COATING

OVERSIZED
HOLE

ADHESIVE
MIXTURE
ALLOWED TO
SATURATE
ADJACENT
WOOD

STUD-BONDED
IN OVERSIZED
HOLE

PIECE TO BE
QUICK-DISCONNECTED

TWO DRILL
BITS MIGHT
BE USED —

— OR A —

= SPADE BIT

TIP

3/8" — IF TIP IS GROUND OFF
THERE WILL BE LESS CHANCE
OF POKING A HOLE OUT
OPPOSITE SIDE

HARDWARE
ITEM

WOOD
SHIM

MARK OUTLINE
ALL AROUND

BLOBS OF THICKENED
MIXTURE

HARDWARE
ITEM REMOVED

CURED
BLOBS

FORM
BALANCE OF
PAD, FILLET
ALL AROUND

HARDWARE ITEM
USED AS FORM

MARK

CURED
PAD

DRILL OVERSIZED HOLES
TO EVEN DEPTH INTO
SUPPORT MATERIAL

HARDWARE PADS

HARDWARE ITEM
BONDED AND FASTENED
ON

ADHESIVE
MIXTURE

MACHINE SCREWS
BONDED TO SUPPORT

Wood screws should be used for wood-to-wood connections only; use flathead machine screws to hold hardware items to the structure. Drill guide holes for machine screws, using a bit one size smaller than the screw size. Oversized holes are most easily drilled using a spade bit the diameter of the oversized hole, with all but ⅜ inch of the tip ground off. This leaves a small hole centered at the bottom of the larger one. Coat the hole with resin, then drive the machine screw in so that its threads catch in the smaller hole. The screw will then be held in position while the adhesive cures.

An alternative is to drill the large-diameter hole first, then drill the smaller hole at the bottom using a smaller bit. About a quarter of the screw should project into the smaller hole. Always remove wood chips and dust from the holes before inserting the screw.

The oversized hole for a #8 or a #10 screw would be 3⁄8 inch in diameter; for a #12 screw, ⁷⁄₁₆ inch; and for a #14 screw, a ½-inch-diameter hole is about right. For rods, studs, and bolts, make an oversized hole about ¼ inch larger than the diameter of the fastener. Larger oversized holes mean a stronger bond, but they interrupt the continuity of more grain than a smaller, filled hole in what might already be a slender structural member.

Be sure to keep the spade bit used to drill oversized holes sharp; dull blades burnish the sides of the hole, inhibiting satisfactory penetration of the resin into the wood, and resulting in a weaker bond.

Holes drilled downward into horizontal material are simply filled with adhesive mixture and ignored for 15 to 20 minutes, allowing the surrounding wood to become saturated. If the fastenings are placed too soon, resin continues to be drawn into the wood, leaving voids. The fastenings displace much of the resin, so prior to their placement, remove some of the resin with a syringe.

When a hole is drilled at such an angle that it cannot be filled with resin, first coat the interior surfaces of the hole completely with resin, using an applicator (such as a pipe cleaner) that will reach to the end of the hole. Next pack a syringe with a thickened adhesive mixture and inject it into the hole so that no air is trapped inside. Fill the threads of the fastening with this mixture, and place the fastening in the hole. The resulting mess can be cleaned away easily with a putty knife.

Bonding the fastenings as described above greatly increases the ability of the connection to resist tensile stress. However, much hardware is primarily subject to shear stress, particularly winches and chainplates. The ability to resist these stresses can be greatly increased by bonding them to the structure with resin. The intervening layer of resin serves the equally important function of closing the avenue for moisture and oxygen to the wood underneath, thereby extending the life of the boat.

To prepare aluminum hardware items for bonding, treat its bonding surface with an acid wash, followed by an alodine conversion coating. Apply adhesive mixture shortly thereafter for bonding. Kits and instructions for this process are available from suppliers of epoxy products.

To prepare stainless steel for bonding, first thoroughly clean the bonding surface of grease and oil, using a solvent and a clean cloth. Use 60-grit sandpaper to remove mill scale and rust. Cover the bonding surface with a thin coating of resin, and sand again with 60-grit sandpaper. Apply adhesive shortly thereafter for bonding.

Bronze hardware preparation is the same as for steel. Bronze relies on a keying effect of the cured resin. To increase this keying potential, drill small, shallow holes in the surfaces of the bronze that will be bonded, where possible, to allow adhesive mixture to rise into them.

Whether to bond hardware to a surface after it has been painted or to paint around the hardware later is the builder's choice. In either case, the bond must be made to a clean resin surface.

HARDWARE INSTALLATION

First, lay out all hardware exactly where it is to go, and mark the precise center of each fastening hole with an ice pick or other pointed tool. Set the hardware items aside, and drill all the holes with a sharp bit as previously described. Mark the drill bit for the depth of hole required, taking into account the thickness of the hardware through which the fastening must pass. Place the hardware again to verify its fit. Screws should just be able to auger into the bottom of the small guide holes. Work from item to item, bonding each as previously discussed. Due to the concentration of adhesive mixture, curing will commence rapidly. In hot weather, there may be only 20 minutes of working time.

If a hardware item will be bonded to a surface that has already been painted, mask the surface around the perimeter of the item with tape. Place the tape so that the hardware just overlaps it and cut around its base, using a sharp blade and just enough pressure to cut the tape but not the surface underneath. Remove the hardware and peel away the narrow strips of tape that lie under the hardware. With a sharp tool, scrape away the paint on the exposed area, which is the bonding surface, to expose the cured resin underneath. The tape protects the surrounding painted surface during the bonding process.

Hardware items bonded at an angle to the supporting surface can be installed on a sloped pad of thickened adhesive mixture. Coat the bonding surface of the hardware item with a release agent to facilitate its removal, then prop the hardware item on some scrap wood at the desired angle, and squirt a couple of blobs of thickened adhesive mixture to support it. Mark the outline of the item on the supporting surface with a pencil and, when the props have cured, pop the hardware item loose. Build the sloped pad, using a syringe to administer thickened adhesive mixture around the edges to form a fillet. Avoid trapping air in the mixture. Use the bonding surface of the hardware item itself as the upper form for the sloped pad. When the sloped pad has cured, mark the center for each fastening and remove the hardware item. Drill oversized holes through the sloped pad so that they penetrate the supporting material equally, and bond as previously described.

CHAPTER 18

Teak Surfacing

In laminated wood boatbuilding, a teak surface for a deck or houseside is an aesthetic decision. It must be thought of as a veneer or wearing surface, rather than as a major structural element. If a good bond can be achieved between the teak and the backing material, the teak can be figured into the required structural thickness. Since teak glues only moderately well, any teak to be laminated should be degreased over the area of its bonding surface with acetone, MEK, or some other solvent.

Teak that will be applied to a plywood structure should be from ⅛ inch to 3/16 inch thick and spaced about 3/32 inch apart. Consider for a moment that teak will probably be left uncoated and unfinished, allowing it to weather to a beautiful silver gray. (It's hard to imagine maintaining a varnished surface this size.) If the wood is not coated, it is outside the envelope of protection offered by the resin, and the wood will try to swell and shrink under changing weather conditions, as one would expect. If it is too thick, it will exert considerable force on the adhesive and on itself—something may give. Some builders speak of using teak up to ⅜ inch thick, with a 3/16-inch space between the strips. The wide gaps allow for more give-and-take between the strips, but one supposes that once there is give-and-take, the bond (or strip) is broken already, at least partially.

Teak strips can be sawn from 2-inch-thick, rough-sawn solid stock. If the rough plank is ripped into 2-inch-wide pieces, the resulting 2 x 2

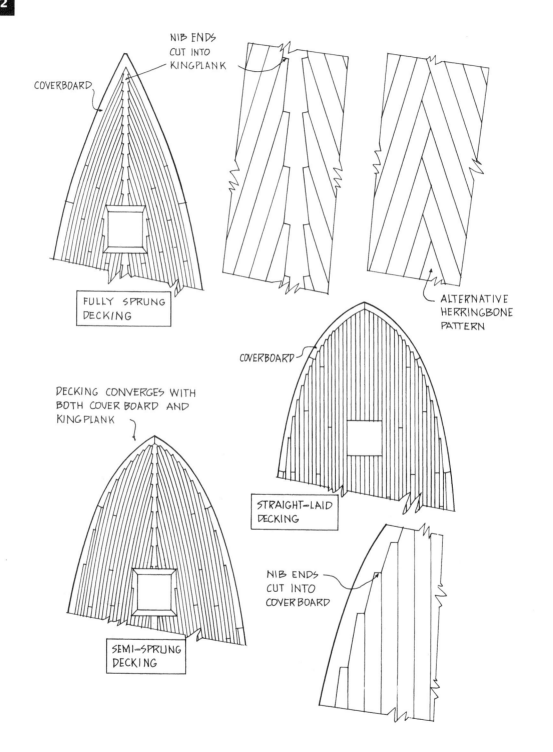

NIB ENDS
CUT INTO
KINGPLANK

COVERBOARD

FULLY SPRUNG
DECKING

ALTERNATIVE
HERRINGBONE
PATTERN

COVERBOARD

DECKING CONVERGES WITH
BOTH COVER BOARD AND
KINGPLANK

STRAIGHT-LAID
DECKING

SEMI-SPRUNG
DECKING

NIB ENDS
CUT INTO
COVERBOARD

sticks can be turned to yield edge-grain strips for use in lamination. The strips can be finished in 1½-inch to 1¾-inch widths.

There are three patterns commonly used in laying out the strips on deck: *fully sprung, half-sprung,* and *straight-laid.*

In all cases, a covering board, sometimes made of a contrasting hardwood, such as mahogany, is bonded along the plan sheerline from stem to stern. The covering board is assembled from sections of solid wood of the same thickness as the deck surfacing and about twice the width of the individual strips. Templates of the deck edge are made to transfer the shape to the covering-board material. The shapes are cut out and fitted together with butt joints for bonding along the sheer.

For sprung decks, margin pieces of a similar material are placed around obstructions on the deck, such as housesides, trunks, and hatches. If a kingplank is used, it is made of the same thickness material as the deck surfacing and is placed next.

In a fully sprung deck, the strips follow the plan sheer to converge at the centerline. Here the strips can mesh in a herringbone pattern or intersect a kingplank that is positioned over the centerline. The first strip is sprung around the outer edge of the deck alongside the covering board, and the deck is covered by working toward the center from alternating sides. This pattern is usually seen on sailboats, which are more apt to have a continuously curving deck from end to end.

A half-sprung pattern will have strips converging toward the centerline but at a lesser angle, so that they also converge on the covering boards. The first strip is placed at the housesides, and the deck is covered by working out toward the covering boards and then in toward the centerline to cover the foredeck and afterdeck.

A straight-laid pattern runs the strips in straight lines fore and aft. The first strip is placed at the centerline and the deck is covered by working out toward the covering boards on alternating sides. Margin strips around hatches and other obstructions are not used normally. This is seen most often on powerboats, which are more likely to have a sharper curve toward the bow and a flatter line toward the stern. Contrary to what some builders say, straight-laid decking is not a sign of inferior construction. The choice is simply a matter of what works best for the boat.

When surfacing material less than about ³⁄₃₂ inch thick is used, it is best to feather the strip ends against the kingplank or covering boards. Thicker material should be cut into the kingplank or covering boards to accommodate the nib ends. The nibs should be cut in about ½ inch to ⅝ inch and feathered back to nothing.

Strips longer than about 12 feet are awkward to handle during installation, so with longer planks butt 12-foot strips end to end with simple butt joints at random locations, making sure they do not line up. Standard practice is to separate butts by five strips.

Teak strips sometimes are placed vertically on housesides, sometimes running from deck to overhang or housetop, or from deck to a molding at windowsill height. They may form a band of surfacing in line with the windows from the sill up to the housetop, and sometimes are seen on trunksides or cockpit coamings. Where the vertical surface curves in the plan view, the strips may have to be as narrow as 1 inch to accommodate the bend.

APPLYING TEAK

To begin the bonding process, seal the underlying plywood with two applications of resin that has been allowed to cure, sanding lightly between and after applications. Coat both the strip and the surface area where it will be bonded with a thickened adhesive mixture. If a dark glue line is desired, add some graphite powder to the mixture. Hold the strips in place with temporary wide-crown staples, set about 8 inches apart down the middle of each strip. The gap between the planks must be maintained at an absolutely uniform distance, measuring the gap with a gauge made of plastic that will not stick in the adhesive.

Apply enough adhesive mixture to bed the strips and fill the gaps between them. There must be no voids remaining in the adhesive, and any visible deficiency in the gap between the strips must be made up.

After the resin has cured, sand the deck to remove all the accumulated mess using 50-grit sandpaper on a rotary electric sander with a foam disc pad. If you have a large, unobstructed deck area to sand, a commercial floor sander (rent one at a hardware store) will save a lot of time. More voids between strips may come to light after sanding the deck and can be filled at this time.

Finish sanding with a rotary sander, using 80-grit sandpaper to achieve a smooth surface. Tight corners and edges will have to be done by hand, using 80-grit sandpaper on a sanding block. When the sanding is complete, there is nothing more to be done. If the surface material becomes damaged, it can be removed with a router and a new piece of stripping bonded in.

CHAPTER 19

Applying the Finish

To prepare the hull for finishing, wipe it with clean, wet rags or a sponge to remove the residue from the curing process. Dry with soft rags, and wipe once again with rags dampened with solvent to clean away any stain or sanding dust that might remain. For a good finish, it will be absolutely necessary to create and maintain as dust-free an environment as possible in the workplace.

An oil-based paint is probably best for wood that is not sheathed with glass cloth because it forms a more flexible coat. A linear polyurethane (LP) paint is best for the completed hull because of its superior resistance to weathering and its toughness when applied over stable sheathing. The fumes are dangerous, however, and the work space must have adequate ventilation. Always wear a fume mask and protective clothing when working with linear polyurethane; safety instructions will be packaged with the paint.

Begin application with a roller, using long, even strokes to yield a uniform coat. A second person can follow along to smooth the surface (called tipping), using a brush lightly wet with paint. The finer the brush, the better the finish. Avoid a buildup of paint in any area, which could cause runs. Use only enough thinner in the paint to permit good flowing. When the paint starts to drag under the brush, add a little thinner to the

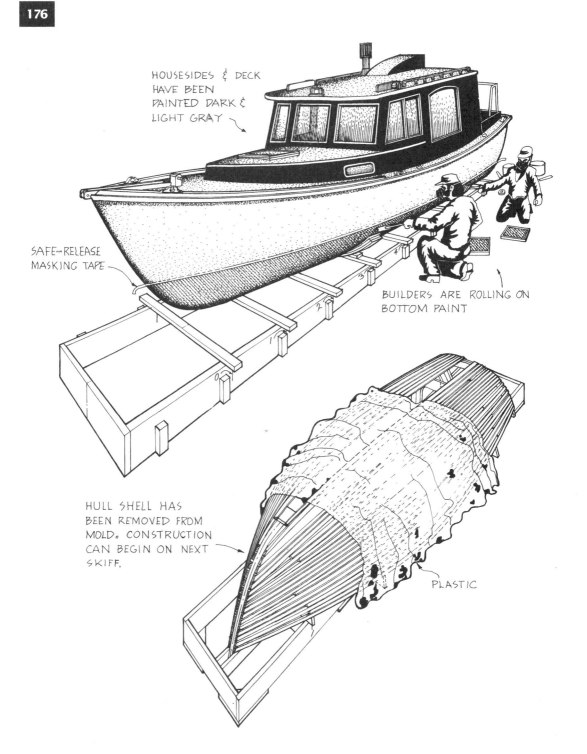

HOUSESIDES & DECK
HAVE BEEN
PAINTED DARK &
LIGHT GRAY

SAFE-RELEASE
MASKING TAPE

BUILDERS ARE ROLLING ON
BOTTOM PAINT

HULL SHELL HAS
BEEN REMOVED FROM
MOLD. CONSTRUCTION
CAN BEGIN ON NEXT
SKIFF.

PLASTIC

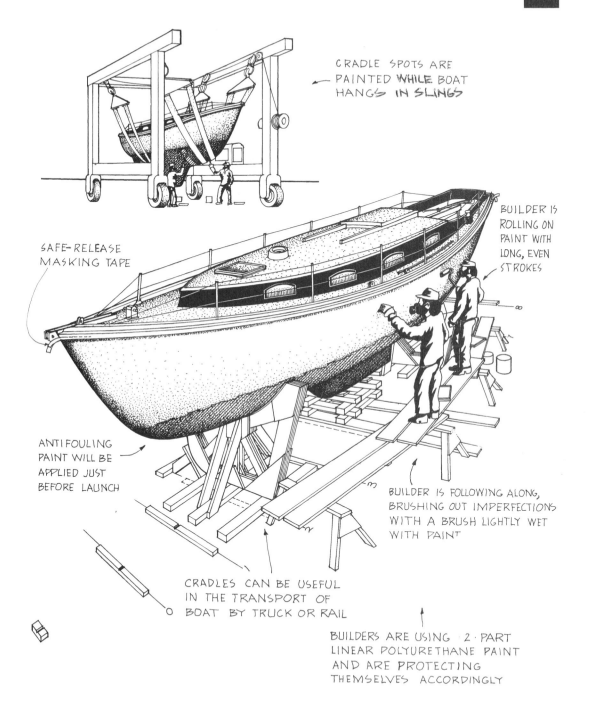

CRADLE SPOTS ARE PAINTED WHILE BOAT HANGS IN SLINGS

BUILDER IS ROLLING ON PAINT WITH LONG, EVEN STROKES

SAFE-RELEASE MASKING TAPE

ANTIFOULING PAINT WILL BE APPLIED JUST BEFORE LAUNCH

BUILDER IS FOLLOWING ALONG, BRUSHING OUT IMPERFECTIONS WITH A BRUSH LIGHTLY WET WITH PAINT

CRADLES CAN BE USEFUL IN THE TRANSPORT OF BOAT BY TRUCK OR RAIL

BUILDERS ARE USING 2-PART LINEAR POLYURETHANE PAINT AND ARE PROTECTING THEMSELVES ACCORDINGLY

roller pan to make up for evaporation. After the surface is sufficiently dry, sand lightly with fine sandpaper to remove any runs or imperfections. Wipe the hull with a tack cloth and repaint with the final coat within 36 hours.

Using varnish on the exterior of the boat means higher maintenance costs in both time and money. Sunlight is the problem; eventually it breaks down the surface coating and separates it from the wood. The speed at which this happens depends upon a number of factors, such as climate, the location of the varnish on the boat, and the quality of the coating. Topsides and housesides generally receive less direct radiation than decks. Toerails and trim, where varnish is seen most often, get lots of direct radiation but probably are the easiest to refinish.

On the other side of the coin, brightly finished wood can be a joy to behold—a literal work of art. The best veneers are chosen for the final lamination of the hull and perhaps are run fore and aft. Extra care is taken with the hull surface to avoid dings and holes because these show through the varnish wherever they are filled or patched. Boats that live on trailers and are kept inside when not at sea, and boats kept in boathouses, are good candidates for exterior brightwork.

Under normal circumstances, a life span of about three years can be expected for exterior brightwork if two coats of varnish are applied over a resin-coated hull—provided a high-quality varnish is used that contains an ultraviolet light filter (UV). By adding a coat of varnish each year, this life span can be extended up to maybe eight years. High-grade synthetic varnish is considerably more expensive than others, but using it lowers long-term maintenance costs when you consider the cost of labor. Using the best varnish is cheaper in the long run.

As mentioned in the chapter on materials, hulls that are finished bright should be sheathed with cloth of 4 ounces or less; otherwise, the weave will show through the finish. Surface preparation is the same as described for paint application, except that extra care should be exercised to ensure that all final sanding of the underlying wood is done with the grain so that no scratches show.

Always start with fresh varnish and the very best brush available. With proper care, a good brush can last years. A fresh can of varnish should not be stirred; *anything* that is placed in it can contaminate it. Wipe the area to be coated with a tack cloth just prior to varnishing. Lay on the varnish with a minimum of brushing, working quickly. Do not allow laps to develop—easy to say but not so easy to do. With some synthetic varnishes, it is possible to apply the successive coat when the previous one has set but not cured, say in several hours. Oil-based varnish must be allowed to dry completely and sanded with fine paper before applying the next coat. In any case, the manufacturer's directions should be followed.

CHAPTER 20

Spars

S pars are built from staves of wood bonded together along their edges to form hollow tubes of the exact sizes and shapes shown on the plans. After the tubes are bonded and cured, sharp edges are rounded and brought to a uniform surface by planing and sanding. The head, partner, and spreader areas have solid wood cores. The partner core runs from the boom and winch hardware down, extending below the bottom of the staves and forming a tenon that fits the mast step. Normally, the step is on the keel, but sometimes it is on deck, with appropriate supporting structure underneath.

Spars are built using tubes of four, six, or eight sides; eight-sided shapes are reserved for large spars. Whatever the spar's shape, the surfaces that receive sail tracks are straight. Unstayed masts and masts for gaff-headed rigs are circular in section. Masts with spreaders are oval or oblong in section, with the long axis running fore and aft.

Alternatively, for small- to moderate-size spars, wood can be layered. One surface of each half is hollowed out so that when the spar is assembled, it forms a hollow tube with four sides. If only two pieces of wood are used, one side of each piece is routed out before the spar is assembled. If more pieces are used, each half of the spar is bonded and cured before any hollowing takes place.

The spar pieces can be hollowed by scoring them with an appropriately set circular saw and removing the remaining material with

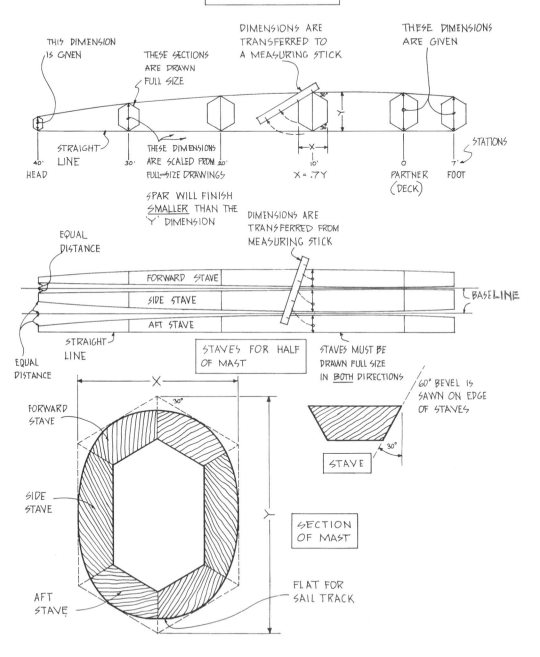

LOFTING THE MAST

THIS DIMENSION IS GIVEN

THESE SECTIONS ARE DRAWN FULL SIZE

DIMENSIONS ARE TRANSFERRED TO A MEASURING STICK

THESE DIMENSIONS ARE GIVEN

STRAIGHT LINE

THESE DIMENSIONS ARE SCALED FROM FULL-SIZE DRAWINGS

STATIONS

40' HEAD

30'

20'

X = .7Y

10'

0 PARTNER (DECK)

7' FOOT

SPAR WILL FINISH SMALLER THAN THE 'Y' DIMENSION

DIMENSIONS ARE TRANSFERRED FROM MEASURING STICK

EQUAL DISTANCE

FORWARD STAVE

SIDE STAVE

AFT STAVE

BASELINE

STRAIGHT LINE

EQUAL DISTANCE

STAVES FOR HALF OF MAST

STAVES MUST BE DRAWN FULL SIZE IN BOTH DIRECTIONS

60° BEVEL IS SAWN ON EDGE OF STAVES

FORWARD STAVE

30°

STAVE

30°

SIDE STAVE

AFT STAVE

X

Y

SECTION OF MAST

FLAT FOR SAIL TRACK

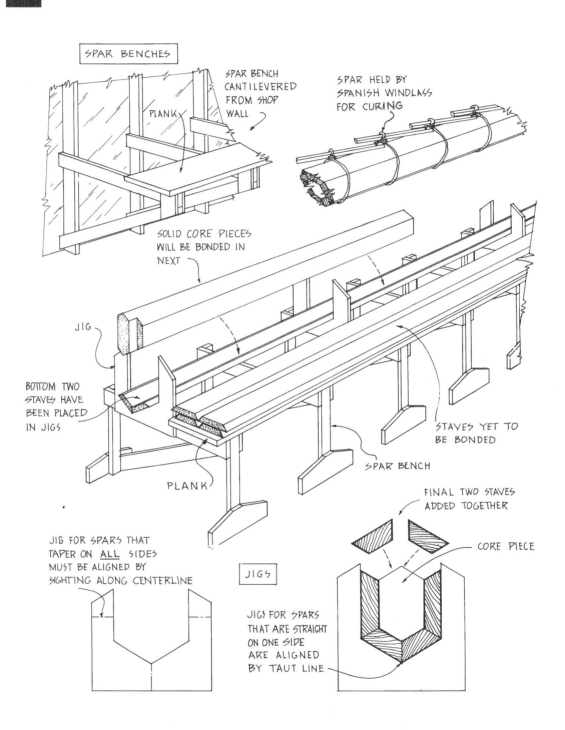

SPAR BENCHES

SPAR BENCH CANTILEVERED FROM SHOP WALL

PLANK

SPAR HELD BY SPANISH WINDLASS FOR CURING

SOLID CORE PIECES WILL BE BONDED IN NEXT

JIG

BOTTOM TWO STAVES HAVE BEEN PLACED IN JIGS

STAVES YET TO BE BONDED

SPAR BENCH

PLANK

JIG FOR SPARS THAT TAPER ON ALL SIDES MUST BE ALIGNED BY SIGHTING ALONG CENTERLINE

JIGS

FINAL TWO STAVES ADDED TOGETHER

CORE PIECE

JIGS FOR SPARS THAT ARE STRAIGHT ON ONE SIDE ARE ALIGNED BY TAUT LINE

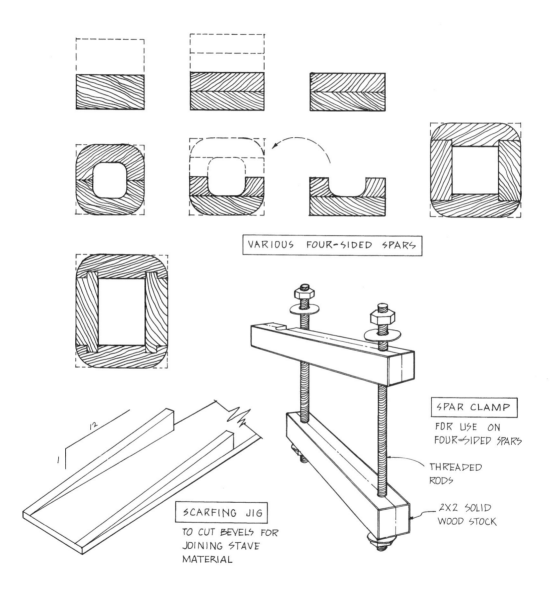

VARIOUS FOUR-SIDED SPARS

SPAR CLAMP

FOR USE ON
FOUR-SIDED SPARS

THREADED
RODS

2X2 SOLID
WOOD STOCK

SCARFING JIG

TO CUT BEVELS FOR
JOINING STAVE
MATERIAL

gouges and chisels. In some cases a hollowing plane is useful. The interior is sanded smooth and coated with adhesive mixture before the spar is assembled.

Spars are constructed most conveniently on a spar bench, the length of the longest spar, made from simple brackets cantilevered off the shop wall, or a row of sawhorses set up at a comfortable working height. Sight along the tops of these supports to a taut line to ensure that the planks added to form the surface will be level. Fasten or stake sawhorses to the shop floor so they will remain steady. Space the supports so that some of them align with arbitrarily assigned lofting stations along the spar. In this way, jigs can be used to hold the spar during assembly and bonding, their shapes having been taken directly from the spar lofting. Square-section spars normally won't need jigs because they are more easily clamped for curing. With circular and oval spars, jigs prevent their staves from skating out of position during curing.

Shapes for spars are shown on plans with their length contracted. Loft these drawings full size, so that the thickness dimension is accurate even though the length dimension is shortened greatly. Position stationlines along the spar at arbitrary spacings. Make a full-size section drawing of the spar at each of these stations using information given on the plans. Take dimensions from these section drawings to plot the individual stave shapes.

Staves for spars more than about 20 feet in length will have to be scarfed using a 1-in-12 slope. Make a simple scarfing jig consisting of a trough of wood just wider than the widest stave, with sloping sides on which the heel and toe of a plane can ride up and down. Quantities of spar clamps are required and can be made up from foot-long pieces of threaded rod and 2 x 2s. Bond and scarf the staves before marking the shapes on them. Let the scarf joints fall where they may.

Mark the stationlines across the outside surface of the staves. For spars that taper equally on all sides, make measurements from a centerline drawn down the middle of the timber. For spars with one straight edge, make measurements from a straight line (baseline) drawn near the edge of the timber. Make these measurements along each stationline.

Join the resulting points by drawing a line with the aid of a stiff batten sprung through the points. Set a circular saw with a carbide rip blade to the indicated bevel angle and carefully cut out each stave.

Plot the shapes for the core pieces to be placed inside the spar onto solid timber and cut them out to a loose fit. Test the fit of the stave and core pieces by dry assembling them in clamps or jigs. When all is well, spread the pieces out on the spar bench and coat the bonding surfaces quickly with a slightly thickened adhesive mixture, using a narrow roller. After the bottom two staves are put back into the jigs, bond the core pieces onto them. Add the side staves, and, finally, add the top two simultaneously. Secure square spars with a spar clamp about every foot. Round and oval spars are held tightly, using Spanish windlasses, also about a foot apart. After curing, plane and sand the spar to remove the sharp ridges and to create a uniform curvature.

Solid spars we won't discuss. Not being made from laminated wood, they are too heavy for the boats illustrated in this book.

CHAPTER 21

Repairs

Wooden boats built by traditional methods gain longevity through the piecemeal replacement of parts. Actually, traditional methods encourage degeneration by design. There are innumerable nooks and crannies for fresh water to pond or creep. The constant working of adjacent surfaces opens routes for the entry of oxygen and moisture, giving rot fungus a congenial environment for growth. Exposed metal fastenings are attacked by the maritime environment, causing corrosion. Traditional wooden-boat design puts a premium on the use of high-quality materials (both wood and fastenings) and the use of preservatives and coatings to extend the life of the boat. At some point, the boat will be attacked by termites or teredo worms, lose fastenings to corrosion, or be involved in an accident. The boatbuilder can replace plank for plank, frame for frame, or any other part to keep the boat young.

The laminated wood boat structure sidesteps many of the problems experienced by a traditional wooden boat by being a monocoque, unitized design, which minimizes the chafing and working of adjacent surfaces. These boats are encapsulated by a tough, protective sheathing and coating that, so long as it remains intact, locks out rot and pests and keeps corrosive elements away from fastenings. Naturally the coating can be dinged, scratched, or gouged, thereby opening unprotected wood to potential problems. Any boat can encounter accidental structural damage. The notion seems to persist that laminated wood boat structures are difficult to repair; in fact, they probably are easier to repair than those of a carvel-planked wooden boat.

It should be noted that once the outside world enters the interior of the wood, all the possibilities for trouble exist that any other wooden boat experiences. This goes for the inside of the hull as well as for the exterior. A warm, unventilated, humid atmosphere inside a boat contributes to the rapid growth of rot fungus. Both termites and marine borers can destroy the structural integrity of a boat without altering its appearance. For this reason, wood not listed as rot resistant should be treated with preservative to offer protection should some of the protective coating be accidentally removed. Antifouling bottom paint is effective only when it is intact. Hulls sheathed with glass cloth in matrix with resin offer a much higher level of protection.

Copper naphtanate and pentachlorophenol (Penta) are commonly used preservatives; both have clear and colored versions. The colored ones permit visual proof of coverage but cannot be painted over. Some preservatives use tributal-tin-oxide as the active agent. Some of these preservatives have components to which glue will not adhere, and all are hostile to life, including yours. Always wear protective clothing whenever applying these preservatives, and work in a ventilated area. Read the manufacturer's precautions carefully.

Minor surface damage can be sanded or planed away so long as no more than about $\frac{1}{16}$ inch is removed. Fill deep cuts or gouges with a thickened adhesive mixture. Long, continuous gouges must be cleaned up by using a chisel to remove material to a neat, even shape; then a new piece of wood can be cut to shape and bonded in. If the gouge has penetrated more than one layer, glue lines will show clearly as the wood is being cleaned up. Sometimes the work will go faster with a router. Excavate down to the last layer to show damage, and shape the edges to form a regular rectangle. Cut the pieces to fit, and laminate them in layers, allowing the final layer to protrude slightly from the surface. This leaves extra material for planing and sanding to a true surface.

If a hole 4 inches or 5 inches across or less has been punched clear through the hull shell, cut out material to form a rectangular shape and replace it with a solid piece of wood set against a backing piece. The backing piece overlaps all sides of the hole and is bonded to the interior surface of the hull shell.

No backing is used if the damaged area is larger than 4 inches or 5 inches. Instead, each layer is stepped back from the previous one in a regular manner to provide a seat for a series of laminations that comprise

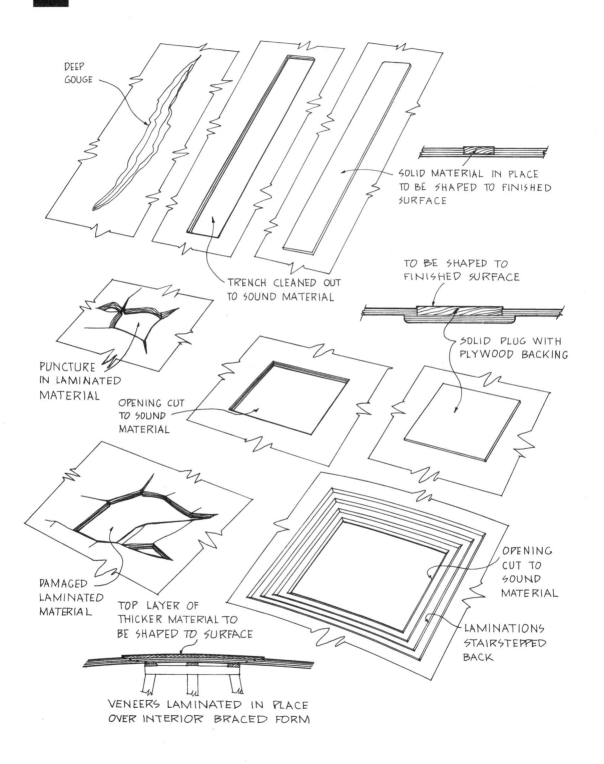

DEEP GOUGE

SOLID MATERIAL IN PLACE TO BE SHAPED TO FINISHED SURFACE

TRENCH CLEANED OUT TO SOUND MATERIAL

TO BE SHAPED TO FINISHED SURFACE

SOLID PLUG WITH PLYWOOD BACKING

PUNCTURE IN LAMINATED MATERIAL

OPENING CUT TO SOUND MATERIAL

OPENING CUT TO SOUND MATERIAL

DAMAGED LAMINATED MATERIAL

TOP LAYER OF THICKER MATERIAL TO BE SHAPED TO SURFACE

LAMINATIONS STAIRSTEPPED BACK

VENEERS LAMINATED IN PLACE OVER INTERIOR BRACED FORM

the patch. Slope the edge of each layer to increase its bonding area. Examine the glue lines to see that they are intact all around the opening. If they are not, more material must be removed. Create a regular, even opening (usually a rectangle running fore and aft). The patch layers can be held for curing with shoring or temporary screws. Temporary staples can be used to hold veneers in place for curing. The outer layers normally will hold the inner layers in place. Fill the holes left by temporary fastenings with resin. Alternatively, drill out the holes and fill them with dowels. As noted before, the outer layer should protrude slightly to allow it to be faired to a true surface.

If the area of damage is extensive enough, the curvature of the hull will come into play. You'll need to provide some temporary support of the correct shape so that the patch can cure fairly with the hull lines. If the lofting is available, shapes can be plotted from it and transferred to lumber or plywood to make a sawn frame. Alternatively, a laminated frame can be made using the opposite side of the hull as a mold.

Sometimes stringers or frames are damaged. If these are merely fractured, they can be repositioned and "sistered" to material alongside. Stringers can be strengthened with solid material of the same size bonded alongside and continuing from frame to frame. If the stringer is laminated, the sister stringer should be laminated to match. Sister reinforcement for laminated frames will have to be laminated in a similar fashion themselves, using the opposite side of the hull as a form (unless the lofting is available). Plywood frames and bulkheads can be reinforced with sawn sister frames of plywood of the same thickness as the damaged material and of sufficient width to cover the fractured area. Before bonding the sister frame, the frame or bulkhead must be returned to its proper position.

If the damage to a frame or stringer is too extensive to allow salvage in the damaged area, then wood must be removed back to sound material. New, solid stringer material must be scarfed to the old with a 1-in-12 scarf angle, sprung into position in a fair curve and held for curing with temporary fastenings. If the stringer is laminated, the laminations must be stairstepped to receive the new laminates. Laminated frames must likewise be stairstepped back to receive laminated material. This time, however, the shape for the new laminated material must be taken from the lofting, or it must be laminated using the other side of the hull as a mold. Remove the damaged part of a plywood frame or bulkhead back to a regular shape, and replace it with new material of the same kind. The new material is butt-joined to the old

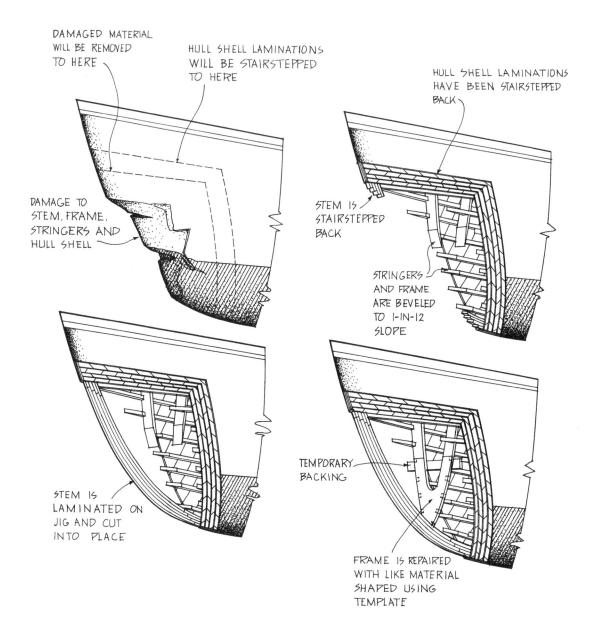

DAMAGED MATERIAL WILL BE REMOVED TO HERE

HULL SHELL LAMINATIONS WILL BE STAIRSTEPPED TO HERE

DAMAGE TO STEM, FRAME, STRINGERS AND HULL SHELL

HULL SHELL LAMINATIONS HAVE BEEN STAIRSTEPPED BACK

STEM IS STAIRSTEPPED BACK

STRINGERS AND FRAME ARE BEVELED TO 1-IN-12 SLOPE

STEM IS LAMINATED ON JIG AND CUT INTO PLACE

TEMPORARY BACKING

FRAME IS REPAIRED WITH LIKE MATERIAL SHAPED USING TEMPLATE

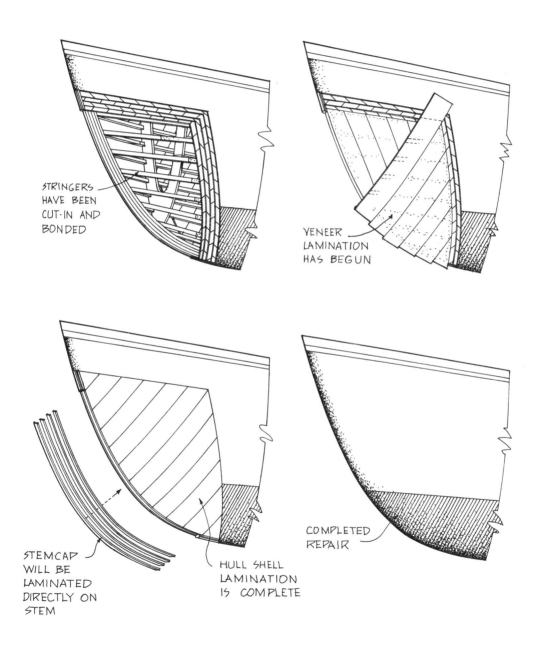

STRINGERS HAVE BEEN CUT-IN AND BONDED

VENEER LAMINATION HAS BEGUN

STEMCAP WILL BE LAMINATED DIRECTLY ON STEM

HULL SHELL LAMINATION IS COMPLETE

COMPLETED REPAIR

and must be "sistered," as previously described, to achieve adequate strength.

Always repair frame or bulkhead material first, so that it can be notched to receive any stringers that may need replacing. Carefully plot the shape of any frame or bulkhead part that must be replaced; these determine the future fairness of the hull. Coat the end grain of any piece of wood that will be bonded with sufficient resin to achieve saturation prior to reapplying adhesive for bonding into position. If this is not done, the wood will draw the adhesive mixture out of the joint before an adequate bond is achieved.

Hull shells that do not have stringers can be repaired as previously described. Damage large enough to involve significant curvature of the hull requires temporary bracing on the interior of the hull shell to support the new shell laminations at the correct curve for curing.

If the sheer clamp and deck beams are involved in the damage, the area affected must be cut back to sound material as before. If the sheer clamp is salvageable, it will be pulled back into shape and sistered onto the interior surface with similar material of the same thickness, which is sprung in and clamped for curing. If the sheer clamp is not salvageable, a new piece must be scarfed in, using a 1-in-12 scarf angle and being careful to follow the fair curve of the deck. If the sheer clamp is laminated, the joints must be stairstepped, as previously described.

If a frame or a bulkhead is involved, it must be repaired first because it determines the shape of the hull. After the repair is completed, notch the frame or bulkhead to receive a new sheer clamp. After the new sheer clamp is in place, it is notched to receive any new deck beam ends that are required. Repair damaged deck beams as described for frames or stringers, taking their curves from the existing deck camber.

Replace the hull laminations first and trim them off at the top of the sheer clamp. Then replace the decking material, allowing it to overlap the side a little. This overlap is later planed off flush with the new hull shell. Where the new decking is butt joined to the old decking, apply a backing of a similar thickness below each joint to increase its strength. The exposed surfaces of new wood must be coated with resin, sheathed, and finished to match the existing hull.

Stem and keel damage can be repaired—but with considerable effort. Where visible fracture and displacement have occurred, the affected material must be removed and replaced. This is because of the difficulty of the ordinary sistering techniques. If the stem is damaged, the wood might have to be chiseled out. If the damage is extensive, the adjoining hull shell, frames, floor timbers, etc., are likely to be affected. It's best to saw out the entire area back to sound material and start over. Solid backbone material is scarfed in at a 1-in-12 angle, and laminated material is stairstepped. Begin repairs with the keel or stem, then repair frames and bulkheads. Next, do stringers and shell planking. Finally, mold laminated floor timbers over the keel.

Where varnished surfaces are involved, the situation becomes a little more complicated. Minor damage can be repaired by masking the area with tape and filling the gouge or scrape with a thickened adhesive mixture, taking care that no voids remain. This filling is close to the color of the varnish and will finish nicely. When extensive areas of new, bare wood are required, the problem is trying to match new varnish to old; otherwise, the entire hull may have to be refinished.

Before applying the new wood laminates, prepare some test panels using various wood samples. Coat these with resin, sheath with 4-ounce glass cloth (if it was used originally), fill the cloth's weave with resin, and varnish. Compare the various samples to the original, and select the wood that creates the closest match. Then proceed with the reconstruction process as previously described.

If damage occurs in areas supporting bonded-on hardware, at the very least the hardware will need to be reclaimed from the background material. A metal-to-wood bond can be broken if the temperature of the adhesive is raised momentarily to 300 degrees F. Remove metal fastenings first, using a soldering gun fitted with a blade tip that fits the screw's slot. Back the fitting out quickly, before the adhesive reasserts itself. Briefly heat the hardware item itself with a propane or welding torch. Pop the hardware item loose with a sharp rap from a hammer. If it doesn't come loose, briefly reheat the hardware and try again.

Variations on a Theme

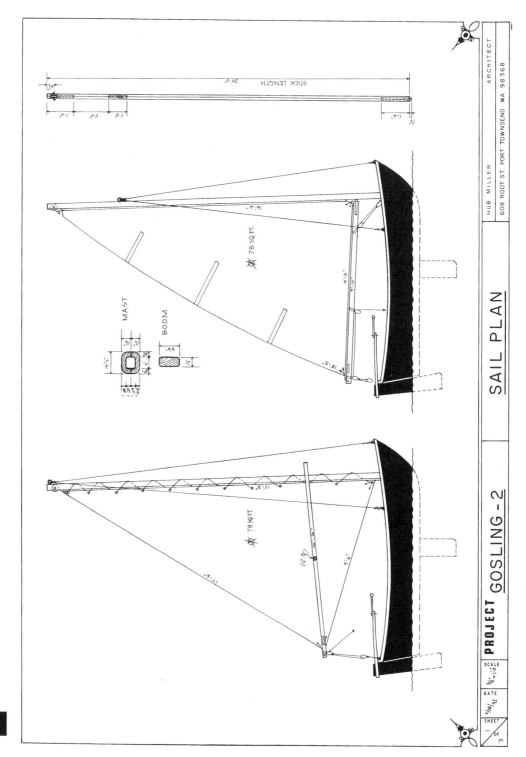

STICK LENGTH
26'-0"

MAST

BOOM

78 SQ. FT.

16'-6"

4'-5"

4'-10"

18'-5"

78 SQ FT.

17'-3"

17'-6"

1½" ⌀

9'-2"

HUB MILLER   ARCHITECT
608 ROOT ST PORT TOWNSEND WA. 98368

SAIL PLAN

PROJECT GOSLING - 2

SCALE
¾" = 1'-0"

DATE
7/28/92

SHEET
1 OF 3

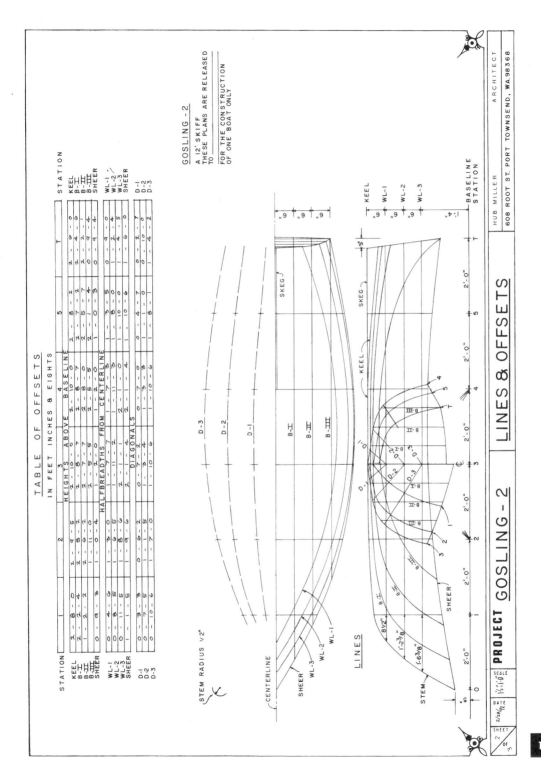

TABLE OF OFFSETS
IN FEET INCHES & EIGHTS

STEM RADIUS 1/2"

GOSLING - 2

A 12' SKIFF
THESE PLANS ARE RELEASED
TO

FOR THE CONSTRUCTION
OF ONE BOAT ONLY

LINES

PROJECT GOSLING - 2   LINES & OFFSETS

HUB MILLER   ARCHITECT
608 ROOT ST. PORT TOWNSEND, WA 98368

SCALE 1/2"=1'-0"   DATE 2/28/92   SHEET 2 OF 3

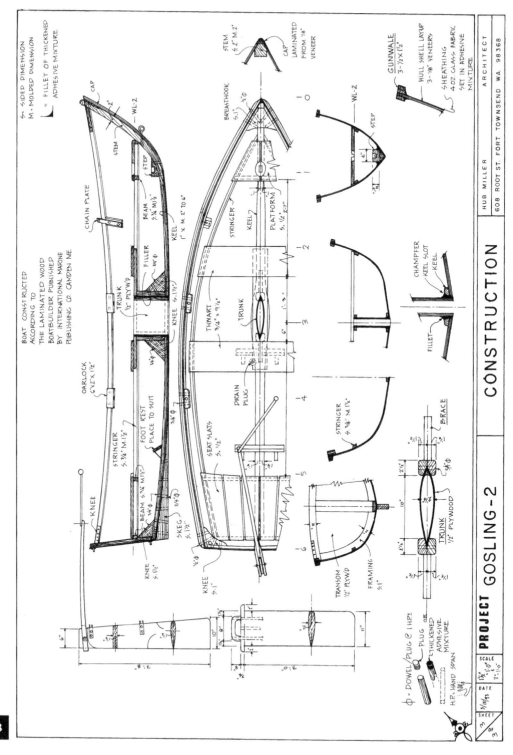

CONSTRUCTION

PROJECT GOSLING-2

HUB MILLER   ARCHITECT
608 ROOT ST. FORT TOWNSEND WA. 98368

SCALE
DATE 3/15/93
SHEET 3 OF 3

198

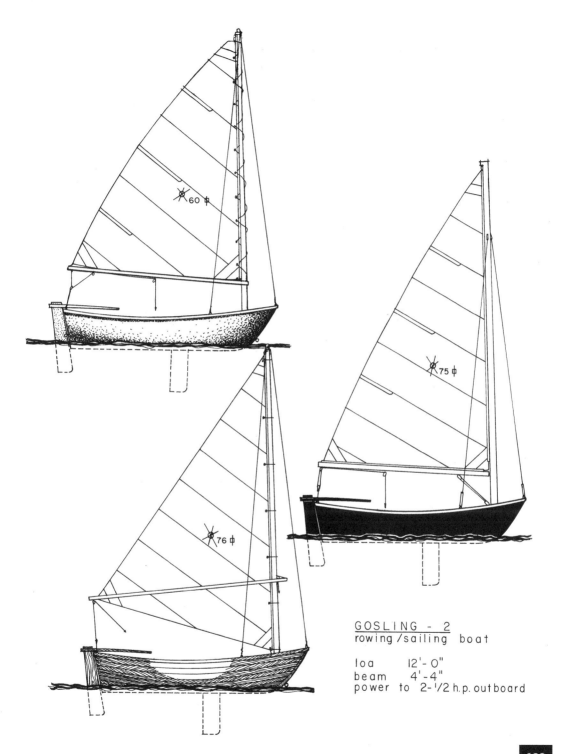

GOSLING - 2
rowing/sailing boat

loa   12'-0"
beam   4'-4"
power to 2-1/2 h.p. outboard

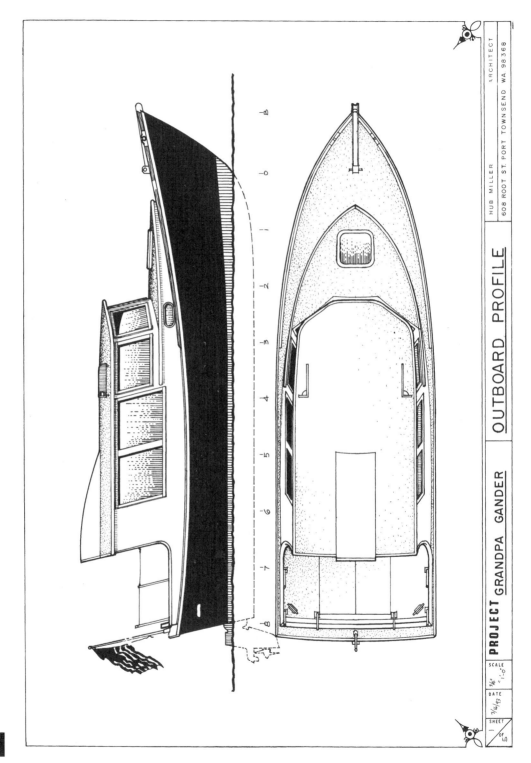

HUB MILLER   ARCHITECT
608 ROOT ST. PORT TOWNSEND WA 98368

OUTBOARD PROFILE

PROJECT GRANDPA GANDER

SCALE ¾" = 1'-0"

DATE 3/14/93

SHEET 1 OF 5

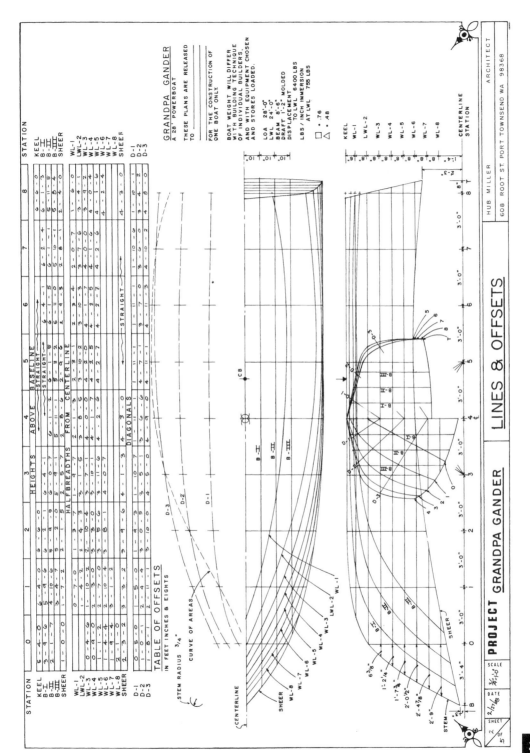

GRANDPA GANDER
A 28' POWERBOAT

THESE PLANS ARE RELEASED TO

FOR THE CONSTRUCTION OF ONE BOAT ONLY.

BOAT WEIGHT WILL DIFFER WITH BUILDING TECHNIQUE OF INDIVIDUAL BUILDERS, AND WITH EQUIPMENT CHOSEN AND STORES LOADED.

LOA 28'-0"
LWL 24'-0"
BEAM 8'-6"
DRAFT 1'-2" MOLDED
DISPLACEMENT 6400 LBS
    TO LWL
LBS / INCH IMMERSION
    AT LWL 795 LBS

□ = .76
△ = .48

TABLE OF OFFSETS
IN FEET INCHES & EIGHTS

STEM RADIUS 3/4"

CURVE OF AREAS

LINES & OFFSETS

PROJECT GRANDPA GANDER

SCALE 3/4"=1'-0"
DATE 2/27/78
SHEET 2 OF 5

HUB MILLER ARCHITECT
608 ROOT ST. PORT TOWNSEND WA 98368

201

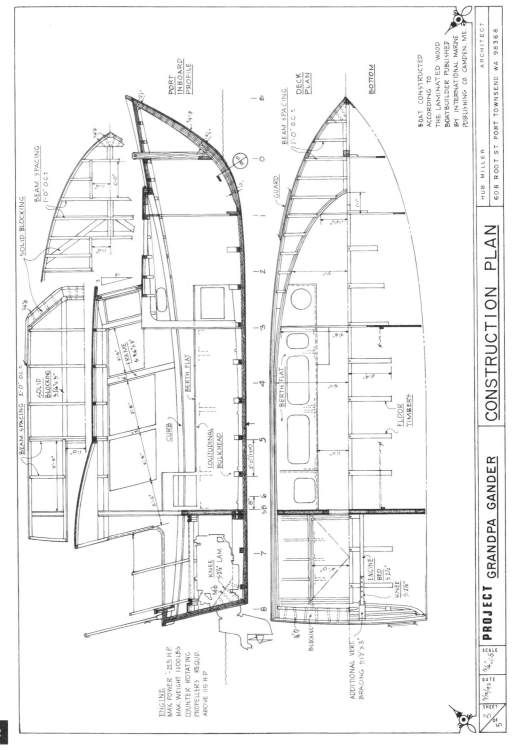

BEAM SPACING 1'-0" O.C. ±

SOLID BLOCKING

BEAM SPACING 2'-0" O.C.

SOLID BLOCKING 1¼" x 1¾" x 5"

FRAME 1¾" x 1¼" x 3"

CURB

BERTH FLAT

LOGITUDINAL BULKHEAD

KNEE 1½" LAM.

PORT INBOARD PROFILE

GUARD

BEAM SPACING 1'-0" O.C. ±

DECK PLAN

BOTTOM

BERTH FLAT

FLOOR TIMBERS

ENGINE BED 1¾" x 2½"

KNEE 1¾" x 2¼"

ADDITIONAL VERT. BRACING 1¾" x 3"

BLOCKING

ENGINE
MAX. POWER - 215 H.P.
MAX. WEIGHT - 1100 LBS.
COUNTER ROTATING
PROPELLERS REQ'D.
ABOVE 115 H.P.

BOAT CONSTRUCTED
ACCORDING TO
THE LAMINATED WOOD
BOATBUILDER PUBLISHED
BY INTERNATIONAL MARINE
PUBLISHING CO. CAMDEN, ME.

HUB MILLER   ARCHITECT
608 ROOT ST. PORT TOWNSEND WA 98368

PROJECT GRANDPA GANDER   CONSTRUCTION PLAN

DATE	SCALE	SHEET
5/15/93	¾" = 1'-0"	3 OF 5

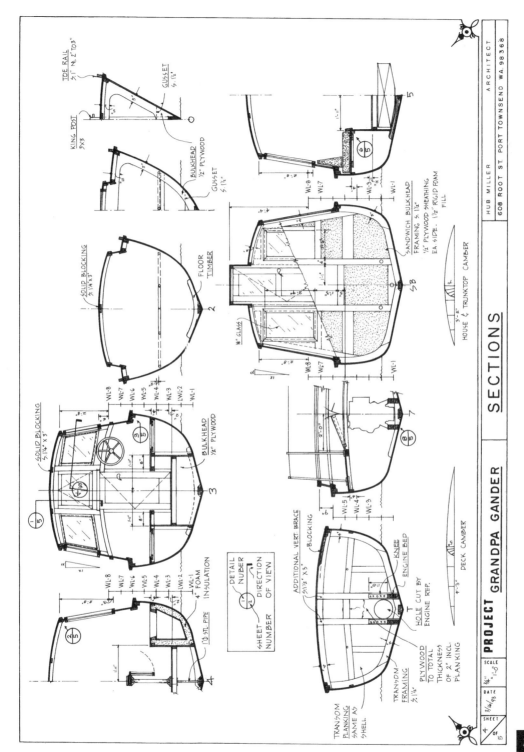

TOE RAIL
¾" Ø, 2" TO 3"

GUSSET
6 ¼"

KING POST
3x3

BULKHEAD
½" PLYWOOD

GUSSET
6 ¼"

SOLID BLOCKING
3 ¼" x 3

FLOOR TIMBER

SOLID BLOCKING
3 ¼" x 3

BULKHEAD
½" PLYWOOD

DETAIL NUMBER

DIRECTION OF VIEW

SHEET NUMBER

4" FOAM INSULATION

1" Ø STL PIPE

PLYWOOD TO TOTAL THICKNESS OF 2" INCL. PLANKING

TRANSOM FRAMING
6 ¼"

TRANSOM PLANKING SAME AS SHELL

SANDWICH BULKHEAD
FRAMING 5 ¼"
½" PLYWOOD SHEATHING
EA. SIDE. ½" RIGID FOAM
FILL

HOUSE & TRUNKTOP CAMBER

¼" GLASS

WL-8
WL-7
WL-1

DECK CAMBER

ADDITIONAL VERT BRACE
6 ¼" x 3"

BLOCKING

KNEE

ENGINE BED

HOLE CUT BY ENGINE REP.

WL-5
WL-4
WL-3

WL-8 WL-7 WL-6 WL-5 WL-4 WL-3 LWL-2 WL-1

SECTIONS

PROJECT GRANDPA GANDER

HUB MILLER   ARCHITECT
608 ROOT ST PORT TOWNSEND WA 98368

DATE 3/10/93

SCALE ¾" 1'-0

SHEET 4 OF 5

203

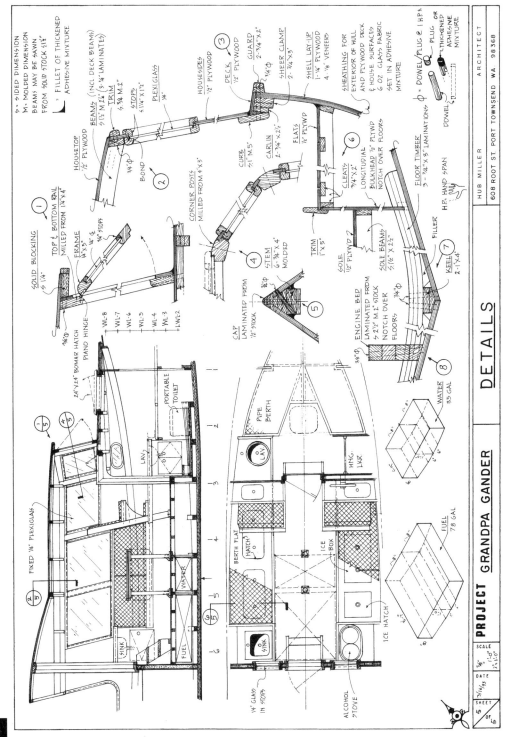

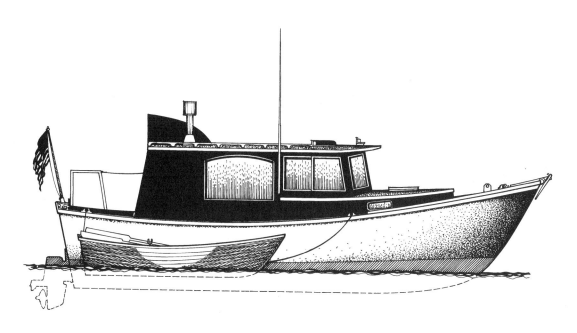

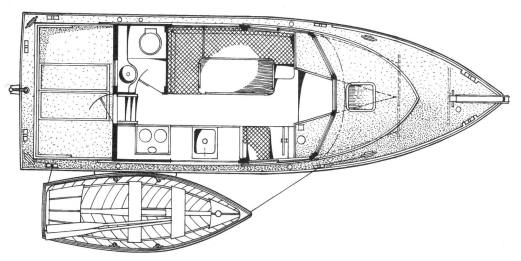

GOSLING - 2
rowing / sailing boat

loa   12'- 0"
beam   4'- 4"
power to 2-1/2 h.p. outboard

GRANDPA GANDER
trailerable power cruiser

loa   28'- 0"
beam   8'- 6"
power to 125 h.p. diesel outdrive
          225 h.p. gas outdrive

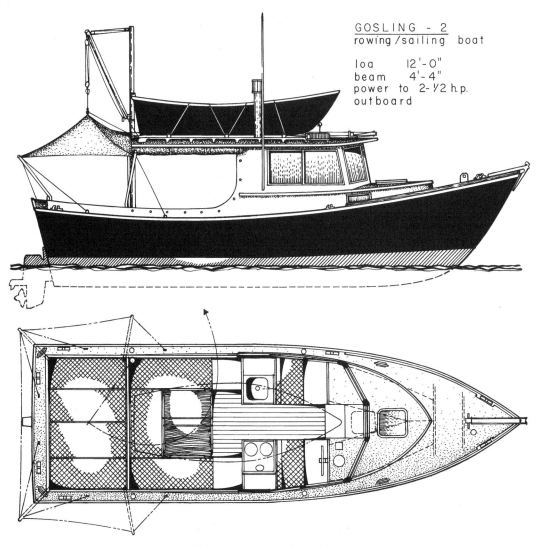

GOSLING - 2
rowing/sailing boat

loa   12'-0"
beam   4'-4"
power to 2-½ h.p.
outboard

GRANDPA GANDER
three-quarter open powerboat w/cargo boom

loa   28'- 0"
beam   8'- 6"
power to 125 h.p. diesel outdrive
            225 h.p. gas outdrive

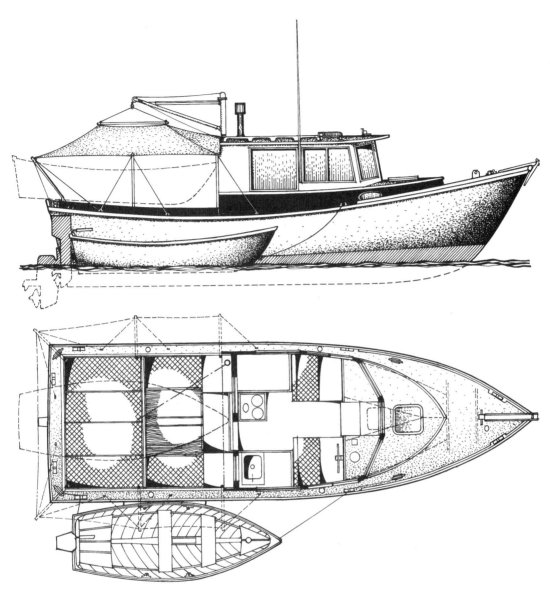

GOSLING - 2
rowing/sailing boat

loa   12'-0"
beam   4'-4"
power to 2·1/2 h.p. outboard

GRANDPA GANDER
half open powerboat w/ tent

loa   28'-0"
beam   8'-6"
power to 125 h.p. diesel outdrive
         225 h.p. gas outdrive

GRANDPA GANDER
kayak tender

loa   28'- 0"
beam   8'- 6"
power to 125 h.p. diesel outdrive
        225 h.p. gas outdrive

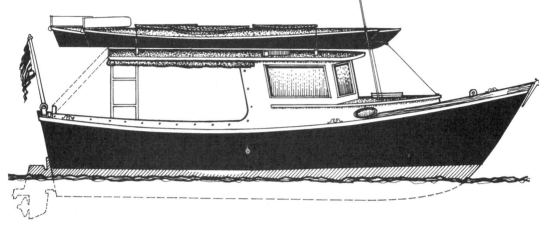

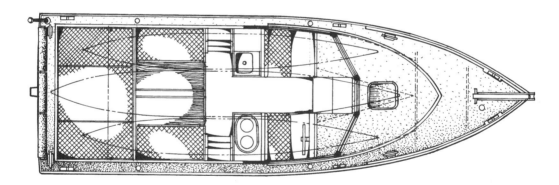

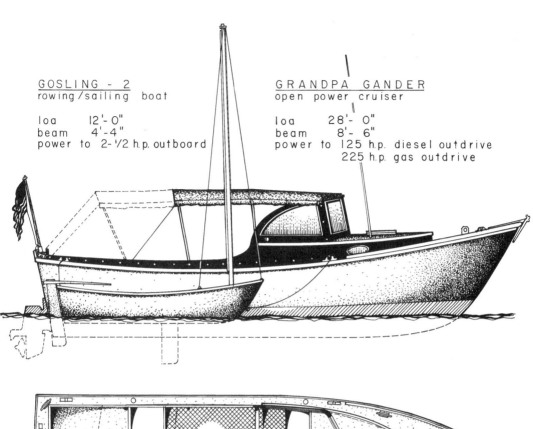

GOSLING - 2
rowing/sailing boat

loa   12'- 0"
beam   4'- 4"
power to 2-1/2 h.p. outboard

GRANDPA GANDER
open power cruiser

loa   28'- 0"
beam   8'- 6"
power to 125 h.p. diesel outdrive
         225 h.p. gas outdrive

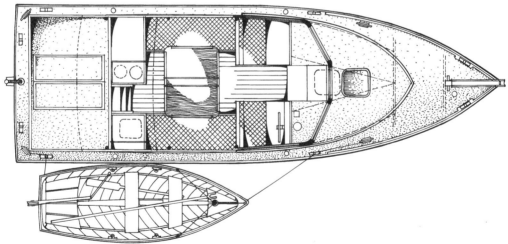

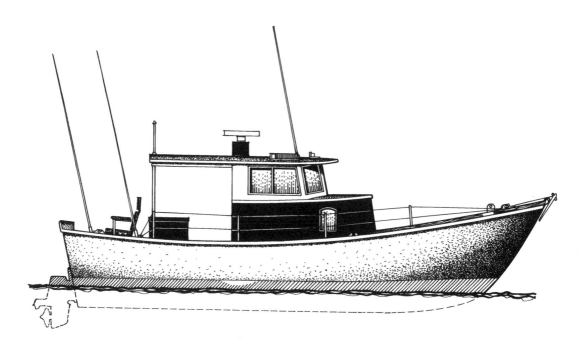

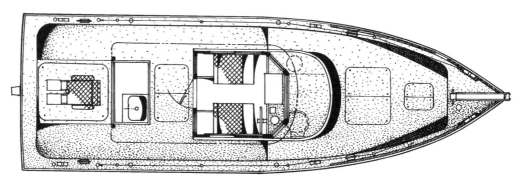

GRANDPA GANDER
fishing boat

loa   28'- 0"
beam   8'- 6"
power to 125 h.p. diesel outdrive
         225 h.p. gas outdrive

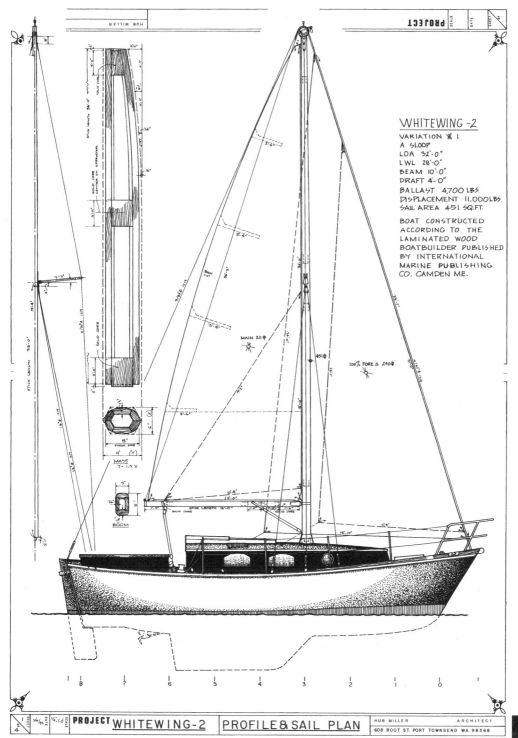

WHITEWING -2

VARIATION # 1
A SLOOP
LOA 32'-0"
LWL 28'-0"
BEAM 10'-0"
DRAFT 4'-0"
BALLAST 4,700 LBS.
DISPLACEMENT 11,000 LBS.
SAIL AREA 451 SQ. FT.

BOAT CONSTRUCTED
ACCORDING TO THE
LAMINATED WOOD
BOATBUILDER PUBLISHED
BY INTERNATIONAL
MARINE PUBLISHING
CO. CAMDEN ME.

MAIN 211 □

451 □

100% FORE △ 240 □

MAST
Y - 1.5 X

BOOM

TABLE OF OFFSETS
IN FEET INCHES & EIGHTS

STATION	0	1	2	3	4	5	6	7	8	STATION
				HEIGHTS ABOVE BASELINE						
BALLAST KEEL				7-1-1	9-2-0	9-2-4				BALLAST KEEL
KEEL	5-0-0	6-3-2	6-6-3	6-7-0	6-7-0	6-7-0	6-5-4	6-0-0	5-0-0	KEEL
B-I	2-2-0	5-8-0	6-2-5	6-4-4	6-5-3	6-5-4	6-2-5	5-7-1	4-4-0	B-I
B-II		4-3-0	5-10-0	6-2-0	6-3-5	6-2-4	5-10-3	5-0-0	3-5-5	B-II
B-III			5-0-0	5-4-4	6-0-4	5-7-6	5-4-6	4-1-3	1-5-5	B-III
SHEER	0-7-4	1-0-4	1-5-4	1-9-0	1-10-5	1-10-4	1-9-6	1-7-4	1-3-6	SHEER
				HALFBREADTHS FROM CENTERLINE						
WL-1					0-4-0	0-2-5				WL-1
WL-2					0-4-6	0-2-7				WL-2
WL-3				0-1-5	0-5-3	0-3-5				WL-3
WL-4		0-7-7	1-8-5	2-7-3	3-1-6	2-7-4	1-8-3			WL-4
LWL-5		1-7-3	3-0-1	3-11-2	4-4-5	4-3-0	3-6-2	2-1-6		LWL-5
WL-6	0-4-3	2-1-4	3-5-7	4-4-6	4-9-4	4-7-4	4-0-5	3-0-3	1-7-1	WL-6
WL-7	0-9-0	2-5-6	3-9-6	4-7-2	5-0-0	4-9-4	4-3-7	3-5-4	2-4-0	WL-7
WL-8	1-0-7	2-9-2	4-0-5	4-8-4	5-0-0	4-10-5	4-5-7	3-9-2	2-9-6	WL-8
WL-9	1-4-7									WL-9
SHEER	1-6-0	3-0-0	4-1-3	4-8-7	4-11-1	4-10-2	4-5-6	3-10-3	3-0-5	SHEER
D-1	0-5-0	1-11-3	2-7-5	2-11-2	3-1-7	3-0-0	2-8-0	1-11-5	0-10-1	D-1
D-2	0-8-7	2-5-6	3-7-2	4-2-3	4-5-2	4-3-2	3-9-7	2-11-2	1-9-6	D-2
D-3	1-0-1	2-9-2	4-0-7	4-10-5	5-3-6	5-1-7	4-7-0	3-8-2	2-6-4	D-3

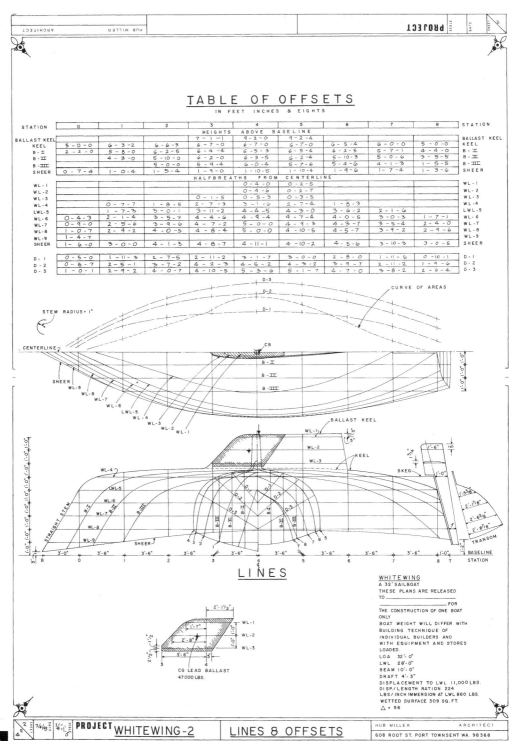

STEM RADIUS = 1"

CURVE OF AREAS

CENTERLINE

CB

BALLAST KEEL

KEEL

SKEG

STRAIGHT STEM

TRANSOM

BASELINE STATION

LINES

CG LEAD BALLAST
47000 LBS.

WHITEWING
A 32' SAILBOAT
THESE PLANS ARE RELEASED
TO _____
_____ FOR
THE CONSTRUCTION OF ONE BOAT
ONLY
BOAT WEIGHT WILL DIFFER WITH
BUILDING TECHNIQUE OF
INDIVIDUAL BUILDERS AND
WITH EQUIPMENT AND STORES
LOADED.
LOA   32'-0"
LWL   28'-0"
BEAM 10'-0"
DRAFT 4'-3"
DISPLACEMENT TO LWL 11,000 LBS.
DISP./LENGTH RATION 224
LBS./INCH IMMERSION AT LWL 860 LBS.
WETTED SURFACE 309 SQ. FT.
△ = 56

PROJECT WHITEWING-2   LINES & OFFSETS   HUB MILLER   ARCHITECT
608 ROOT ST. PORT TOWNSENT WA. 98368

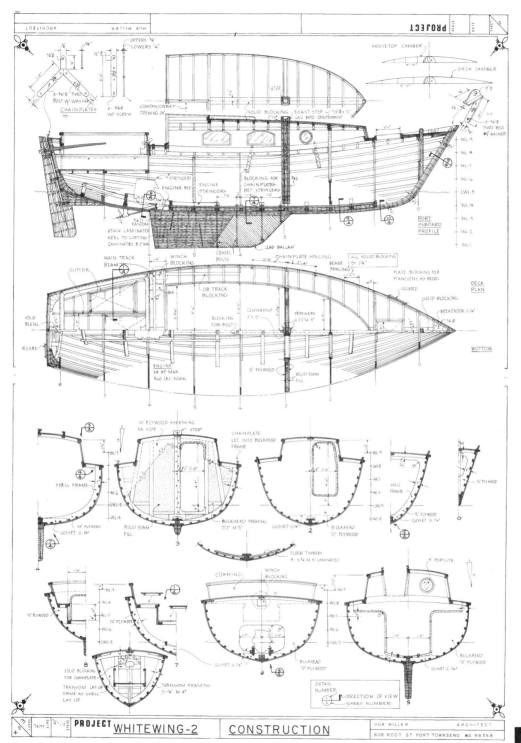

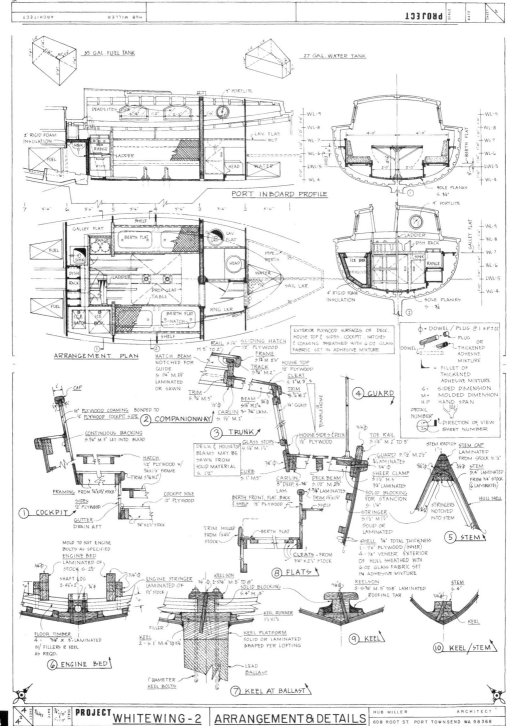

35 GAL. FUEL TANK

27 GAL. WATER TANK

4" PORTLITE

DEADLITES

2" RIGID FOAM INSULATION

RANGE

LADDER

FUEL

HEAD   WATER

PORT INBOARD PROFILE

WL-9
WL-8
WL-7
WL-6
LWL-5
WL 4

WL-9
WL-8
WL-7
WL-6
LWL-5
WL-4

LAV. FLAT
WL-7

BERTH FLAT

SOLE PLANKS S. 3/4"

4" PORTLITE

GALLEY FLAT

SHELF

BERTH FLAT

LAV. FLAT

SINK

RANGE

DISH RACK

FUEL

HEAD

PIPE BERTH

DROP-LEAF TABLE

LADDER

WATER

SAIL LKR.

HNG. LKR.

BERTH FLAT

ICE BOX

SHELF

ICE HATCH

HATCH

4" RIGID FOAM INSULATION

LADDER
DISH RACK
ICE BOX
SINK
RANGE
GALLEY FLAT

WL-9
WL-8
WL-7
WL-6
LWL-5
WL-4

SOLE PLANKS S. 3/4"

ARRANGEMENT PLAN

EXTERIOR PLYWOOD SURFACES OF DECK, HOUSE TOP & SIDES, COCKPIT, HATCHES & COAMING SHEATHED WITH 6 OZ. GLASS FABRIC SET IN ADHESIVE MIXTURE

DOWEL / PLUG @ 1 H.P. O.C.

PLUG OR THICKENED ADHESIVE MIXTURE

DOWEL

= FILLET OF THICKENED ADHESIVE MIXTURE

S.= SIDED DIMENSION
M.= MOLDED DIMENSION
H.P.= HAND SPAN

DETAIL NUMBER

DIRECTION OF VIEW
SHEET NUMBER

② COMPANIONWAY

③ TRUNK

④ GUARD

RAIL S. 1/4" SLIDING HATCH
M. 5" TO 2"   1/2" PLYWOOD FRAME

HATCH BEAM NOTCHED FOR GUIDE
S. 1/4" M. 2 5/8" LAMINATED OR SAWN

TRIM
S. 3/4" M. 3"

BEAM S. 1/4" M. 2 5/8"

TRACK 3/4" PLYWOOD
S. 3/4" M. 2"

CLEAT S. 1" M. 1 1/2"

TRIM S. 3/4" M. 3/4"

1/4" GLASS

CAP

1/2" PLYWOOD COAMING BONDED TO 1/2" PLYWOOD COCKPIT SIDE

CONTINUOUS BACKING S. 3/4" M. 3" LET INTO BLKHD.

HATCH 1/2" PLYWOOD W/ 3/4"x1 1/2" FRAME

TRIM S. 3/4" M. 2"

FRAMING FROM 3/4"x1 1/2" STOCK

COCKPIT SOLE 1/2" PLYWOOD

① COCKPIT

SIDES 1/2" PLYWOOD

GUTTER DRAIN AFT

3/4"x2 1/4" STOCK

BEAM S. 1/4" M. 2 5/8"

CARLIN S. 3/4" LAM.
S. 1/4" M. 2"

GLASS STOPS S. 1/4" M. 1 1/2"

DECK & HOUSETOP BEAMS MAY BE SAWN FROM SOLID MATERIAL S. 1 1/2"

CURB S. 1" M. 5"

HOUSE SIDES & DECK 1/2" PLYWOOD

BERTH FRONT, FLAT, BACK & SHELF 1/2" PLYWOOD

TRIM MILLED FROM 1 3/4"x4 1/2" STOCK

BERTH FLAT

CLEATS - FROM 3/4"x2 1/4" STOCK

⑧ FLATS

TOE RAIL S. 1 1/2" M. 2" TO 3"

GUARD S. 1 1/2" M. 2 1/2"
4 LAMINATES 3/4" ∅

SHEER CLAMP S. 1 1/2" M. 3"
3/4" LAMINATES

SOLID BLOCKING FOR STANCION S. 1 1/4"

STRINGER S. 1 1/2" M. 1 1/2" SOLID OR LAMINATED

SHELF

SHELF

DECK BEAM S. 1/2" M. 2 5/8" 4-3/4" LAMINATES
TRIM 1 1/2"x1 1/4"

3/4" ∅

3/4" ∅

STEM RADIUS

STEM CAP LAMINATED FROM STOCK S. 5/8"

STEM S. 4" LAMINATED FROM 3/4" STOCK (6 LAMINATES)

STRINGERS NOTCHED INTO STEM

HULL SHELL

⑤ STEM

SHELL 3/4" TOTAL THICKNESS (1 - 1/4" PLYWOOD (INNER) 4 - 1/8" VENEER) EXTERIOR OF HULL SHEATHED WITH 6 OZ. GLASS FABRIC SET IN ADHESIVE MIXTURE

MOLD TO SUIT ENGINE BOLTS AS SPECIFIED

ENGINE BED LAMINATED OF STOCK S. 2 1/2"

SHAFT LOG 2 - 4 1/4"x2"

ENGINE STRINGER LAMINATED OF 1/2" STOCK

3/4" ∅

KEELSON S. 2 - 5 3/4" M. 5" TO 9"

SOLID BLOCKING S. 5 1/4"

KEELSON 2 - 5 3/4" M. 5" TO 9" LAMINATED ROOFING TAR

STEM S. 4"

FLOOR TIMBER 4 - 3/4" x 3" LAMINATED W/ FILLERS & KEEL AS REQD.

KEEL 2 - 5 1" M. 4" TO 10 1/2"

KEEL RUNNER 1 1/2"x1 1/2"

FILLER

KEEL PLATFORM SOLID OR LAMINATED SHAPED PER LOFTING

LEAD BALLAST

1" DIAMETER KEEL BOLTS

3/4" ∅

KEEL

⑥ ENGINE BED

⑦ KEEL AT BALLAST

⑨ KEEL

⑩ KEEL/STEM

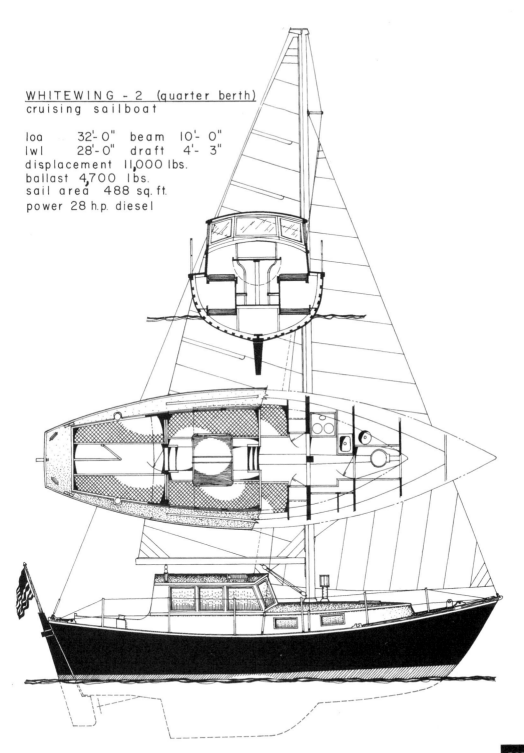

WHITEWING - 2 (quarter berth)
cruising sailboat

loa   32'- 0"   beam 10'- 0"
lwl   28'- 0"   draft 4'- 3"
displacement 11,000 lbs.
ballast 4,700 lbs.
sail area   488 sq. ft.
power 28 h.p. diesel

215

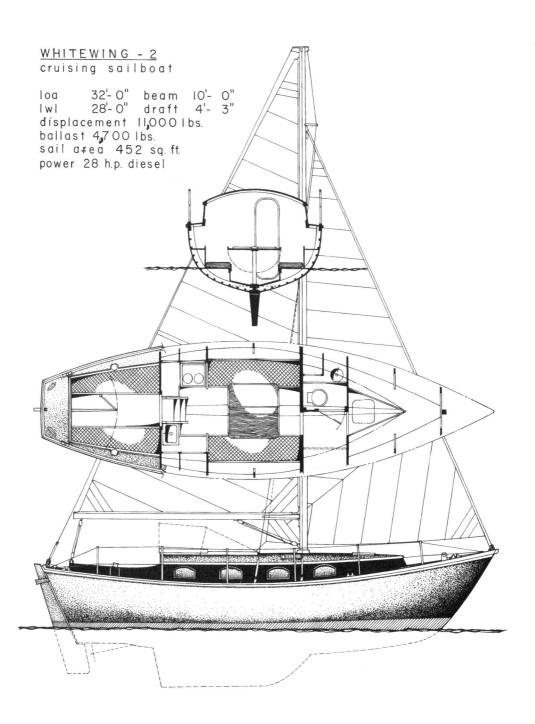

WHITEWING - 2
cruising sailboat

loa   32'- 0" beam 10'- 0"
lwl   28'- 0" draft 4'- 3"
displacement 11,000 lbs.
ballast 4,700 lbs.
sail area 452 sq. ft.
power 28 h.p. diesel

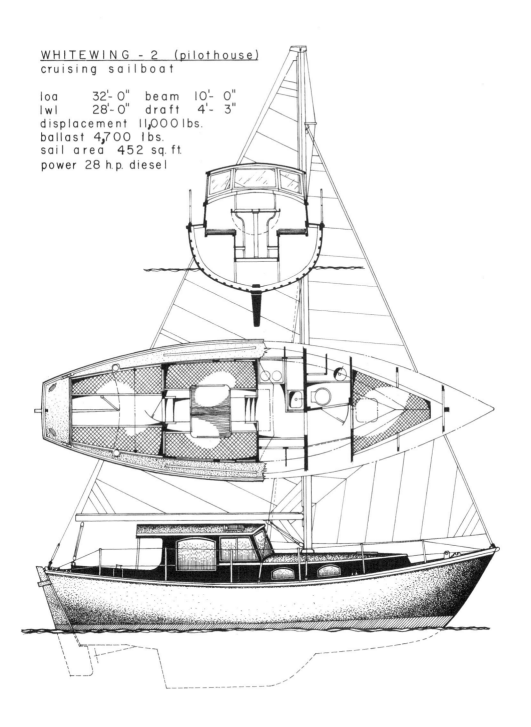

WHITEWING - 2 (pilothouse)
cruising sailboat

loa   32'- 0"   beam 10'- 0"
lwl   28'- 0"   draft 4'- 3"
displacement 11,000 lbs.
ballast 4,700 lbs.
sail area 452 sq. ft.
power 28 h.p. diesel

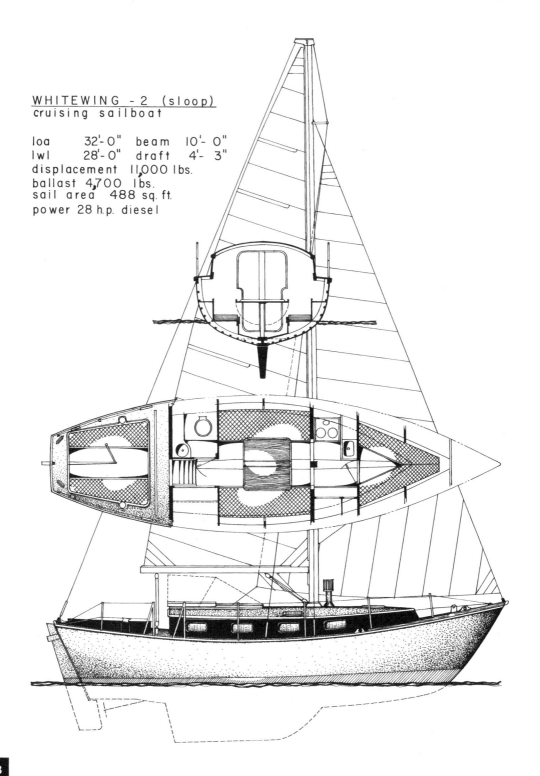

WHITEWING - 2 (sloop)
cruising sailboat

loa   32'-0" beam 10'- 0"
lwl   28'-0" draft 4'- 3"
displacement 11,000 lbs.
ballast 4,700 lbs.
sail area 488 sq. ft.
power 28 h.p. diesel

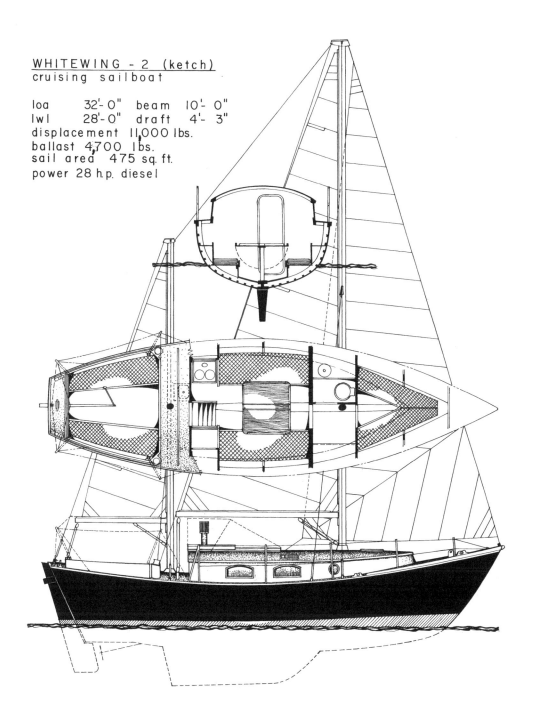

WHITEWING - 2 (ketch)
cruising sailboat

loa   32'-0"   beam   10'- 0"
lwl   28'-0"   draft   4'- 3"
displacement 11,000 lbs.
ballast 4,700 lbs.
sail area 475 sq. ft.
power 28 h.p. diesel

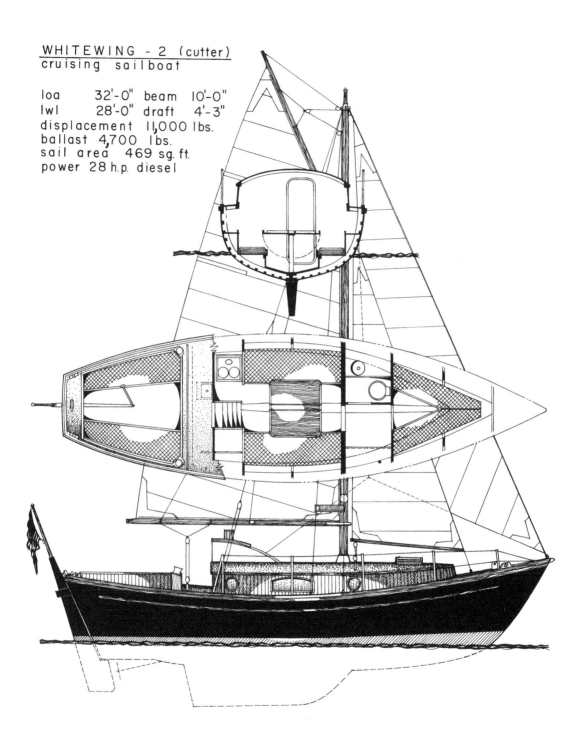

WHITEWING - 2 (cutter)
cruising sailboat

loa   32'-0" beam 10'-0"
lwl   28'-0" draft 4'-3"
displacement 11,000 lbs.
ballast 4,700 lbs.
sail area 469 sq. ft.
power 28 h.p. diesel

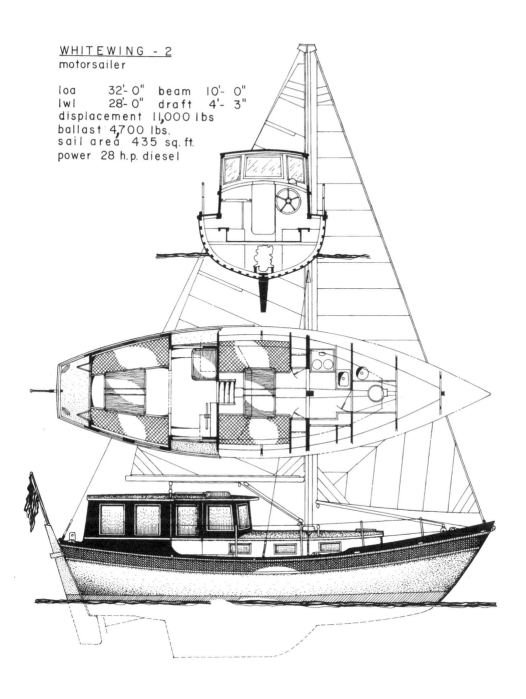

WHITEWING - 2
motorsailer

loa   32'- 0"   beam 10'- 0"
lwl   28'- 0"   draft 4'- 3"
displacement 11,000 lbs
ballast 4,700 lbs.
sail area 435 sq. ft.
power 28 h.p. diesel

HOW TO ORDER PLANS

The working drawings included here are legible enough to work from, but if you'd like full-size plans, or are interested in other designs, please write:

Hub Miller
P.O. Box 1984
Port Townsend, WA 98368

Bibliography

Buehler, George. *Buehler's Backyard Boatbuilding.* Camden, Maine: International Marine, 1991.

Crosby, William F. *Amateur Boat Building.* New York: The RUDDER Publishing Co., 1941.

Gougeon, Meade. *The Gougeon Brothers on Boat Construction.* Bay City, Michigan: The Gougeon Brothers, latest edition.

Guzzwell, John. *Modern Wooden Yacht Construction.* Camden, Maine: International Marine, 1979.

McIntosh, David C. "Bud." *How to Build a Wooden Boat.* Brooklin, Maine: WoodenBoat Publications, Inc., 1987.

Nicolson, Ian. *Cold-Moulded and Strip-Planked Wood Boatbuilding.* London: Stanford Maritime, 1983.

Parker, Reuel B. *The New Cold-Molded Boatbuilding.* Camden, Maine: International Marine, 1990.

Taube, Allen. *The Boatwright's Companion.* Camden, Maine: International Marine, 1986.

Varney, Michael. *Amateur Boat Building.* London: John Murray, 1950.

Wittman, Rebecca J. *Brightwork.* Camden, Maine: International Marine, 1990.

Index

If you enjoyed **The Laminated Wood Boatbuilder,** *you may be interested in the following books from the International Marine library. Prices subject to change.*

Boatowner's Energy Planner: How to Make and Manage Electrical Energy on Board
Kevin and Nan Jeffrey

A detailed exploration of onboard energy systems, including marine alternators, portable generators, solar panels, wind and water generators, battery management, AC shore-power hookups, and system controls and accessories for both DC and AC electrical service, with just enough theory to make all the options crystal clear. "A valuable addition to any boat maintenance library." *Offshore.*

Paperbound, 7⅜" x 9¼", 288 pages, 77 illustrations, $21.95. Order No. 60234P.

Refrigeration for Pleasureboats: Installation, Maintenance, and Repair
Nigel Calder

Here is the ultimate refrigeration resource for power and sailboats. "Iceboxes, compressors, condensers, expansion valves, everything you were wondering about." *WoodenBoat.*

Hardbound, 7⅜" x 9¼", 160 pages, 220 illustrations, $24.95. Order No. 60255H.

Boat Joinery and Cabinetmaking Simplified
Fred P. Bingham

Drawing upon more than 60 years' experience as a boatbuilder, cabinetmaker, and designer, Fred Bingham has revamped his classic *Practical Yacht Joinery* to appeal to a whole new generation of boatbuilders. "One almost has the feeling that the author is right there, advising and encouraging, showing how to use a tool, helping lay out deck beams, pausing to tell how he did a job on such and such a boat." *Small Boat Journal.*

Paperbound, 7⅜" x 9¼", 256 pages, 475 illustrations, $24.95. Order No. 60356P.

Yachtcraftsman's Handbook: 50 Woodworking Projects for Boats
Garth Graves

Clear photography and drawings, and concise but friendly step-by-step instructions explain how to build handsome, functional furnishings and appointments for your boat. "Graves tries to teach the reader how to think, before going on to teach him or her how to do. And that is where this book differs from many other 'project books'. . . . A reader with basic woodworking skills and a desire to produce some quality custom items will find its information quite valuable." *WoodenBoat.*

Hardbound, 7⅜" x 9¼", 224 pages, 308 illustrations, $29.95. Order No. 60229H.

Brightwork: The Art of Finishing Wood
Rebecca Wittman

A rarity among boating and boat maintenance books: a beautiful how-to book, with 59 lush four-color photographs. "A first-class and highly readable text that should be mandatory reading for anyone who owns or is contemplating owning a wood-trimmed vessel." *Sailing.*

Hardbound, 8" x 9½", 192 pages, 59 four-color photographs, $29.95. Order No. 60129H.

The Rigger's Locker: Tools and Techniques for Modern and Traditional Rigging
Brion Toss
Illustrated by Robert Shetterly

An all-new collection of useful ideas, undeservedly obscure knots and splices, and tips on everything from working safely aloft to splicing wire, splicing braided rope, splicing rope to chain, rigging self-tending headsails, and even preventing the eternally irritating problem of keeping that drawstring from disappearing into the waistband of your sweatpants.

Hardbound, 7⅜" x 9¼", 224 pages, 237 illustrations, $24.95. Order No. 60126H.

The Nature of Boats: Insights and Esoterica for the Nautically Obsessed
Dave Gerr

The Nature of Boats is the ideal companion for old salts, boatyard crawlers, boatshow oglers, and landlocked dreamers. It's packed with understandable explanations of the difference between initial and reserve stability, of how torque and horsepower work, of traditional boatbuilding materials versus high-tech, of rudder control, of speed powered by sails versus engines, of flotation and trim. Dave Gerr examines sail and power boats from every conceivable angle to create a book that's not only fascinating and fun, but also extremely useful.

"Fascinating potpourri of information about today's boat's, modern and traditional; reminiscent of the work of Culler, Lane, Davis, Atkin, and many others of an earlier era." *WoodenBoat.*

"Gerr understands those of us afflicted with a passion for boats. Furthermore he trades on our insatiable appetites for nautical tidbits. And he does it well. Gerr has a talent for describing complicated concepts in simple terms." *SEA*.

Hardbound, 7⅜" x 9¼", 432 pages, 253 illustrations, $29.95. Order No. 60262H.

Boat Trailers and Tow Vehicles: A User's Guide
Steve Henkel

Densely illustrated with Steve Henkel's clear drawings, this book is packed with information showing adjustment, towing, launching, maintenance, and repair procedures. It describes how to choose the right style and type of trailer for a particular boat and trailering venue; how to choose the best tow vehicle; how to troubleshoot and repair the electrics and wheel bearings; how to correct sway and stability problems while towing; and much more. Detailed appendices include trailer towing regulations by state; trailer towing ratings for cars, vans, and pickups; and a product source list.

"A book like this has been long needed. . . . [It covers] subjects that often take boaters several years to learn. It's a good investment." *Trailer Boats*.

"The best single source guide I've seen. Commonsense advice, and nicely organized." *American Sailor*.

"A no-fluff practical primer that can help the trailer boater steer a safe course along the highways to the high seas." *Sailing*.

Paperbound, 7⅜" x 9¼", 144 pages, 50 illustrations, $14.95. Book No. 60264P.

Gently with the Tides: The Best of *Living Aboard*,
edited by Michael Frankel

Fueled by 17 years of the best letters, articles, and firsthand accounts from *Living Aboard* journal, *Gently with the Tides* is a powerful testimonial to the lure and romance of living aboard a boat. Most of all, it's a high-octane dream-feeder for liveaboard aspirants. It will help them decide whether to, it will tell them how to, and, most important, it will fill their dreams with why to.

Paperbound, 7⅜" x 9¼", 256 pages, 16 illustrations, $14.95. Order No. 60374P.

Look for These and Other International Marine Books
at Your Local Bookstore

To Order, Call Toll Free 1-800-822-8158
(outside the U.S., call 717-794-2191)

or Write to International Marine/TAB Books
A Division of McGraw-Hill, Inc.
Blue Ridge Summit, PA 17294-0840.

- -

Title	Product No.	Quantity	Price

Subtotal: $_____

Postage and Handling
($3.00 in U.S., $5.00 outside U.S.): $_____

Add applicable state and local sales tax: $_____

TOTAL: $_____

❏ Check or money order made payable to TAB Books

Charge my   ❏ VISA   ❏ MasterCard   ❏ American Express

Acct. No.: _____ Exp.: _____

Signature: _____

Name: _____

Address: _____

City: _____

State: _____ Zip: _____

International Marine catalog free with purchase; otherwise, send $1.00 in check or money order and receive $1.00 credit on your next purchase.

Orders outside U.S. must pay with international money order in U.S. dollars.

If for any reason you are not satisfied with the book(s) you order, simply return it (them) within 15 days and receive a full refund.